Tastes Like

Home

Tastes Like
Home

My Caribbean Cookbook

Cynthia Nelson

IAN RANDLE PUBLISHERS
Kingston • Miami

First published in Jamaica, 2011 by

Ian Randle Publishers

11 Cunningham Avenue

Box 686

Kingston 6

www.ianrandlepublishers.com

© 2011 Cynthia Nelson

National Library of Jamaica Cataloguing-in-Publication Data

Nelson, Cynthia

    Tastes like home : My Caribbean cookbook / Cynthia Nelson

    p. : ill. ; cm.

Includes index

ISBN 978-976-637-519-5 (pbk)

Cookery, Caribbean

I   Title

641.59729   dc 22

Props and Food Styling by Cynthia Nelson

All photographs © 2011 Cynthia Nelson

Cover and Book Design by Ian Randle Publishers

Printed and Bound in Malaysia

Contents

Foreword • ix

Acknowledgements • xi

Introduction • xiii

Generic Ingredients Guide • xv

Part 1 – Food Memoir • 1

Home is Where the Flavour is • 3

Craving the Taste • 5

Me and My Mauby • 7

Market'n Skills • 10

Making Roti – No Longer Stressful • 13

Mothers Make Memories • 16

Backyard Discovery • 18

The Prize in My Rice • 20

Proper Food • 22

Making a New Dish • 25

Nothing Sweeter than Salt fish • 28

Discovering Different Dhals • 30

What I'm Eating • 33

The Many Ways of Okra • 36

Oh, to be a Kid Again • 39

Nuts for Coconuts • 42

Me and Eggplants • 44

I Like it Like That • 47

Gimme My Plantains • 49

The Laws of Tea • 52

Feasting at Festivals • 54

Time for Conkies • 57

Gets Better with Age • 60

Christmas Rituals • 63

I Like it Hot! Hot! Hot! • 66

The Essence of Choka • 69

A Golden Love for the Golden apple • 71

Hard at Work • 73

Two Ingredients: One Love • 76

My True Love – Curry • 79

A New National Dish? • 81

Holi Hai! • 84

It's All About the Bakes • 86

An Acquired Taste • 89

Part 2 – Recipes • 91

Good at Breakfast • 93

Entrées & Special Occasions • 125

Condiments & Sides • 201

Snacks & Drinks • 223

Sweet Treats • 263

How-to-Guide • 319

Glossary • 329

Index • 331

For Susan

Foreword

I am a Guyanese American living in a small college town in the American mid-west who returns to his Caribbean home with some regularity. One of the joys of my return trips to the Caribbean is the region's food. These memories fortify me during winters and the other moments of despair experienced by immigrants.

For the past three and a half years, I have kept a weekly date with Cynthia Nelson's column "Tastes Like Home" in the on-line version of Guyana's *Stabroek News*. I find the columns educational. They reinforce and nourish my Caribbeanness. The vividness of the prose and the excellent photographs that accompany these columns rekindle my memory and always leave a good flavour in my mouth. In some cases these columns have introduced me to new foods and encouraged me to try them. Such has been the case with her recipe for sautéed banana flowers. I am so happy that Cynthia is bringing her body of work together in this publication.

Tastes Like Home is destined to become an important work on Caribbean cultural expression. Food is one of the significant manifestations of Caribbean creativity. The foods we eat are homage to the creativity of our ancestors who had to struggle with food shortages, poor cuts, and inadequate storage facilities. As Cynthia Nelson has shown over the past several years, our ancestors have created a distinctive and delicious world-class cuisine. This creativity has continued across generations, and this book is a celebration.

Contemporary Caribbean cuisine integrates culinary memories and practices from old-world sending societies in Africa, Asia, and Europe with the resources and techniques of the Americas. In *Tastes Like Home*, Cynthia provides a personalised and eloquent journey through this history. The book also serves as a survey of what is the current and guide for what is emerging in Caribbean society. In *Tastes Like Home,* Cynthia Nelson has also made the case that Caribbean cuisine helps to maintain linkages between Caribbean people in Diaspora and their home societies. It also helps to win new friends for the Caribbean.

The memoir style used by Cynthia also provides an insight into the way culinary traditions are developed and shared in the Caribbean. Follow the shopping guides and the recipes and you will be connected with the extended Caribbean family and the joy of preparing and sharing a meal. You can hear and feel in this book the pleasure that comes from experiencing Caribbean food in the home and outdoors. Cynthia's book extends Austin Clark's *Pig Tails n' Breadfruit*—a pioneering work on the Caribbean culinary tradition.

Tastes Like Home is a valuable text and contributes to our understanding of the emergence of the Caribbean people. It reaffirms our common heritage and identifies the common emerging destiny. This publication joins S.R. R. Allsopp's, *Dictionary of Caribbean English Usage* as a pivotal statement on our Caribbean identity.

Vibert C. Cambridge, Ph.D.
Professor, School of Media Arts and Studies
Ohio University
Athens, OH 45701
November 1, 2008

Acknowledgements

Almost from the beginning of my weekly *Tastes Like Home* writings, I have been encouraged to write a cookbook. I've received many emails with the word "urgent" in the subject line from people desperately saying, "I cannot locate your cookbook!" only for me to have to tell them that I don't have one. What moved me however were the countless messages I read from second and third generations of people of Caribbean parentage wanting to learn more about the foods of their parents' home. Also instrumental in my writing of *Tastes Like Home,* the cookbook, has been the men and women married to spouses of Caribbean heritage who'd write often requesting recipes to surprise their mates or to share with their children. So, when I received an offer to write this book, I knew there and then that nothing would give me more joy than to share the tastes of my home.

Tastes Like Home – the column, the photography, the blog, this book – would not have been possible without the unconditional and unwavering love, support, encouragement, dedication and editorial eyes of my dear friend Susan. There were times when I felt that the task of this book was too much and that I'd never finish it but she was always around, cheering me on. Thank you Susan, I hope I can do the same for you some day.

Thanks Mommy for letting me stand at your side and watch as you prepared our meals daily. And what delicious meals and traditions you passed on. I am forever grateful. I love you.

Auntie Betty, your adventurous spirit in and out of the kitchen has been infectious and utterly inspiring. My life is richer because of you. I miss Uncle Freddy.

I'd like to thank my editor at *Stabroek News,* Cheryl Springer for sharing the vision and being a fan of *Tastes Like Home.* Thanks for your professionalism and your friendship.

Thanks to Christine Randle Wray and the dedicated team at Ian Randle Publishers for transforming my words, thoughts and photographs into a book that I hope will bring pleasure and joy to many.

My friends Bhavana Padiyath, Stella Ramsaroop, Suganya Balasubramanian, Sue Gordon, Tuty Alexander and Jennifer Sweeny-Tookes, I thank you all for making the time in your already busy lives to offer invaluable feedback on this book. Oh, I need to add here a special thank you, again, to Susan for all the hand-modelling. With the exception of filling the dhal puri dough, my gal pal was kind and patient enough to model for me while I took the photographs. I had her grating coconuts, clapping hot roti straight from the tawah....Can you imagine if I had to pay her how staggering the bill would be?!

Finally my heartfelt thanks to the many faithful readers of my column and blog, www.tasteslikehome.org your comments, support and encouragement have been motivating and inspiring. Your input will continue to inform my work. Thank you!

Introduction

This book is a gift from my kitchen to the kitchens of Caribbean people who want to remember the tastes of home, and also to the kitchens of non-Caribbean people who are interested in learning a little something about the rich diversity of Caribbean life and Caribbean food.

I have always been amazed about how much of our history is told in the recipes we swap with each other. As I have talked with people all over the world about Caribbean food they always seem surprised about the cultural diversity of our region. Long before the trendy term "fusion food" was coined, we were cooking and eating a fused cuisine. Our culinary heritage is, in part, shaped by our colonial history. Our fore-parents who came to these shores, whether as masters, servants or slaves, brought with them their food cultures. The broad range of these cultures is evident in our cuisine today. We are quite literally, a rich melting pot of African, British, Chinese, Dutch, French, Indian, Indigenous, Portuguese, Spanish and other cuisines. As you read this book you will see these culinary influences, and as you try the recipes in this book you will be able to savour the world in our cuisine.

I have also been constantly amazed by how much our connections with each other are renewed and strengthened when we sit down around a table and enjoy the meals we grew up with. Ask anyone who has travelled what they miss most about home and they will say, "The food!" And that is exactly what I missed most about living away from my homeland, Guyana. Now, I have only moved from one part of the Caribbean to other parts of the region. Nevertheless there were tastes of Guyana I missed even as I was creating a new home and revelling in the new tastes of my new home in Barbados. As I have embarked on my journeys and corresponded with Caribbean people living throughout the region and all over the world I found that my experiences, though very much mine, were far from unique. Each of us told our biography through our taste memories, through the dishes that had been handed down to us by our parents, through the new ingredients and cooking methods we learnt as we traveled.

My own taste memories and recipe creations were the inspiration for my weekly newspaper column *Tastes Like Home* and now for this book. In the first half of this book I have gathered together a collection of some of these columns. They're often personal memories that provide the reader with greater insight into Caribbean food and Caribbean life. Many focus on a particular ingredient. For example you will find out about the myriad of ways we use okra, and which type of plantain works for which type of recipe. Some focus on special festivals. Christmas, Diwali, Eid are just three festivals that immediately show how diverse the region is and I'll tell you a little something about the joys of being able to celebrate all of these festivals. Many of the memoirs focus on a particular dish or a variety of dishes. And in telling you about choka, or Chinese cake, or pepperpot I'll share with you the importance of these dishes to Caribbean life and culture. You will also get the opportunity to meet my family, my mom Barbara, my sister Pat, my brother Eon, my Aunties Golin and Betty, my late Uncle Freddy, my cousin Shantie, even the newest member of our family, little Ethan. These are people I love and so, because the story of food is always the story of love, it is obvious that these people are up front and centre in my stories about Caribbean food.

In the second half of the book I have collected a range of Caribbean recipes. In thinking about which recipes to put in this book I have tended to include the recipes for dishes that my Caribbean friends have said "Hey Cyn, my mum used to make this, but I never got a recipe, help me out nuh!" and for dishes which my friends from other parts of the world have read about in my columns and have wanted to try. Hopefully each and every one of you will try these recipes and savor the dishes that appear on Caribbean tables.

For me, the best part about being a foodie is sharing – sharing my life through food. And cooking for others is about baring your soul, letting down your guard, opening yourself – something that is not always easy.... This book is your invitation to my table, where family and friends gather to swap stories, gaff (Guyanese term for having a chat and reminiscing), and to revel in the tastes of my Caribbean home.

Generic Ingredients Guide

In the Caribbean we are fortunate to get fresh produce daily; therefore, most if not all of the ingredients suggested for use in this book are of the fresh variety that means in particular, the vegetables, herbs and coconuts. You will notice that certain generic terms are used for some ingredients; this is so that the cook using this book can adapt those ingredients to the ones they regularly use in their kitchens. The recipes were written with the following ingredients in mind.

Oil – Canola oil or vegetable oil

Hot pepper – scotch bonnet variety

Butter – unsalted, unless otherwise stated

Lard – vegetable shortening

Tomatoes – beefsteak or salad variety

Potatoes – Yukon gold or Idaho

Sugar – brown sugar (Demerara sugar), however granulated sugar can be substituted unless the recipe specifically states which sugar to use

Bay leaves – fresh

Shrimp – baby shrimp (small); use whatever size you have available to you

Ginger – fresh root ginger

Onions – Spanish, white or red

Part 1

Food Memoir

Home is Where the Flavour is

Twas the season – my bags were packed and I was heading home to Guyana for Christmas, my first in eight years. I armed myself with a list, not of Christmas gifts, but of the food and dishes I wanted to eat, to taste, to re-awaken memories and to reconnect with my homeland.

For a foodie or food-enthusiast such as myself, going home for Christmas was a journey of food appreciation and re-discovery. I wanted to absorb everything in sight. I wanted to go to the source – the markets, to see, smell and taste what freshness is like. I wanted to visit the eating places I remembered such as Coal Pot, Salt and Pepper and Arapaima, now called The Main Street Qik Serve.

One Sunday morning I went shopping with my brother, Eon, to Bourda Market. He took me to the stall he buys from regularly. Back in the day, I remember always asking the price of things before I made my purchase but now as I found myself caught up in the glory of the abundance price seemed to be less of a factor. Issued with a list from my mother and sister, I filled the shopping bags forgetting about poundage, bundles or units;

I even wanted to get things that were *not* on the list. I found myself caressing the bunch of red-head eschallots inhaling the gentle onion flavour; stroking the length of the fine, green bora; rubbing the white-skinned eggplant and fighting the urge to grab the sweet-fig banana and eat it. I did not want to leave the market. It was an ironic moment for me because before moving abroad, I never liked going to the market and now here I was standing, reluctant to leave.

In making my food wish list, there were some things I had not remembered to put down and duck curry was one of them. So the week following my jaunt to Bourda Market, my sister, Pat and I set out for Mon Repos Market on the East Coast to get some fresh duck that would have just been killed, plucked and roasted until almost black. As I got out of the car, my nose tingled with the deep, delicious, smoky scent of roasted poultry. It's a scent that I associate with the country areas of Guyana – it conjured images of clay and mud firesides with roaring fires, large blacked pots boiling and sada roti cooking. I breathed in deeply. Men were busy plucking chickens and ducks, while others were roasting the birds over the open flames of a makeshift grill – the sizzle and crackle adding to the liveliness of the atmosphere. We stopped at the first stall, bought a couple of ducks and waited patiently as the butcher gutted and chopped them up. It's true – we eat with our eyes, while my tummy was not yet filled with the duck curry, my heart was filled just standing there taking in the sight, sounds and smells of home.

Next came "the night of three cook-ups", at least that's what I am calling it. Each Old Year's night and every Christmas Eve night, my mother makes cook-up rice, with the works: tripe, beef, pigtail, sometimes adding chicken. My brother and sister continue the tradition in their respective homes. Now, in order to remain in good favour with my brother and sister, I am not going to discuss which one was better. By mid-afternoon, my brother had finished cooking and so his was the first I ate – all beef with red beans along with some steamed okras. It was delicious. In the evening about eight o'clock, I ate my mother's cook-up; man dah woman should market de ting and teach a class on how to cook cook-up rice, de ting taste wicked – black eye peas with the works. I was a little worried because my sister was coming over later and bringing some of her cook-up for me and I was full, full, full. However, as the evening wore on I found I had room for a little more, so, about midnight I ate some of my sister's food: pigeon peas with chicken and salt meat – another winner. My mother has taught her children well and *she* has *not* lost *her* touch.

I'd forgotten the about the constant feeding that takes place when you go home. You could just finish eating a plate of food, just finish swallowing the last mouthful and someone asks, "You want some more? Are you sure? Eat nuh! You know you don't get dis kind ah food steady! Look, we gat…. And they will list a set of things. Something on the list will catch your attention and before you know it – you're eating, *again*.

Of the 27 items on my food wish list, I managed to eat only 10 but I ate other things that were not on the list such as katahar, hassar, Chinese fried rice and chow mein. It was impossible to eat everything on the list in 11 days.

Packing up to leave was difficult, I knew I could not take all the food in Guyana, but you can't blame a girl for trying. I put a few things in my suitcase: hassar, gilbaka, grey snapper, katahar, cheese rolls, patties, pine-tarts, black pudding and achar. As I said, just a few things to keep the memories alive for a little while longer. Maybe I should start making my list for my next trip.

► Cook-up Rice, 137–139
► Hassar Curry, 160–161
► Katahar Curry, 165–166

Craving the Taste

The aroma of 'married man's pork' (sweet basil) and thyme fills the kitchen as I lift the lid of the steamer. Gently, I place the black pudding I had reheated onto a plate, slicing it and adding some sour. It is as fresh as the day it was delivered – a little over a week ago. I sit down to eat.

I put the first piece into my mouth and as I chew, I cast my mind back to my mother's house where everyone would gather, each with a little plate full of black pudding, the house would be quiet as mouths were full and chewing. Every now and then, a comment was made about how good the black pudding tastes; someone asking if there's more; people eyeing the plates of those, like me, who are slow eaters. If you spot someone staring, you pull the plate closer to your chest.

I laugh now as I put another piece of black pudding into my mouth because I did not have to share mine with anyone. I can eat to my heart's content. But by the third piece, the black pudding is losing its taste – not that it has gotten cold or that it is flavourless but because the atmosphere that made it so attractive, so tasty, and so desirable was no longer there. In some way, it had lost its appeal.

In many ways, taste is relative; taste is subjective. Taste is *not* just the physical reaction to something in our mouths or the sensation created by having something in our mouths, often, taste is atmospheric, environmental and yes, psychological.

The creation of a distinctive mood (atmospheric) influences our taste. The surroundings and conditions in which we live and operate (environmental) contribute to our sense of taste. The way our minds function (psychological) impacts our taste. And these are the factors that contribute to our missing food from home. Let's face it, in New York there are large West Indian Markets, London, and yes in many other cities where there are large populations of Caribbean people. If you're a Guyanese living in Trinidad it is *almost* as if you're home. Here in Barbados, we can get quite a few staples from home. What is it then that makes those of us living abroad crave the foods of home? It is the atmosphere and the environment that plays on our minds.

The black pudding and souse is spicier when you're having it at your favourite "black pudding lady" surrounded by friends and drinking a beer. The dhal is tastier when you're drinking it at Shanta's. The fried fish is hot and fresh when eating it at the White Shop after work. If you live in the country, there is nothing quite like sitting on the steps and eating. Get the picture? It is the company we long for, the shop at the corner, the vendor that sells only on Saturdays and the family we miss.

I always marvelled at some things:

Have you ever noticed how the food you buy as takeout tastes different than if you were eating it right there at the restaurant, shop or snackette? I remember how much sweeter, juicer and refreshing the cane juice would be at Bourda Market after lugging around shopping bags for about an hour; the juice we ordered to take home never seemed to taste the same way.

At school we would buy green mango with pepper and salt and this thing tasted so good. One mango never seemed to be enough and if you shared it with a friend, there was always a debate about who was going to get the seed. The salt and pepper was like no other – raw pepper ground into the salt so you could see flecks here and there. Mommy would buy green mangoes for us. My sister, Pat, would prepare the pepper and salt (often with pepper sauce). We'd race to peel a mango and after a slice each, we would give up on the mango – it did not taste as nice as the "mango lady's" at school.

Then there was the Chinese fried rice and cucumber. Whenever we bought Chinese food the quarrel was always over the cucumber – not the meat or the rice but the slice of cucumber. We always ended up dividing it between us. Being the smart women that we are, we decided that whenever we were going to order Chinese food that we would cut up cucumbers in advance, that way we would not have to delay the process of eating. The food would arrive and we would each have more than enough cucumbers but did it taste the same as the one that came with the food? No way!

In some ways, we can never perfectly capture those wonderful tastes from our past. They are memories caught up in the moment, in the place, in the people. And that is true whether we live home in Guyana or Jamaica, or we live abroad. Still, we *can* savour those memories – in our minds. And we can enjoy the adventure of making new taste memories – such as, where is the new hang out snack spot in GT? Who is the new "souse lady"? Or what is it like to explore the tastes of our new homes in Boston, Brixton or Bridgetown? And what is it like to experience good ole Guyanese black pudding whilst sitting in my apartment in Barbados? Well that last one I can answer right now, excuse me a moment…Mmmmm, just as I thought, it's delicious!

► Sautéed Bora and Shrimps, 188–189
► Sautéed Squash, 194–195

Me and My Mauby

When last did you have a nice big glass of ice-cold, home-made mauby – the frosty beads of water on the glass from the coldness, the ice twirling in the glass, the heady scent of the ripened bark mixed with clove and cinnamon, the slight froth at the top indicating that it's been properly brewed? When last did you have such a drink of mauby?

Mauby was the one beverage I requested my mother make for me on my recent trip back home. Before I even reached Guyana, the bark was boiled with the cinnamon, clove and her secret ingredient – cracked nutmeg. She'd spent time brewing the mauby daily and sweetening it until it was right, perfect, and *ripe*.

I took my first sip and then I titled my head back and drank non-stop until the glass was empty. "Mommy, this mauby tasted soooo gooood; you make the best mauby." She smiled, modestly. My mom gets shy with compliments, although her mauby-making skills are almost legendary.

I remember as a child the fantastic annual fairs we had at Sacred Heart Church. Mommy used to be in charge of one of the food stalls and she was also one of the main persons responsible for making the mauby and ginger beer. They would be bottled in recycled sterilised rum bottles and when the golden sun of the afternoon shone on them, they looked like liquid gold.

The mauby and ginger beer would be the first items to be sold out. Sometimes, only the ginger beer managed to make it to the fair because people would be calling at least two days leading up to the fair to reserve their bottles of mauby. It was *that* good and in such high demand.

The Knights of the Blessed Sacrament (KBS) boys, (altar boys) loved to come and visit "Auntie Barbara" because she always had treats for them. Gavin, Matthew and Dexter were the regulars. On weekends mommy made mauby, coconut buns, sweet bread and cassava pone (whenever she could motivate my sister or I to grate the cassava).

Mauby has always been a big part of Guyanese food culture. There was a shop on Lamaha Street, between Carmichael and Main streets, opposite the then Transport Board offices that used to sell mauby daily. The owner was Mr Balgobin but he was always referred to as the Mauby Shop Man and his shop, known as the Mauby Shop. I remember passing the shop and seeing it overcrowded with people, mostly men I think. Some would be sitting on stools inside the shop, others, standing outside with large plastic tumblers filled with mauby in one hand and holding in the other, tennis roll and cheese or dhal puri or cassava ball or egg ball.

By mid-afternoon all the mauby would be sold out. I know this because on my way home from school I would stop at the shop hoping to buy some of this famous mauby but alas, there would be none. I used to stare up at the large oak barrel with a tap attached to the bottom wondering how all that mauby could be finished.

I can't recall when, but I know I did eventually get to drink the mauby from The Mauby Shop.

What is mauby? What is this thing, this drink that quenches our thirst in such a flavourful and satisfying manner?

Mauby is made from the bark of a small tree, *Colubrina elliptica*, and grows in many parts of the Northern Caribbean, such as Puerto Rico and Guatemala, and South Florida.

As popular as mauby is in the Caribbean, for many, it is an acquired taste. It is the *finish,* the after taste, of the drink with its slight bitter taste that turns some people off. The key, I believe, to making good mauby lies in the ripening of the drink. In other words, allowing it enough time to develop its flavour and brewing it daily. It is also important to know when to stop the process of ripening so that the mauby does not become exceedingly bitter; two days, a full 48 hours, is good time to strain the mauby and refrigerate it to be served.

The best mauby recipe is the one that has been handed down to you or the one you got from the person whose mauby you enjoy the best. People put a variety of things in their mauby, I've seen some recipes that include putting orange peel, star anise and Angostura® Bitters. I've noticed also that immediately after the steeping process, some people add some of the cooled liquid (their desired strength) to water, sweeten with sugar, add ice and serve right away. Everybody does things their own way I guess.

Mauby syrup is a big seller here in Barbados however, even eating establishments that offer mauby on the menu often serve the syrup version. It will never taste the same as home-made but at least you will have some essence of it. I'm not knocking it because for years, that's what I've been drinking.

The trip home changed it for me though, after tasting the spicy, almost fruity like flavour of home-made mauby, I find it difficult to drink the syrup version. So I got on the phone last weekend and had my mother talk me through the process with her recipe.

I started my process last Saturday midday, strained it off on Monday evening and enjoyed a glass of my own home-made mauby on Tuesday.

This was my first attempt; it is not as good as my mother's but its better than any I've had in years. I won't make it every weekend but I will make it once a month perfecting my mauby-making skills. Who knows? Maybe one day I'll bottle the stuff.

Thanks mom, for the recipe and the memories.

▶ Mauby, 250–251
▶ Cassava Pone, 264–265
▶ Pound Cake, 300–301

Market'n Skills

When I was younger I never liked going to the market. Supermarkets? Yes, but the market, uh uh. And yet, every week, my mother would send me to the market. I swear the woman was punishing me.

What was it about going to the market I didn't like? Well, I had bag issues. After shopping, the bag was really heavy and I always walked home. Walking slowly, I would shift the bag from one hand to the next. Sometimes I wondered if I would ever reach home and, as I continued to walk, I would daydream about later in the day when I would be curled up reading a book off in some imaginary faraway place where I would not have to go to the market!

I found market bags to be large and unattractive and I don't know which was worse – having to walk with a bag to the market or dragging the heavy bag home. Both had their own degrees of distress for me. I didn't like holding things in my hand and, after all, I was an attractive young lady and you never could tell when a young man might whistle at me. So I used to fold the bag as small as I could, trying to make it as tiny as a change purse, but it never worked.

Another reason I did not like going to the market had to do with the vendors. They probably figured because I was young, I did not know anything about shopping. So, they never let me choose any of the produce and would sometimes give me sub-standard things, even though I'd point to what I want. I'd reach home and get a lecture, *again*, about what to look for when shopping for vegetables or fish or shrimp: Tomatoes should be firm, never to be squeezed, only caressed gently to find any of the faulty soft spots. The skin of an eggplant should be smooth not wrinkled; the pumpkin – thick and deep-orange in colour, not thin and pale. The "white-belly" shrimp should be glossy, shiny and pink, not swollen and white; the gills of fish should be pink-red, the flesh firm and the skin glistening with its natural elements, perhaps even breathing.

My mom always had "rules" when it came to market shopping. "Don't stop and buy at the first stall", she'd say meaning that, invariably, the first stall would have the item overpriced "to catch people just like you." Mommy's advice was to walk around, making a mental note of which vendor's produce looked good and the price. She told me to only start buying as I made my way back to the front of the market.

In retrospect, I understand the wisdom of her advice.

Not buying at the first stall provided an opportunity to peruse what was on offer, ask a question, and get more information without committing yourself.

I learnt to shop *and* pack – I'd place the heavier items at the bottom of the bag and the more delicate things such as tomatoes, eschallots etc. at the top.

Since I'd start shopping from the back of the market, and the bag got increasingly heavier, I would also be approaching the entrance to make my exit home.

Here's yet another reason I did not like going to the market, after shopping and walking home with the heavy bag, you had to clean the fish and shrimp you bought! Already tired, you had more work to do. So I'd help to "pick shrimps" (clean shrimp) and clean and cut-up a variety of fish. I learnt how to peel and shred katahar, seed and cut karaila, sprinkle with salt and squeeze it to extract the bitterness. I am grateful that I know how to do those things; they are skills I could only have learnt by doing

and being in an environment where such chores existed.

Here in Barbados, I don't go to the market often. I go to the supermarkets. The times I've gone to the market, however, (as recently as last weekend) I found that I could not employ one of my mother's major rules of not stopping to buy at the first stall. Here's why.

At weekly markets, such as the one here in Barbados, timing is important; demand is more than supply and relationships can mean everything.

Arriving at 6.30 a.m. so that you can get all the things you need is a must, it's amazing the difference that 15 minutes later can make. It could mean no tomatoes, no eschallots, no bora or having to settle for something that is not as fresh.

There will always be more demand than supply at weekly markets. The one I go to is serviced by a small number of farmers who try their best to cater to a city with a growing population. So, I throw out my mother's advice about not shopping at the first stall – when I arrive and I see that the first stall has one of items on my list, I check it for quality and make my purchase right away, I do not have the luxury of walking around and then coming back to buy. Of course, it would be different if I had a relationship with the vendor, in other words, if we were friends or if I were a regular customer.

You see, once you make a connection with vendors, life can be good; as a regular customer, you're special. Being special means you are guaranteed certain things. Vendors, now your friends, will turn away *new* customers and tell them that "all done" while there are two parcels of the requested items clearly in sight!

I miss not having a daily market. Even if we had a daily market I would probably still shop weekly, I have a hectic schedule. Nevertheless, a daily market offers you some things a weekly market can't – you get abundance and variety and you don't have to rush out of bed early on a Saturday morning after a hard week of work just to get to the market before everything has gone.

I don't know if I like going to the market any more now than when I was younger. I know what I *do* like about a market – the freshness of the food, the education from conversing with the vendors, the sounds, and the sense of community. Supermarkets and mega markets are the rave these days, they beat markets on convenience every time but if most of us are honest, we would prefer that our food come from the butcher, the fisher folk, or the vegetable and ground provision vendor at the market.

Making Roti –
No Longer Stressful

In almost every cook's life there is one dish or one food that tests them in ways unimaginable. The preparation, which might seem simple and easy to those who've mastered it, is often a source of frustration and anxiety for those who've spent months and even years trying to *at least* make it resemble what the dish is supposed to be like.

For me, roti was that food – paratha roti or oil-roti as it is known to us Guyanese. Despite the variety of things I could already make as a child and teenager, my inability, to make a proper roti meant that I had not yet earned my cooking stripes. It was the test that I had to pass. And I was determined to not just pass the test but to excel at making that elusive, ideal roti. The ideal roti meant that it should be rolled to a perfect circle and not in the shapes of the maps of the world; the ideal roti should be cooked so that it has only a few tiny brown spots that flake and crack as you clap; and I, as the ideal roti maker, should be able to clap the roti straight from the tawah to release the leafy layers that make it fluffy.

The first phase of my roti-making test had to do with kneading the dough. When I first started, this was the part I hated the most. I had to knead the dough not only to make it soft and pliable, but so that all the flour in the bowl would be fully incorporated. In other words, there should not be any remnants of the mixture; the bowl must be clean with just the ball of dough. I never seemed to be able to get this right no matter how hard I tried. And, like any good teacher, my mom used to inspect my work.

As I was gradually getting better, my mom would leave me alone in the kitchen to make the dough for the roti and I have to shamefully admit here that I would cheat. I would make the big ball of dough, take it out of the bowl and scrape all the remaining bits of mixture and dry flour, discard it, put the dough back into the bowl and continue to knead in my perfectly clean bowl.

Eventually, after much practice and watching my mom, aunt and cousin every opportunity I got, I was able to knead the dough incorporating all the flour and bits.

Armed with this confidence, I eagerly volunteered whenever I visited my aunt's house to help make the roti but my cousin

Shantie, who was masterful at making roti in her family, did not trust me to knead the flour so I was relegated to oiling the roti (something I already did at home). This was my favourite part of the roti-making process anyway. There was no pressure to roll in particular shapes and I guess I loved this part the most because it was like playing with play-dough. All you had to do was roll the dough, rub some oil on the surface, make a cut from the center to one end of the dough, roll it to form a layered cone cup, punch down the pointed end and voila, done. Another test passed.

Still, one of *the* most trying times was yet to come – rolling the dough to form a perfect circle in order to cook the roti. This stage, for me, was fraught with frustration, disappointment and a feeling of inadequacy. Why could I not get the dough rolled round?! It often came out square or in shapes like pieces of a jigsaw puzzle. I watched my mother, my aunt and my cousin over and over again. Sometimes I came close to getting the circle but not often enough.

In the latter part of my teenage years, I rebelled, debating with my mom the necessity of having the roti rolled round when it was going to be torn and eaten anyway; it is not like the shape of the roti would change the taste. Boy, who tell me to say that? My mother lectured me for weeks. Stage not yet passed.

I was willing to give up the whole roti-making venture at this stage but my mother was determined that I know how to make roti so we ploughed on to the next stage – actual cooking. I think she figured that I'd get the round-rolling as I continued to make roti.

The main thing about the actual cooking process was heat control. And it's really a matter of personal choice and standards set by individual families. Most of my family likes the roti to have just a few tiny light-brown spots that crack and flake when you clap the roti. Others prefer the roti not to have any spots at all. I like it both ways. I passed this stage after a number of trials and errors. I always used the first roti as a sort of tester to gauge the heat. I still do.

One of the really intimidating parts of roti-making was clapping the roti. While I had watched in awe the many times that the women in my family would use their bare hands to lift the roti from the hot tawah and start clapping it mid-air, I was never enthusiastic about doing it myself. As a matter of fact, I had no desire to do that part; but alas, if I were to earn my roti-making stripes and by extension by cooking stripes, I had to learn to clap roti.

Thankfully, my mom let me use the spatula to turn the roti and to remove it from the tawah, she also gave me room to let the roti rest a few seconds before I would begin clapping. The first time I clapped a piping hot roti, I swear that my hands were going to be swollen, burnt and marked forever – they weren't. As time went by I learnt that I only had to make about three claps and that would be good enough to release the fluffy layers. I learnt the importance of not letting the roti cool before clapping it – the air trapped in the roti would dissipate without the layers separating.

Today, I am happy to report that yours truly has earned her full cooking stripes from the family, especially my roti-making stripes. As I stated above, I have mastered the art of kneading the dough with the bowl being clean and void of any remnants (without cheating). Oiling the roti is still my favourite part of the process; and rolling the dough to make a perfect circle – why, I won't have it any other way, thanks to my continuous practice. The trick is to make a round disk of the dough before rolling it, flouring the rolling surface really well and turning the dough at 90-degree angles only and flipping it over also.

So adept have I become at making roti I have even started teaching a Bajan friend of mine how to make it. We'll see how she passes the tests.

▶ Paratha Roti, 176–179
▶ Sautéed Pumpkin and Shrimps, 192–193

Mothers Make Memories

The month of May brings Mothers' Day and Mothers' Day brings meals…and memories.

I believe that Mothers' Day is everyday. What perhaps makes the day we *choose* to mark as her day different or special, is that we try to relieve our mums of all household duties for that day, especially the cooking.

Ask anyone what they're doing for mothers' day and they'll tell you that apart from buying mum a present, (often to be used in the kitchen) they're taking her out to lunch with the family. That's the centrepiece of the day, the meal.

But why is having a meal on Mothers' Day so special? What does it really mean or say? Why can't an extravagant gift be enough? Because a meal is a symbol of love, it signifies family and togetherness and we often identify one person that embodies this – a mother.

In her book, *The Surprising Power of Family Meals*, Mariam Weinstein, says, "A family meal is important because it gives children reliable access to their parents. It provides anchoring for everyone's day. It emphasizes the importance of the family, nonverbally." I think when we gather for family meals, such as on Mothers' Day it reminds us that we are a part of something special – a family.

Mothers are remarkable creatures of resourcefulness, especially in the kitchen. They can stretch, adjust, "and make things do." Growing up, I'd watch my mother add potatoes to a stew to 'stretch the meat' or add vegetables to scrambled eggs to make us feel as if we're having a lot - or maybe, that was her smart way of getting us to eat our vegetables, hmmmm….Such ingenuity is not just born out of the need to provide but also to nurture and love.

Mothers spend endless hours shopping, chopping, mixing, baking… all with one aim – to nourish their loved ones, body and soul.

My mother always made everything from scratch. In those days, not many things came in cans, were pre-cut, already shelled or marinated. Rotisserie chickens were not being sold in supermarkets, there was no sandwich-deli section, in-store cafeterias or any of the conveniences that the modern day cook can fall back on. She worked and then headed home to cook.

At meal times, we catch up on each other's lives, we argue, we make up, we advise, we console, we give thanks, we share, we toast one another, we remember why we like or don't like these gatherings, memories are recalled. It's the memories that we cherish, the memories that live on.

I remember...

When it was my 7th birthday and I was allowed to sit at the head of the table

When my sister said that she was changing her religion, and my mum almost choked (being a staunch Catholic and all)

When my mum made my favourite meal *(which at the time was fried rice and baked chicken)* because I'd come first in class

When we all cried at the table because it was the first Christmas since our parents divorce and my brother was promoted to sit at the head of the table

When my siblings and I toasted our mom on the great job she had done as a single parent

I remember when...

Meal time is bonding time; it is the glue that keeps the family together. And so every Mother's Day that families gather for that special meal, at home or in a restaurant, what they are doing is toasting, celebrating, congratulating, cuddling, and loving the woman who has helped to make their journey through life, memorable.

Happy Mothers' Day Mommy!

Backyard Discovery

It often takes being away from home to appreciate some things, particularly some foods. In this case, I am talking about the versatile breadfruit. It has never been a favourite of mine nor have I ever craved it. In fact, I knew little of the many ways it can be prepared until I came to Barbados.

I'll never forget the morning I turned up at work and found the newsroom, studios and editing suites empty, not a member of staff in sight. "Is there an impromptu staff meeting?" I wondered. I checked the conference room, empty. I came down the stairs, and headed to the kitchen to make myself a cup a tea. As I turned the corner towards the kitchen I could hear their voices. It was like a party. People were standing, sitting, some with glasses of soft drinks in their hands, others with cups of tea and coffee but what caught my eyes was what they had in their other hand – something the colour of cream, I noticed that some people were sprinkling salt on it and eating it.

Mr Cooke, the security guard came up to me and offered me a piece of what everyone else was enjoying. The outer skin of the piece he held out to me was jet black but the mound of flesh, golden yellow. I didn't know what it was but I stretched out my hand nevertheless. "What is it?" I asked. "Roasted breadfruit," he said. I never knew breadfruit could be roasted. Mr Cooke sprinkled some salt on my piece of breadfruit and encouraged me to take a bite.

The flesh in my mouth was warm, soft, creamy, slightly sweet and salty. The smokiness of the charred skin added to the experience as I brought the roasted breadfruit to my mouth again. "Cookie, (that was our nickname for Mr Cooke) I have never had this before and it tastes so good." He smiled and walked away. That was my introduction to one of the many ways breadfruit can be cooked and eaten.

Prior to this experience, the only ways I had eaten breadfruit were boiled and sliced or as chips. Soon, I would learn that breadfruit can also be pickled, mashed, and creamed.

And, though I'm yet to experience it, I've also heard about this great way in which Barbadians roast and serve breadfruit which is different from how Mr Cooke did it for us at the office. The breadfruit is slowly roasted on an open flame, cored and butter or salt meat inserted so that the added flavours permeate the flesh of the breadfruit. I can't wait to try it this way.

The breadfruit was brought to the Caribbean not under the most propitious circumstances. It was brought here by Lieutenant William Bligh at the behest of our colonial masters in their quest for cheap high-energy food to feed the enslaved. Bligh, of course, was at the center of the infamous Mutiny on the Bounty that has been made into many books and films. This wonderful fruit, now an integral part of our cuisine, is native to the Malay Peninsula and the Western Pacific Islands. It thrives in the tropics so it grows abundantly in this region and elsewhere.

Breadfruit is rich in starch and is often described as potato-like. It is particularly prized in the Eastern Caribbean Islands where it is boiled, sliced, and served with sautéed salt fish, onions, tomatoes, garlic and fresh herbs. In Guyana, we do a boil and fry – the breadfruit is boiled until cooked yet still firm, and then sautéed with tomatoes and onions. We also like it made into chips. Bajans (a local term for Barbadians) make a really good pickled breadfruit that is served with black pudding and souse. They also make breadfruit coucou (boiled, mashed and creamed). This is different from the Bajan national dish of coucou which is made with cornmeal and okras. Jamaicans like to serve breadfruit roasted and sliced. It's a must-have with the Sunday meal.

Breadfruits can be cooked and eaten green and ripened. When it is green, the fruit is hard and the interior white and starchy. Ripe, it is soft and the inside cream-coloured or slightly yellow. It's the ripe ones that are roasted and made into coucou. The green ones obviously can stand up to the rigors of aggressive boiling, slicing and pickling.

Most of the dishes we make with breadfruit, in these parts, are savoury but while doing research, I also learnt that there are numerous sweet dishes that can be made with the fruit. Again, it's testament to its versatility. For example, the breadfruit can be candied; the Filipinos enjoy it cooked with coconut and sugar. As with any ingredient, there are numerous dishes and methods of preparation that are characteristic to different areas.

Since eating the roasted breadfruit, it has become one of my favourite ways to have it, prior to that, if you had asked me if I like breadfruit I would have had to say no. It just goes to show, if our minds and palates are open just a little more, we may discover a world of flavours and dishes that are right in our own backyard.

It's a tasty world out there, enjoy!

▶ Boiled Breadfruit, 130–131
▶ Fried Salt fish, 110–111
▶ Breadfruit Chips, 231

The Prize in My Rice

It was the first day of January 2006 and I was invited to lunch by some of my Barbadian friends. A feast was set: baked ham and chicken, pot-roasted duck, stewed lamb, pepper-pot, macaroni pie, rice and peas, jug jug, potato salad, coleslaw and garden salad. For dessert: fruit pizza, ice cream, cake, trifle and fresh fruit.

With prayers complete, the hosts ushered all present to form a line and make our way around the table. The woman in front of me gasped as she took a spoon of rice and peas. I glanced up thinking that something was wrong but when I looked at her there was a bright, beautiful smile spread across her face. She leaned over to me and whispered, "I found the prize!" I smiled politely because I had no idea what she was talking about. My eyes followed her hand as she took another spoon of rice and peas and then I saw it: a piece of salt meat, pigtail to be exact. I smiled knowingly.

Rice and peas in Barbados would not be true-true rice and peas without a lil' piece of pigtail in it. Pig-tails – salt-cured, somewhat smokey and full of flavour – are there to impart salt and flavour and is truly prized by us salt-meat lovers.

For as long as I can remember, salt meat – whether it was pigtail or salted beef – has always been viewed as a secret flavour enhancer in foods such as rice and peas, peas and rice, pelau, cook-up rice, oildown, stewed peas and many other Caribbean dishes. I know that some people put it in pepperpot also. What gives this piece of salt meat its prized status is that it is consumed in small quantities because its role is more of a flavour enhancer as opposed to something to be eaten in large quantities such as a regular serving of meat.

One day, last December, while in Guyana, I cooked rice and peas, with pigtail of course. My brother, Eon, called to say that he was passing by for some food. Since I was not going to be around when he visited, I left strict instructions with my mom, "Please tell Eon to ensure that he leaves a piece of pigtail for me!" That's how seriously I take the matter of the prize in my rice. And I am not alone; it is just that I can declare it publicly.

Back here in Barbados, I've have seen women in a kitchen "fight" for the salt meat that was cooked in the rice and peas, eating it before dishing out the food and serving their guests. Just the other day my friend and I were whispering conspiratorially about setting aside the salt meat while serving ourselves at a large gathering she hosted.

I've watched some people "eye" the salt meat in the rice and peas if they come upon it but shy away from taking it, perhaps self-conscious about eating such fare in public.

Since living in Barbados, I've discovered another way that people eat pigtails. They barbeque them!

Rhandi Fitzpatrick owns a popular food stall at the top of Broad Street in the heart of Bridgetown. She does a brisk business of barbeque, especially pigtails, and she told me how she makes her barbequed pigtails. She starts by washing off the salt on the tails and then sets them to boil for approximately one and a half hours. At the end of this first boil, the water is discarded and fresh water added to the pot for another round of boiling. This time however, some sugar is added to the water to help "cut out the salt."

The tails are then drained and patted dry before making their appearance on the grill. They are grilled until completely heated through. (Remember they would have been cured and already cooked after being boiled for at least three hours). An expert brushing with the right amount of a commercial barbeque sauce to which secret spices have been added, is done about three to four times. If you like, a little more sauce can be added when you make your purchase.

The barbequed pig tail is smokey, with just the right amount of salt and a hint of sweetness. The meat literally falls off the bone as a result of the long cooking. Barbequed pigtails are definitely to be had in moderation. It's really good, but it's not good for you if you over do it. Once in a while it's good to treat yourself to one.

When I'm shopping in the supermarket for pigtails for my rice and peas or cook-up rice, I always get the slender ones. I don't like fat pigtails. The meat must be pink (a sign of freshness) and if it's is a little charred from roasting, all the better. When eating it, I particularly like the lower part of the tail.

As Caribbean people, we do love a piece of salt meat. For us it is like real food, simple food, our version of Creole food. I remember going to Stabroek Market back in the day and as soon as you entered the gate that leads to the area where they sell the fish and shrimp, there was a stall on the left hand side that would have this very pink salt meat exhibited for purchase. I was always fascinated by the colour and always wondered why people only bought the meats in small quantities. It was not until years later that I understood the role of salt meat in the food – a prized flavour enhancer. I wonder if that stall is still there…

▶ Rice and Peas, 184–185

Proper Food

Here in the Caribbean when we talk about proper food, food to give you stamina, food to make your muscles strong, we mean eating some good ground provisions. We're talking about cassava, eddoes, sweet potatoes, yams and all those other foods whose fruits grow buried deep in the earth.

This food is proper food because it is given to us from the earth. Yes, yes, yes, yes we know that all the other vegetables and produce are produced by the earth too, but they are grown on trees and vines, whereas these provisions grow in the deep, dark, damp soil. There's something real and true about food you dig from the earth.

My one experience digging for sweet potatoes was many years ago and I'll never forget it. It was during the August holidays and my sister, Pat, and I went to spend some time with one of our aunts, Auntie Golin. She lived at Friendship on the East Bank of Demerara and had a farm. Auntie Golin and her husband used to rear chickens and ducks. They also planted sweet potatoes and lots of vegetables. I remember plucking bora from the tree to put in chow mein and fried rice one day...but I digress. One morning, Auntie Golin decided that we (Pat, me and her children) each would go and get our own breakfast. What this meant was that we would head out to the sweet potato patch and dig up sweet potatoes. Whichever sweet potato we dug up would be what we would have for breakfast. I had no idea how we were supposed to prepare this sweet potato to eat it.

pot to cook. In the meantime, we showered and got ourselves ready for breakfast.

Some of us sat around the table, alright the girls sat around the table and the boys took up various positions in the house and outside by the hammock. I noticed that Auntie Golin was not cutting up anything or frying or stewing anything and I began to wonder how we were going to eat these sweet potatoes.

Soon the sweet potatoes were finished cooking and Pat, and my cousin Sandy and I were the first to receive the sweet potatoes. With a knife, Auntie cut open the sweet potatoes, it was piping hot, the steam forming wisps of smoke. She gave us each a fork, plopped a dollop of butter in the middle of the hot potato and told us to mash and mix the potato with the butter and then eat it. For a kid, it was a treat to watch the butter melting on the hot sweet potato and as I pressed down with the fork each time, the melted butter would drizzle down into the hot flesh of the potato. All I remember is that I had never had anything so creamy and tasty, ever. Thanks for such a delicious memory Auntie Golin.

That day, the simple sweet potato with just a dollop of butter was a perfect food. And the more I think about it, the more I begin to realise that ground provisions generally *are* a perfect type of food – you don't need to eat a lot of it to be satisfied, it sustains you for a very long

I remember being on my hands and knees and digging with all my might and then "finding" a sweet potato – though I'm sure one of my older cousins did the initial digging to help me along. With each of us armed with a sweet potato that we had proudly dug up ourselves we headed back to the house where we washed off the mud from the sweet potatoes. A large pot of water was already boiling. Auntie Golin placed all the sweet potatoes into the time, you never have to worry about storage and quick spoilage, and they are versatile.

No wonder ground provisions are so important to Caribbean cooking. They're important in national dishes. Some ground provisions come together with plantains and coconut milk to make one of our Guyanese national dishes, mettagee. They're also used to make Grenada's national dish, Oildown. Ground provisions are so important that in some Eastern Caribbean countries, you haven't really had you're meal if you haven't had ground provisions.

If I had to pick a particular ground provision as a favourite, it would have to be cassava. There is nothing creamier than a good boiling cassava, not the kind that takes forever to cook and is stringy. I fell in love with cassava while at school. There was a lady there that used to sell the best cassava balls I have ever eaten and then she started to make something called cassava puff; it was the same sort of mixture like the cassava ball but instead of being round it was oblong and the center was filled with sautéed minced beef. It was so good. I also like my cassava boiled and fried (fried with lots of onions, tomatoes and fresh herbs).

I have realised that ground provisions take on different colours and proportions depending on where they are grown. Take Barbados for example, because of the limestone soil, the cassava here is very clean and light skinned. It is also not as thick as the ones in Guyana. The eddoes here are very small, often the size of an egg or a little larger. The sweet potatoes here are particularly tasty. The yams are different, they are huge and the texture not as smooth as the ones in Guyana but they are nevertheless tasty.

All in all, ground provisions are good food, simple food. They might not be very attractive to look at with all the mud stuck to them, the shapes are often strange, some of them are even hairy. But there's nothing like ground provisions when we want to build ourselves up, get a taste of home or get in touch with our roots (pun intended).

▶ **Mettagee, 169–171**

Making a New Dish

Cou-cou

One of the exciting things about living abroad is learning about the foods of the country in which you're living; and there's nothing quite like the thrill of trying to make those dishes in your own kitchen. Ever since coming to live in Barbados I had wanted to learn how to make Cou-cou.

Cou-cou or Coo-coo is a dish made of corn meal and sliced okras that are cooked together until the mixture is firm; the Cou-cou is then molded in a buttered dish, carefully inverted onto a plate or platter for presentation and served with a stewed fish or meat sauce. When the Cou-cou is served with flying fish, it is the national dish of Barbados.

It took a whole year of living in Barbados before I got even a taste of the national dish, and it was not because of any reluctance to try it on my part (actually I dropped numerous hints about wanting to eat the dish, but they all fell on deaf ears). Rather, I kept hearing how difficult and time consuming it is to make and that only certain people can make it (usually referring to grandparents). So the first time I had it was in a restaurant. It was a Saturday

and so they were serving traditional Barbadian fare. I asked my dining companion if this is 'It' you know, the proper stuff – if the texture and flavour were right. The response I got was that it was not bad at all for a restaurant making a local dish but, I was assured, home-made was even better.

It would be years before I attempted to make this dish called Cou-cou. Frankly, I was intimidated by all that I had been hearing and didn't know if I was up to the task. First of all, finding a recipe was not easy and as many, of you can attest getting a recipe from cooking gurus can be virtually impossible. They are great cooks and so all they say is: put a little bit of this, boil it until it looks soft, you will know when it is finished. When you ask for specifics, they are vague and show you various hand measurements that you do not comprehend.

Now you don't need me to tell you that you do not mess about with someone's national dish. Nothing makes people more incensed than when some "foreigner" tries to make their food and pass it off as the real thing. So it was with reverence, timidity, and

a light sprinkling of cooking confidence that I approached making this dish. Armed with the requisite ingredients, and recipe I found online from popular Barbadian Chef, Peter Edey, I set about making Cou-cou.

The first time I made it, I was extremely nervous. I took care to precisely measure the ingredients and follow the recipe exactly. I stood at the stove stirring the Cou-cou for more than an hour and a half. It was then that I truly understood why many people were no longer making the dish, it is time consuming and demands your total attention so that it does not get lumpy or be scorched at the bottom. The end result of my first attempt was better than I had expected, but I vowed not to make the dish again for a long time, it takes too much time.

Nevertheless, a year later I had a second go at making Cou-cou, I was less nervous. By this time, I had learnt that I did not have to stand there all the time watching the coucou, as long as the cooking temperature was correct and I understood that this cooking process was about absorption. It took the same length of time to cook but I did not have to physically stand over the pot and watch it do its magic. The results were better than my first attempt. I felt good, my Cou-cou-making confidence was gradually increasing.

This past week my thoughts turned to the packet of cornmeal in my pantry and I thought, why not make some Cou-cou, I have okras in the fridge and so I set about making Cou-cou, again.

Armed with more confidence, I sliced my okras, soaked my corn meal, set the kettle to boil, chopped up my onions, garlic and herbs and set about making some Bajan Cou-cou. The taste was very flavourful. I like okras and the texture they give to this dish makes it creamy but *not* mushy. I used canned mackerel in tomato sauce that I jazzed up with lots of onions and fresh herbs to eat with the Cou-cou. As the old Bajan proverb says: "Yuh got to eat de coucou fuh de sake o' de sauce". It is great by itself, but to truly experience Cou-cou you have to have it with a sauce.

One of the key things about making Cou-cou is knowing when it's done. The method I follow is to look for when the mixture breaks away clean from the pot or sauce pan but I've just learnt that I can also insert the spoon in the center of the Cou-cou and if the spoon stands up in the pot and removes easily from the mixture, then the Cou-cou is done.

Cou-cou is one of those dishes that came to us from Africa through slavery. It was fed to the enslaved because it was filling and inexpensive. Today, Cou-cou is eaten widely in the Caribbean; while it is a part of Barbados' national dish, each island has its own version of a similar cooked cornmeal dish.

I've come to realise that "Cou-cou" perhaps refers to the *method* of cooking because there is green-banana Cou-cou, breadfruit Cou-cou etc. According to my Bajan friend, Adele, anything that is boiled, mashed, grounded and cooked in this way can be called a Cou-cou. In Guyana, we have an African dish, Foo foo, whereby starchy vegetables such as plantains, breadfruit, cassava etc. are boiled, seasoned and pounded in a mortar and pestle, formed into a ball and served with a fish or meat stew. Like the Cou-cou, Foo-Foo refers to a method of preparation.

I cannot conclude without telling you one of the folk beliefs of the Cou-cou stick, a wooden paddle. It says, "When the rain is falling and the sun is shining simultaneously, it means that the devil and his wife are fighting for the *coucou* stick."

I used a modern day wooden spoon *and* a whisk; I wonder which one they would fight over.

▶ Cou-cou and Flying Fish in Tomato-onion Sauce, 140–141

Nothing Sweeter
than Salt fish

Growing up I never liked salt fish. I couldn't stand the smell of it. It's not that it smelt bad or anything, it was just that I did not like the smell and so I never really ate it.

Fast forward many years later and I was in Jamaica at the University of the West Indies Cafeteria and staying true to my tradition of always trying the local foods wherever I travel. I found myself with a plate of ackee and salt fish in front me. I started eating the ackee by itself, it was okay, and then I speared a piece of salt fish along with the ackee, wow, my mouth came alive. The soft, delicate, creaminess of the ackee melding with the saltiness of salt fish along with the crunch of sweet sautéed onions and the slight tart of the tomatoes made for a heck of a taste party with the various textures and flavours. No wonder it is the national dish of Jamaica.

When I had just moved to Barbados, I used to wander the aisles of the supermarkets and inspect the shelves for things that reminded me of home or ingredients I could use to create a taste like home. Once I picked up a packet of boneless salt fish, I had no idea what I was going to make with it, all I knew was that Mom likes salt fish and just that thought alone was enough to comfort me.

The packet of salt fish stayed in the fridge forgotten, until one day, riddled with guilt of wasting food and knowing how many people would love to have a piece of this salt fish, I set about cooking it. I boiled it more than once discarding the salty water each time; then I broke it up into little pieces, chopped up some onions, tomatoes and fresh thyme and fried it all up. I ate the fried salt fish with dhal and rice. Hmmmm I thought, this is not bad after all. Since then I've been having salt fish in a variety of ways, in the Bajan fish cakes which I absolutely love, in buljol which I had for the first time here in Barbados and fried up.

Salt fish was first introduced to the Caribbean during the sixteenth century. Vessels from North Amercia would come bringing lumber, and pickled and salted fish, and they would return with molasses, rum, sugar and salt. And since that time, salted, dried fish – salt fish, has become a popular and integral ingredient in our cuisine. We Caribbean people love a piece of salt fish and that is demonstrated in the variety of dishes in which it is *the* main ingredient.

A traditional Sunday morning breakfast meal in Antigua & Barbuda is sautéed salt fish with eggplant, tomatoes and herbs.

Barbados' fish cakes made of fizzled salt fish and flour, seasoned with herbs and hot peppers, are made into a batter and deep fried. A traditional Bajan feast would not be the same without some fish cakes.

Salt fish is one half of a dynamic duo that makes up Jamaica's national dish of ackee and salt fish. The two are sautéed together with tomatoes, onions, hot peppers and fresh thyme.

Trinidad & Tobago's buljol is a flavourful pickle-like dish of shredded salt fish with diced tomatoes, sweet peppers, hot peppers and green onions (eschallots), lemon juice and a few drizzles of oil. This twin-island republic also makes a salt fish fritter called Accra which is very similar to the Bajan fishcake.

In Guyana there is also a salt fish choka, similar to the buljol but not as wet. The salt fish in this dish is either pounded in a mortar and pestle or it can be whirled a few times a food processor; hot peppers, green onions and fresh thyme round out this dish.

All across the region we have sautéed salt fish served with breadfruit, ground provisions, roti, rice, bread and, of course, we all make the all-time favourite - bakes and salt fish.

The main thing about cooking salt fish is de-salting it. There are a variety of ways to do this and each cook has his or her own method.

My sister, Pat, usually boils the salt fish with cut limes. Many people boil it *without* limes, more than once, draining the water each time and adding fresh water to boil again, they repeat this process 2 to 3 times. Each time, the salt fish is boiled anywhere from 5 to 7 to 10 to 15 minutes. The length of time to boil depends on the thickness of the fish and the size of the piece of salt fish being boiled. What I do is soak the salt fish overnight in water, drain it the next morning and shred it to bits or loosen it to make whatever dish I am preparing. Now if the piece of salt fish I am using is thick, then after draining it from the overnight soak, I will boil it once for about 10 – 15 minutes and then prepare it.

Salt fish has a long shelf life and all the nutritional goodness of the fish is preserved in the salting process. As with most curing processes the ingredient being cured matures and gives a rich, deep flavour that is distinctive and delectable.

These days, the smell of salt fish does not bother me in the least and I like cooking it. As an adult I now understand the scent – it is an intense aroma of the sea and the curing of the salt fish locks in all that seaworthiness. I think of it as one of those ole time, traditional ingredients that lends a certain degree of hominess to any dish.

▶ Bajan Fish Cakes, 224–225
▶ Buljol, 101–102
▶ Fried Salt fish, 110–111

Discovering Different Dhals

It's a stewed pulse that's flavoured with a variety of spices. It can be drunk as a soup, ladled over rice and eaten or devoured with shards of hand-ripped roti. It is dhal and it is one of my favourite comfort foods to have with rice and achar; a meal that's testament of how simple food can be flavourful, filling and satisfying.

All my life, the dhal I've eaten and known has been the split-peas variety that's chunkayed (tempered) with oil-roasted geera (cumin seeds) and sliced garlic. That was, until I started blogging about food. As I would visit some blogs I'd see various dishes of dhals such as Indira of Mahanandi's, tomato dhal and Sandeepa of Bong Mom's Cookbook's, mango dhal. I became excited at the prospect of making and trying these new dhals as well as the countless other dhals that I'd seen from other members online. So I did what any food writer would do, I researched, cooked, tasted and decided to write about it.

The first thing I learnt was that dhal, also spelt dal or dahl, is a term that refers to pulses (peas and beans) which have been stripped of their outer shells and split. Dhal is also the spicy peas-stew that's made from these split pulses.

The split pulses (dhals) come in a variety. There is Toor dhal which is similar to the split peas we are familiar with but the Toor dhal pulses are smaller. Chana dhal is the same chick peas/garbanzo peas we have but in this case, it is split and does not have that outer coating. Kala chana is a variety of chick peas that is smaller than the regular channa and is brown. I've never seen this type in our region. Another type of dhal pulse is the Mung dhal which refers to the mung beans. Urad dhal is black lentil or black gram; this pulse originated in India and is highly prized in that country. Masoor dhal is the red lentils, the colour is of a deep orange and they are tiny and thin. They cook up quickly. Rajma dhal we know as kidney beans. The yellow and green split peas that we get all the time here in the Caribbean are called Matar dhal. From experience, I've found that the green split peas cook up quicker than its yellow sibling.

The process of making dhal is very simple. It starts by boiling the peas in water with tumeric (some people leave this out or substitute with a little curry powder), salt to taste and hot pepper. Once the dhal is cooked - the peas having melted whether naturally, or aided by a dhal gutney (wooden masher), then it's time to chunkay (temper) the dhal. This is also known as tadka.

Tadka is the garnish for the dhal, for us it would be the frying of the cumin (geera) seeds and sliced garlic in oil. Some other ingredients that are used for chunkaying the dhal include asafoetida, fresh or dried chili pods, cayenne powder, cilantro, mustard seeds, onion seeds, and garam masala among others.

The spices or ingredients used to chunkay the dhal vary according to the pulses being used, individual tastes and by region. And so in the Caribbean we like the combination of geera seeds and sliced garlic. It's what we know and are accustomed to.

To chunkay the dhal, the raw spices are fried in oil, think of it as a wet roasting. The sliced garlic is added last as it cooks quickly (and you don't want to burn it). This spice-infused oil is then added to the cooked dhal (we usually stir in the chunkayed ingredients) and then serve.

Armed with my new knowledge and confident in my ability to cook dhal, it was time to get busy in the kitchen. I did so by making five different dhals starting off with the familiar ones, spinach dhal and okra dhal. To make the spinach dhal, I used the yellow split peas (Matar dhal), half way through the peas cooking, I added the spinach and continued to cook the dhal as usual. I used geera and sliced garlic to chunkay.

The okra dhal was made with the green split peas, which, as I mentioned before, cooks up faster than the yellow split peas, so I thought it best to pair it up with okras which also cook up quickly. By the time I had finished making this dhal, I just wanted to stop everything and sit down with a bowl and spoon but no, I still had three more dhals to make. To chunkay, I used geera and sliced garlic.

Next it was time for the red lentils (Masoor) dhal. The first time I made this dhal was a couple of years ago; I was pleasantly surprised with the speed with which it cooked. This time I made it as I would the plain yellow or green split peas dhal. The difference with these peas when cooked had to do with the texture. While

it cooks up quickly is does not melt to a creamy consistency, it has a fine texture.

I was now down to two dhals, two I had never attempted before. I started with the tomato dhal, using the yellow split peas (Matar dhal) and followed the recipe by adding to the peas, tomato chunks, diced onions, hot chilies, tumeric and ripe tamarind, all to cook at the same time. To chunkay this dhal, I oil-roasted black mustard seeds, geera, garlic and dried chilies.

Finally, it was time for the mango dhal. This dhal required a two-part cooking that was going to come together for a union that was designed by the dhal gods. The yellow split peas were cooked separately and then added to a pan where mustard seeds, dried chilies, tumeric and green mangoes were sautéing, some water was added to cook through the mangoes, a teaspoon of sugar.

Finally it was time to taste.

Spinach dhal - the flavour of the spinach had completely permeated the dhal with the split peas content in its supporting role. The cumin and garlic tadka was perfect as both aromatics usually work well with spinach and split peas in other dishes. It is a deliciously mild dhal with silky leaves of spinach.

Okra dhal – okras is one of my favourite vegetables and to pair it up with dhal, which I love, is truly a treat. I found that the okras in this dhal were not as assertive as the spinach in the spinach dhal. Both ingredients balanced themselves out equally. And the cumin and garlic tadka while you knew it was present was not as bold. This is a dhal where everything played evenly and very well together.

Masoor (red lentil) dhal – a very mild tasting lentil and by extension, a mild flavoured dhal though tasty. The next time, I will definitely try a different, bolder tadka combo.

Tomato dhal – there are not enough good things to say about this dhal. The peas, tomatoes, onion, tumeric, hot chilies and tamarind all melding together to create a dhal that had me doing a lil' jig as I tasted it again and again. There's no doubt about the star in this dhal – the tomato. Equally important but not as prominent was the ripe tamarind that made its presence known. The ever so slight edge tamarind gives to the dhal is remarkable. This was also the first time I had tasted mustard seeds in a dhal, and immediately I was introduced to a flavour I'd never had before, now I'm thinking that I want to chunkay all my dhals with mustard seeds.

Mango dhal – this dhal was another great treat. The cooked mango gave the dhal a smooth creamy texture. My friends who assisted in the tasting said this dhal was their favourite. I liked it very much too and will be making it over and over but of the five dhals, the tomato dhal was my favourite.

▶   Dhal, 142

▶   Mango Achar, 211

What I'm Eating –
Weekday Food and Weekend Food

Do you remember that when we were growing up there was a clear distinction between weekday food and weekend food, nowadays the lines are completely blurred.

Weekday food was simple fare. It was simple for a number of reasons – it took less time in the kitchen, it fit in the need to stretch a dollar and it also fit in with the assumption by grown ups that you needed a different kind of sustenance when you were at work or school. During the week we always ate vegetables and seafood – shrimp or fish.

Weekend meals were plenty-ingredients; fancy-dancy dressed up dishes that were created when there was more time to cook, to experiment, to entertain and to take delight in after a hard week at work or school. That's when we'd make Spanish rice, potato salad, fried rice, baked chicken, macaroni pie, duck curry, dhal puri, roast pork, pot roast etc.

Even the beverages we had were different. During the week, my mother insisted that we drink water. On the weekend, we got to have sweet drinks – home-made fruit juices (no bottled drinks for us). Home-made meant that Mom knew exactly what was going into the

drink, and it was a smart way to monitor the amount of sugar we consumed.

Whenever Mommy cooked something that was considered a weekend food during the week it was like a treat. I remember being totally elated one afternoon when I opened the karahi and found curried chicken, one of my favourites. She used to do this for us every now and then – treat us to weekend food during the week – we loved being surprised by it, and I think that Mom enjoyed the looks of pleasure on our faces as well.

Weekend cooking is where I started to hone my cooking skills. I had a pact with Mom that I would relieve her of the cooking on weekends. The kitchen became mine on weekends, particularly Sundays (since Saturday was always cook-up rice day and my mom makes a *fantastic* cook-up rice).

I enjoyed those weekend cooking ventures - planning the menu during the week, prepping some things the night before, and starting early on the Sunday morning. My family loved my food and Mom was glad for the break from the kitchen. But one day, my brother, Eon, made an outburst that stopped me in my tracks and hurt my fledgling chef's heart. One Sunday morning he said to mother, loud and clear for me to hear, "Mommy, why Cynthia got to cook on Sundays? She always tek long in de kitchen because she got to mek about 50-million things." Ungrateful little boy! I'm glad to hear now that he spends just as long in the kitchen because he is always experimenting with new dishes and perfecting his favourites. 50-million things! Ha!

Years later, having moved to Barbados, I had to adjust my food. No longer was there weekday food and weekend food. In many ways it was a different food culture. For starters, when I had just arrived, the abundance and variety of vegetables to which I was accustomed and familiar with was not readily available and when it was, it was pricey. Also, the bounty of imported Caribbean seafood that we now get in Barbados was not available when I came here nine years ago and so I adjusted. Pork, beef, chicken, lamb and veal became regular weekday food. Vegetables, when consumed, consisted of carrots, cabbage, cauliflower and broccoli. I quickly learnt that macaroni pie and baked chicken were everyday fare.

Sunday lunch, as it is called here, often comprises of all the weekday dishes with the addition of baked pork, and stewed lamb.

These days, things have changed yet again. With the influx of farmers from other Caribbean territories into Barbados, a variety of vegetables are readily available at the weekly markets. Fish and shrimp from other Caribbean neighbours are stocked in the supermarket freezers. However, my weekday cooking has not gone back to the days of my growing up. Yes, there are vegetables everyday but now I have them with beef, chicken, pork, lamb or veal – whichever meat I feel like having on any given day.

Nevertheless, I still try to make weekend food special simply by the method of preparation and cooking – lots more baking and roasting takes place on the weekends. I always try to make a different rice dish and I use the weekends to also test out new recipes. And I pay particular attention to the presentation on weekends, sometimes that makes all the difference to my meal. So while I may serve rice and peas, the crockery I choose to present it in will draw ooooooohs and ahhhhhhs. So, on my weekend table you can find something familiar, though dressed up differently, something new or something you have not had in a long time.

I know that we are all busy and that it is difficult for some people to cook during the week but on the weekends, we can try. It does not have to be the "50-million things" I was accused of making when I was younger; it could be a couple of things using my new strategy: something old style, something new style and something with real style. And if you have children, even better. Let them come and help you even if it is just to sit and watch or set the table. We all have memories of being in the kitchen with our parents. Some of my favourite weekend cooking memories are Saturday afternoons' baking sprees. Those afternoons were spent grating coconut, beating eggs, mixing buns and cakes and baking bread, all to stock up for breakfast and snacks for the upcoming week. I loved those Saturdays and though I do not have children to bake for, I bake on Saturdays and share with my friends.

Have a good weekend everyone and do enjoy your weekend food.

▶ Baked Chicken, 126–127
▶ Roast Chicken, 186–187
▶ Vegetable Rice, 198–199
▶ Macaroni and Cheese Pie, 167–168

The Many Ways of Okra

Some people love it, some people hate it and some people just can't make up their minds about it. But me? I love my okras. It's also familiarly known as lady's finger, bhindi and gumbo.

Okra fans love this vegetable for its flavour, quick-cooking and without a doubt, its silkiness. The haters object primarily to this same silky nature, calling it slimy. But there's slimy and there's *slimy*. There's the slimy that comes from not understanding the vegetable and how to prepare it and then there's the slimy/silkiness that finishes off the dish perfectly – it's the slimy/silkiness that makes callaloo callaloo, makes gumbo gumbo, and makes okra slush okra slush. And then there are those people who can only eat okras when they are prepared in certain dishes as a necessary but not understated ingredient as exemplified in the Bajan cou cou.

As I was sorting through some of my photos recently, it struck me how many of them contained okras and how much we in the Caribbean use this vegetable whether it's steamed, fried, curried, stewed or mashed. I even heard once that it's good for pregnant women to eat a lot of okras as it aids in the smooth delivery of babies. True or false I have no idea!

Here's what I do know – some of the ways this vegetable is cooked and enjoyed.

Steamed – with the stop and bottom snipped off, steamed okras are enjoyed atop a plate of cook-up rice or any dish.

Sautéed – sliced into rounds and cooked with onions, garlic, tomatoes and fresh herbs, okras are an appetizing dish; cooked with shrimp or saltfish makes it even more appealing.

Curried – dropped whole into curried fish, okras make the curry silky and provide another texture to the dish. They can also be curried by themselves.

Fried – cut into half-inch rounds, bathed in buttermilk and coated in cornmeal, it's a snack you can't stop popping into your mouth until all's gone. In the southern states of the USA it is known as Southern Popcorn.

Stuffed – slit lengthwise and filled with a highly flavourful mix of spices and masala, the okras are fried uncovered.

Cooked in – is one of the more popular ways we use this vegetable. You will recall Barbados' national dish, Cou Cou, in which okras were used to provide the textural silkiness that is required for that dish as well as the flavour it imparts.

In fact, okra seems to feature in a number of Caribbean dishes. One of Trinidad and Tobago's national dishes, callaloo, would not be what it is without okras. Callaloo is a thick soup made of dasheen or eddo leaves, salted beef or pork, okras, coconut milk, crabs, water and fresh herbs. It is traditionally served with Sunday Lunch and it is also eaten throughout the week.

Mettagee, a national dish of Guyana, made with ground provisions (tubular and root vegetables) cooked in coconut milk also includes whole okras.

Barbadians also make something called okra slush where they boil the okras with onions, thyme and salt meat until everything melts and get thick. It is eaten as a side dish.

My favourite way to have okras is sautéed and I learnt how to perfect this method by watching the women in my family. If they planned to cook okras, early in the morning, the okras would be sliced into rounds, spread on a baking sheet or something with a wide flat surface and placed in the sun. My mom explained that this was so that the moisture from the okras could be extracted.

Onions, garlic, tomatoes and other fresh herbs would then be chopped fine and sautéed in hot oil. The okras are then added and the heat reduced to medium as they cook uncovered. No salt was added until the dish was just a minute away from completion. Adding the salt at the end was ingenious, here's why. When salt is added to certain ingredients, it aids in the release of moisture from that ingredient and lengthens the time before it caramelises (gets brown). So, by adding the salt at the end of cooking the okra means that it prevents the release of any moisture that will yield the sliminess that most people can't tolerate.

When shopping for okras, you want to ensure that they are bright green in colour, and that they are tender but not soft. At the markets in Guyana, I remember the vendors would gently break the bottom tip of some of the okras to show buyers that it was young, fresh and not hard. Of course it is not possible to check all the okras for tenderness before you purchase them. However, when you are ready to prepare them to cook, you will know as soon as you cut into them whether or not they are tender. If they're not, they'll offer some resistance to your knife. Discard the hard okras because they are not going to cook.

In terms of storage, my mom always bought okra the day before she was going to cook it that way it never went into the fridge. I, however, buy it at the weekend and cook it during the week. I usually, wrap mine in a paper bag and store it in the crisper or I'd wrap them in paper-towels, store then in a perforated bag and put them in the crisper, all this in an effort to stave off additional moisture.

Recently, I've taken to cooking my rice with vegetables and yes, you guessed it, I make okra-vegetable rice. I slice the okras into half-inch thick rounds, lightly sauté them with onions and thyme add washed rice and measured boiling water and cook the dish, first letting everything boil and then turning the heat to simmer. My vegetable rice comes out fluffy, flavourful with just a hint of silkiness. And that's the joy of okra it is an ingredient that adds as much texture as it adds flavour. If you have never had okras before, try it, taste it, enjoy it, revel in it, and take joy in it. Umm ...I really like okras, can you tell?

▶　Okra in Tomato–onion Sauce, 174–175

▶　Okra and Salt fish, 172–173

Oh, to be a Kid Again

Small days, still on my mind

There used to be a Guyanese song some years ago and the chorus went "small days are still on me mind." Small days, that's what we call childhood and when the August holiday, or what those in the North call the summer vacation, rolls around we tend to think about the fun we had during our own small days.

I was reading Barbados' *Nation* Newspaper the other day in which they proudly displayed a photograph of two little boys doing some small days activity – roasting breadfruit and having a good time playing

As I stared at the photograph, I cast my mind back to my small days and treats we had…two in particular came to mind – gooseberry syrup and marbles made from kuru.

Gooseberry syrup – there was a tree just outside our house that, when in season, it would be laden with its plump, pastel-green berries clumped in bunches. The branches would bend gently from the weight of the fruit begging to be plucked. The tree was tall and slender and, since it offered little opportunity for climbing, my siblings, friends from around the neighbourhood and I would gather at the bottom tree. We'd stare up, blinded by the

sun and shake that tree as hard as we dared. Loud peals of laughter could be heard as the gooseberries fell to the ground, on top of our heads and on our faces. We would get down on our hands and knees and fill our pockets; and we girls would turn up the hem of our dress or shirt to make a bowl and fill it with gooseberries.

We'd take most of our stash to my Auntie Betty and she would make the gooseberry syrup for us. We'd help her take off the stems and then she'd wash them clean and place them in a sauce pot with water, sugar, cinnamon and cloves and let it boil until the gooseberries would be cooked and reduced to a thick, tart but sweet syrup. While the syrup was cooking, of course we had to occupy ourselves so we'd go back to the tree, get some more goose berries and have them with pepper and salt.

Marbles – there is a fruit we call kuru. It is round and grows as large as seven inches in some cases. The outside ranges in colour from green, to cream to yellow. Once removed, the skin reveals a deep cream-to-yellow coloured flesh that is then eaten either by removing with a paring knife or as we did, with our teeth.

Eating kuru was not so much about the fruit, it was about the seed, the marble; here's why, there was a game called marbles or as I've heard my cousins, say, gam. So the larger the kuru, the more they're prized because it means that you will have a big marble or goobly as it was fondly called.

This game was for us the little ones as much as it was for the older kids, meaning those in their late teens. It required good skills of averaging, precision hitting and a lot of courage not to give up when the older cousins and their friends would be winning and teasing you mercilessly about your lack of skill.

The game, though simple in its construction, was not easy to execute. To describe it simply, there were three holes made in the sand, not in a straight line but zigzagged, and at varying distances from each other. The aim was to stand at a designated start line and try to get your marble into the first hole by throwing or rolling it. The first person to get their marble into the holes going forth and back to the start line wins the game.

If, and it always was the case with us the smaller children, your marble missed getting in to one of the holes, then the person who got theirs in the hole shot your marble with theirs as far away from the hole as possible to impede your progress (think of shooting pool). You would then have to try to get your marble in the hole from wherever yours was shot to. This is why the size of one's marble was important

because if your marble was large then you have a great chance of shooting the other marbles far away.

We took this game seriously in terms of arming ourselves with a cache of marbles. We'd respectively beg our moms to buy lots of kuru and instruct them to look for the big ones. Once we'd finish eating the flesh off the kuru, we spent hours getting it clean, smooth and shiny by rubbing it on the concrete to take away any bits of flesh remaining. Depending on who you were playing against, you'd select which marbles (in terms of size) you'd use.

Those were some good days. And there were other treats we enjoyed eating as well, like ginipes (Barbadians call them ackees, not to be confused with the Jamaican ackee). Like gooseberries, ginipes are grown in bunches, they are small and round, the outside is green and the inside is a rich salmon-colour, you pop one of these babies into your mouth after removing the top of the skin and the flesh melts in your mouth! We – my siblings, friends and I – would each buy a bunch and remove the tops of each ginipe to reveal the flesh. Then we'd hold up the bunch of ginipes, caps-off and compare which one of us had the best bunch of bulbs.

Tamarind balls, sugar cakes, green mangoes with pepper and salt, and mitai were all part of the fun-in-the-sun August holidays treats. Now as adults when we eat these things or see them, we can recall some story related to it or better yet, point to some scar on our hands, feet, knees or elbows that we got from those small days adventures.

▶ Gooseberry Syrup, 288–289

▶ Guava Cheese, 290–291

▶ Flutees, 284–285

▶ Nutmeg Ice Cream, 292–293

▶ Soursop Ice Cream, 309

▶ Paynoos, 296–297

▶ Stewed Guava, 312–313

▶ Tamarind Balls, 316–317

▶ Channa, 236–237

▶ Egg Balls, 242–243

▶ Cassava Balls, 234–235

Nuts for Coconuts

Coconut is a perfect gift from nature. It's one of those fruits that we cook, eat, drink, wear, use as adornments and don't tell me you're too young to have heard of a coconut fibre mattress.

Nothing cools you down like coconut water. I like it when the coconut has a soft jelly – the vendor will split open the coconut for you after you've drunk the water, slice off a piece of the outer shell which you'd use as a spoon to scoop out the jelly. Oh, can you feel that soft, sweet jelly slithering across your tongue?

When you hear the sweet sounds of coconut being grated, you know you're in for a tasty treat. I say this because nowadays, people are so busy that they're using all sorts of short cuts, so to hear someone actually grating fresh coconuts to create a dish is something to savour. Sure, there is the packaged grated coconut in the supermarket freezer but it's not quite the same as using the fresh stuff.

I like coconuts in sweet as well as savoury dishes. However, as I was making a list of the things I like with coconut, the sweet stuff outweighed the savoury. Normally I don't generally have a sweet tooth, I guess with coconutty things I make the exception.

The savoury dishes I love with coconut are cook-up rice, pelau, coconut choka and certain curries. Saturdays in Guyana is always cook-up rice day. In our home, my sister, Pat or I were always tasked with grating the coconut which we didn't mind at all because it was done in no time. What we hated was having to grind the coconut to make coconut choka. Coconut choka is made by removing the flesh from the hard shell, roasting the flesh on an open flame, scraping off some of the charred bits, and grating it on the finest side of a box grater. Then, using a stone grinder (lorha and sil – think of a flat version of a mortar and pestle) the grated coconut along with garlic, pepper, and a piece of green mango is ground until it is almost a paste which is then formed into a ball. It's often eaten with dhal and rice. I love coconut choka but I hate doing the hard work it takes to make it.

With the exception of the coconut choka, most of the savoury dishes only require the coconut be grated in order to extract the cream or milk to cook with. However, the sweet treats used the grated coconut itself. Some of the sweet coconut treats I like are: coconut ice cream, sugar cake, coconut buns, conkies, sweet bread (also known as coconut bread) and salara.

Whenever I want to have any of these treats I make them. I no longer purchase them because in the past, I have been frustrated at the lack of coconut in these coconut treats. It seems there are pretenders out there, people who hardly add any coconut at all. Their pre-packaged not-so goodies should come

with a warning label, "No coconuts were harmed in the making of this sweetbread." I've bought salara that seems to have been merely sprinkled with coconut, lightly dusted even. Then there are another set of pretenders, or coconut criminals as I call them, who dedicate their efforts to extracting every ounce of moisture from the grated coconut. All you get is a dry husk that could choke you if you're not careful. There's nothing more disappointing than yearning for something and finding only fake and flakey imposters instead, especially when you live away from home. So in order to defeat the coconut criminals I have resurrected cooking skills learnt when I was a child.

I've told you before that when I was growing up, Saturday afternoons were always baking time in our home and so a lot of these things I learnt to make from my mom, especially the buns. When I moved to Barbados, I perfected my coconut bread-making skills.

Though I could make coconut buns from since I was small, I learnt to make salara only since I moved to Barbados. When I lived in Guyana, I was actually not a big fan of salara. When you live away, *everything* about home becomes more important and more intense.

The first time I made salara, I couldn't believe how easy it was. I have to say, it turned out very well, especially since it was my first time making it. When I gave my friend, Susan, a slice of the salara, she bit into it and whispered "Cynthia, I've never tasted anything so delicious before." This was the first time she'd eaten salara. The coconut was sweet, flavourful and moist. I liked how it stuck to the dough and some of the filling even seeped out as it was being cut. My favourite way to eat a slice of salara is to unfurl it so that I can get direct contact with the coconut filling. And the colour! Gosh I love that deep red colouring. When I made the salara again for this article, I went to town on the red food colouring.

I can't take it anymore; that preceding paragraph has been a torture. I'm going to have a slice of salara right now.

▶ Coconut Shortbread Cookies, 278–279

▶ Coconut Drops, 274–275

▶ Coconut Sweetbread, 314–315

▶ Coconut Ice Cream, 276–277

▶ Salara, 306–307

Me and Eggplants

An Undefined Relationship

If I said to you that I don't like something and that I can *only* eat it cooked 3 ways and yet I purchase it *every week* at the market, you'd have to conclude that I really *do* like it wouldn't you? If you know the answer, tell me because I'm not sure.

Eggplants or bolangers or bigan as we call them in Guyana have never been among my favourite vegetables. As a child, there was only one way I could eat them – prepared as a choka – fire roasted, mashed and seasoned with peppers, garlic, green onions, salt and a drizzle of oil. Of late however, I've added two other ways I can eat eggplants, fire-roasted and curried dry and as biganee – sliced, dipped in a spiced split peas batter and fried. Eaten with a dollop of mango sour, chutney or achar, you'd want to eat biganee everyday.

My general dislike for this vegetable (considered a fruit, but that's for another time), stemmed from the way my mother cooked it and it was not really the method of cooking but rather the way in which she cut it up to cook. Mommy liked (still does) the eggplants to be sliced lengthways with about half-inch thickness to the slices. She'd then sauté them with lots of onions, garlic, tomatoes and fresh herbs. Sometimes she'd even add a piece of saltfish, smoked herring, shrimp or even thinly sliced potatoes. Serve her this with rice or roti and my mom would be in food paradise. As attractive as the dish looked, I could never bring myself to swallow that soft, spongy-textured-when-cooked vegetable.

But as kids growing up, at least in my time, you had to eat what was put in front of you. I remember one day – and this would have been before I was 10 years old – I was handed my plate of food with a mound of sautéed eggplants on the side. I picked up the eggplants with my hand and squished it as hard as I could between my tiny fingers to make it more like a paste. I barely nibbled at the food. Truth be told the squishing was my way of letting the eggplant know how much I hated it and wanted to hurt it.

Once my mom went through a phase of preparing sautéed eggplants to be eaten with bread for Sunday-morning breakfast! Yuck! I was so glad that I was not alone in my hatred of this thing. My sister, brother and I would push it around our plates, reach for the butter on the table and be content. I think mommy finally got it that her children did not share her passion for the eggplant and so whenever she cooked eggplants, it was always for herself and she'd make other food for us.

Years later though, still in my teens, I visited my uncle and his family who, at that time lived in the country. One morning for breakfast we were all served with sada roti, eggplant choka and steaming, freshly brewed cups of tea. When my plate was put in front of me, I did not realise immediately that it was eggplant; I just saw a smooth-textured dollop of something with green onions and bits of hot pepper. It smelt wonderfully smokey and aromatic. I asked my cousin sitting next to me what it was and was told that it was bolanger choka. My enthusiasm faded. Bolanger? I hate this vegetable. But I was taught politeness and therefore, tore a piece of roti and gingerly dipped into the choka. I tasted it. Hmmmm, I thought, this doesn't taste like eggplant and it's not spongy and it tastes nice. I tore another piece of roti and dipped, tore and before I knew it, my plate was clean! Not a trace of the eggplant choka. And so was born the first way in which I could eat eggplant. I liked the smokiness from the fire roasting, the delicate sweet flavour of the garlic that was inserted into the eggplants as they roasted, the almost creaminess from

mashing it and the light crunch from the green onions with notes of heat from the chilies. It is still my favourite way to eat eggplants.

And so throughout the years, that was the only way I would eat eggplants, until very recently. There's an ongoing event that takes place in the food-blogging world, in which every month, a particular food ingredient is chosen and the challenge is to come up with various interesting ways to cook and present the ingredient being profiled. This past July, the ingredient was eggplant. While there were many fantastic creations, there was one in particular, that grabbed my attention not because the photograph was drool-worthy, but because the first method of preparation required that it be fire roasted! And you know how that's the first step to eggplant choka so my interest was peaked. The recipe went on to instruct that the flesh of the roasted eggplant

be mashed and then sautéed with oil, ginger, garlic, green onions, geera, chilies, tomatoes, tumeric and masala. Read that line again and tell me that the flavours from those ingredients don't entice you.

I set about making the dish immediately and all I have to say is this: I now have another way to eat eggplant. Notice the theme here – fire roasting and mashing.

And finally, the biganee (eggplants sliced thinly and dipped in a spicy split-pea batter and fried). Biganee has been around in my life since I was a child growing up, still I never ventured near it because of my distaste for the eggplant. However, as I prepared for this article, I set about making some. I figured it couldn't hurt, especially since the eggplant has to be sliced thinly, encased in a batter and then eaten with some sour or chutney. And would you know, we have a winner, another way that I like and can eat eggplants. I also made some eggplant croquettes – baked eggplants where

the flesh is pureed with bread crumbs, garlic, parsley and parmesan cheese. The mixture is made into little patties and breaded with an egg wash and bread crumbs and fried. I fire-roasted my eggplant (big surprise) instead of baking it and made the croquettes. They were delicious and I'll definitely make them again whenever I am entertaining but I don't think it's moved into position yet, it's still a trio: choka, roasted curry and biganee.

So, if I told you that I don't like something and that I can *only* eat it cooked three ways and yet I purchase it *every week* at the market, you'd have to conclude that I really *do* like it won't you? Help me define this relationship.

▶ **Eggplant-Potato Curry, 152–153**
▶ **Eggplant Choka, 198–109**
▶ **Biganee, 228–229**
▶ **Sada Roti, 119–120**
▶ **Mango Sour, 214–215**

I Like it Like That

Home cooks throughout the world are renowned for their ingenuity and creativity. They often take the little they have and turn it into a gourmet meal. They know how to take small amounts and stretch them to feed the entire family. They were among the first to understand what it is to eat seasonally because it meant the produce would be in abundance then and it made economical sense. My mom would always say, for example, "Not me. I ain't buying any tomatoes this week, not at that price. The doctor did not order me to buy tomatoes so if I don't eat any this week, I'm not going to die." Ah, such wisdom.

There are some dishes for which it would have been clear to anyone looking on that my mom was strategising in the kitchen in order to make a little stretch for all of us. These dishes might have been ways of economising, but to this day, these are some of my favourite dishes.

The dishes that stand out in my mind when I think of my mom "stretching" things begin with bora (aka yardlong bean and snake bean) and potatoes. Whenever this vegetable was cooked in our house it was either with shrimp, or shrimp and potatoes. Mom would slice the potatoes thinly and sauté it with the bora, carefully timing the dish so that the potatoes would not break up completely and the bora would not be overdone. To this day to me this is one of the best ways to eat bora. For me to eat the bora without the potatoes seems as if something is missing from the dish. Of course I can say things such as, "I like how the potatoes absorb the flavour of the bora and texturally the bora and potatoes compliment each other etc." But the simple truth is I just like it like that.

Curried chicken and potatoes. As a matter of fact most meat or poultry curries and stews had potatoes cooked in. I particularly liked when mom would not peel the potatoes but scrub the skin clean, cut them into wedges and cook them in the various dishes. If I don't put potatoes in my curried chicken, I feel as if I'm eating too much chicken. Silly, I know, but that's the way I like it.

Canned corned beef and potatoes was another stretcher which I still love to this day. The potatoes are sautéed with lots of onions and tomatoes and cooked through then a few minutes before they're done, the corned beef is added and heated through. Served with rice or roti, this is a dish that satisfies a part of your soul. Well at least for some of us Caribbean people, and I like it like that.

Now I know this one might seem strange – chow mein with steamed rice. I think we (well at least I did) saw chow mein as some sort of dish to be eaten with something else, especially with the chow mein being cooked with lots of vegetables and meat or chicken – it would be too rich to eat by itself so rice presented itself as a natural accompaniment. Some good ole starch on starch!

While these days, I don't cook chow mein often, whenever I do, I cook a little rice to go with it. Hey, don't knock it till you try it. I like it like that.

This next dish I am going to tell you about is not only a stretcher but an excellent fast-food dish that's filling and satisfying– egg curry. Mom used to make it with potatoes or eddoes. I prefer it with eddoes as the gravy has that nice thick, creamy consistency. And in case you are wondering, the potatoes or eddoes were placed in the curry as the stretcher. So we'd be served a whole egg and some potatoes or eddoes. I love egg curry but don't make it often, I don't know why…but whenever I do I put either potatoes or eddoes in it. I like it like that.

As I look back, I marvel at the talent of home cooks back in the day and the meals they were able to create. The days when they had only one ingredient or one plus another and would marry them or have them accompany each other. Out of that, a dish is created. In many ways, they are the first recipe developers we know but we call them a different name: mom, dad, aunt, uncle, grandma, grandpa etc. It also shows how our tastes and desires for some things in particular ways were developed.

I've often wondered though what taste desires drove my brother one night as he made dinner for a tired and hungry household. Everyone agreed that it should be something quick and easy. There was canned corned beef so we figured okay, he's going to fry that up with some onions and tomatoes and we'll have it with rice. Little did we know that that was too simple for Eon. Here's what he did, he curried the corned beef and if you think that it stopped there you are sadly mistaken. To the curry, he added a can of baked beans! I tell you honestly, we ate it because we were all tired and hungry, I can't remember the taste because I have blocked it out. The memory of him actually making it is enough to last me till the end of my days and I like it like that.

▶ Egg Curry, 150–151

Gimme My Plantains

Any Which Way

"Boil em, mash em, put em in a stew…"
Sam Gamgee, The Lord of the Rings, The Two Towers.

Sam was talking about his beloved taters – potatoes, but I love my 'tains, plantains that is. You can boil em, fry em, mash em, stew em, roast em, bake em, curry em – anyway you cook em, I'll eat em.

Although I like plantains any which way, I'd say that I find the plantain most versatile when it is at its starchiest - when it is green. When I lived in Guyana, one of our neighbours owned a ground provision stall at Stabroek Market and each Saturday, I'd tell their eldest son, Ashraf, to bring green plantains for me. And so every Saturday evening, I'd eat what we call "boil and fry" boiled green plantains cut into rounds that were then sautéed with lots of onions, tomatoes and fresh herbs. I always had it with a cup of tea.

There are lots of other ways I enjoy green plantains. As chips I slice them thinly into rounds or lengthways, pan fried until golden brown and crisp. How about sliced into wedges, fried and served with fried eggs? Like a lot of people I like plantains this way for a hearty breakfast. Foo-foo is another one of my favorites – boiled in salted water, pounded to a paste in a mortar with pestle with some freshly ground black pepper, a pat of butter and shaped into balls. And there's nothing better than green plantains in hearty, thick soups with other ground provisions such as sweet potatoes, cassava, and eddoes.

"Turning plantain" is when the plantain is moving from green to ripe. The skin usually has a two-toned colour, light green to cream. Turning plantains are used pretty much the same way as green plantains, only they don't hold up well in terms of crispness if chips are attempted. Nevertheless, a turning plantain can be just the right ingredient to make a great dish fantastic. For example, when making foo-foo, a regular reader of my articles, Geralda, advised not to use all green plantains, she said to include a couple of turning plantains, which I did and it certainly aided in the texture and moistness of the foo-foo I made. Thanks for the tip, Geralda.

When a plantain is ripe, it loses most, if not all starchy character and its sweet persona emerges. At this stage, you truly want to enjoy the plantain as naturally as possible. Just boiling it and slicing and eating it as is, is pure delight. But if you want to make it richer, creamier and offer a depth of flavour, just drop a pat of butter on the boiled-peeled-sliced hot plantain and let the butter slide, slither and caress it…bliss.

Timing is important when it comes to cooking ripe plantains with other ingredients and to make certain dishes. Added too early to the pot and the plantain will cook to mush, and overwhelm the dish with sweetness; added at the right time, however, will result in a soft but firm plantain whose sweetness offers depth to the dish. Take for example, mettagee, the ripe plantain should be added five to eight minutes before the dish is completed. If you're going to put it in soups, cut it into large chunks and add it about five minutes before the soup is done.

When you have a very ripe plantain the skin turns black. Some people who are unfamiliar with plantains may be tempted to throw it away at this stage. Don't! We plantain fans know that this can be one of the best ways to eat plantain. At this very ripe stage, all the cooking process is doing is coaxing the sugar out of the plantain, to fluff up the texture and caramelise, heightening its sweetness. Anytime fried ripe plantains are on the offer in any food gathering or setting, it is the one thing that everyone argues about – who has more pieces than whom. It's like a precious commodity. Even now as grown adults when we visit mom and she's fried ripe plantains to accompany our meal, all are gone in one sitting. My sister, brother and I even watch each other carefully to see how much of the ripe plantain the other is taking and we have no shame to say aloud, "By the time you're finished, there'd be no more plantains left!" You'd feel the rest of the food on the plate is immaterial.

There's an art to frying ripe plantains, if you're not careful, you can end up eating oil-soaked plantains. From experience, I've found

that cooking them in a non-stick skillet is best, that way you can use just a slight drizzle of oil. While some may opt to use oil spray, I won't, because when the pan gets hot that spray will start to colour. Another key factor is the heat; you want the pan hot, but not smoking hot. If it's smoking hot, you'll just burn the plantains. Don't forget, it's about coaxing. If you want your fried ripe plantains to have some complexity, as soon as you take them out of the pan, give them a light sprinkling of some good fine sea salt or any good finishing salts you have. I've had it with a gentle squeeze of lemon juice *and* salt as well but I found it a little edgy for me. I don't want sweet, salt and sour in my fried ripe plantains, salt and sweet works just fine for me.

Plantains are known not only for their versatility but also their ability to fill. That's why it's considered a ground provision; once you have a plantain meal you have fuel to last the day. We in the Caribbean believe plantains give stamina and make you strong like a lion! While we may not have a lion to prove it, we certainly have

a tiger in one of our star cricketers, Shivnarine Chanderpaul. I was there at the Bourda Cricket Ground in 1994 as he walked onto the field for his test match debut (England versus the West Indies). Chanders, Shiv, or Tiger as he is fondly called, walked towards the pitch, swinging his bat which looked heavier than he was, his head lost beneath his helmet and the roar of the crowd all around him. Someone sitting behind me said, "All he needs to do is eat some good ground provisions, like some plantains you know, and that will give him body, strength, stamina!" That my dear reader, is how much we believe in what the plantain can do. If you're a cricket fan you know that these days Shiv has great staying power once he occupies the crease. Now, if only we can get the entire team to eat more plantains... alright, alright, it was just a thought.

▶ Boil and Fry Plantain, 99–100
▶ Plantain Chips, 256
▶ Fried Ripe Plantains, 208–209
▶ Plantain Foo-Foo, 182–183
▶ Boiled Ripe Plantain, 202–203

The Laws of Tea

Thou shalt enjoy tea-tea

In the Caribbean any drink made with hot water, sugar and milk we call tea. Cocoa, coffee, Milo, Ovaltine, Horlicks, hot chocolate, Bournvita, Lipton all of these are tea. If you want to ask someone for a nice cup of tea you'd better be clear if you want Milo-tea, coffee-tea, Ovaltine-tea or, my favorite phrase, tea-tea – tea-tea is the one the rest of the world calls tea – Darjeeling, Earl Grey, Pekoe or maybe just a little bag of Typhoo.

Everyone knows that the British have made tea a national obsession. George Orwell went as far as to create eleven golden rules for making tea. Maybe it was that British fixation that gave birth to our own Caribbean interest in tea. But, like everything we got from the British, we changed the rules to suit our taste. We have our own rules for drinking tea.

It seems my mom has been the guardian of the tea laws in our family. When I was growing up tea making in our home could be very frustrating and, I'm not ashamed to say, there were often moments of resentment - at least on my part. My mother was frustrated with my sister and me and our inability to make her a good cup of tea according to her tea laws, and we were frustrated that our efforts never seemed good enough. Mom liked her

tea strong, two level teaspoons of sugar, milk and the temperature to be very warm, never hot, warm! But she didn't want it at room temperature either! She'd instruct us that the boiling water be poured into the cup, half-full and left to steep. Sugar and milk would then be added followed by some tap water to cool down the tea. Stir, discard the tea bag, and serve. Seems simple enough huh? It never was!

Pat and I seemed to constantly mess up the tea, we'd sometimes forgetfully add more hot water in the cup than was necessary so by the time we added the sugar and milk, there was no room in the cup for the extra water to cool down the tea. Then we seemed not to know when exactly the tea had steeped enough for the strength of flavour mom desired. And then there was the milk and sugar issue. Sometimes we'd not put enough milk in the tea and mom would ask, "The cow's dead?" or if we put too much milk, "This tea is white like an angel's bed-gown!"

There were other laws of tea handed down by the women in my family. For example, you had to have some kind of tea to start your day, even if you didn't eat anything for breakfast you *had* to have tea. You could have any type of tea for breakfast except Milo-tea. The *only* time we were allowed to have Milo-tea was at night before going to bed. We were told that Milo-tea makes you sleepy so only have it a night. I honestly don't know if there was any truth to that, I think we psychologically felt sleepy because we were told the Milo-tea would make us sleepy!

When it came to milk, the guidelines were as follows: for regular green tea, canned evaporated milk as it made the tea creamier; this same milk also worked for Milo, Ovaltine, Hot chocolate, cocoa, Horlicks and Bournvita. Herbal teas were drunk without milk, if any milk was added, it was always pasteurized and only a few drops. Coffee was had with the powdered coffee creamer. However, we kids were generally not allowed to drink coffee. It was only on Christmas mornings that we were allowed to have coffee.

Apart from all the established commercial teas, in the Caribbean we also have bush tea. Bush tea is a combination of leaves from various fruits and vegetable trees that are sun-dried and sold in bunches at markets all across the region. It is believed to rid the body of many ills and offer cures in place of treatments by modern medicine, from colds to stomach aches, from swollen joints to headaches. You name it and someone of my mom's generation will say, "You need to drink some bush tea." Well, the only bush tea she ever made for us was lemongrass tea, which, I love, love, love. Mom used to call it fever grass tea. We never had it often because it was a scarce

item. When this tea is being made, the aroma envelopes the kitchen, you feel all warm inside and just content to stand against the wall and slide down to the floor and sit and wait for the tea to be done. There never seemed to be enough, each one of us got only one cup.

Mom also taught us about a natural cocoa-chocolate tea which she had been introduced to by her Barbadian friends. I wish I could buy this cocoa stick and send one for each of you. It is locally made in the Eastern Caribbean islands – St Vincent and the Grenadines and St Lucia are noted for their cocoa sticks. Guyana also makes cocoa sticks. You make the cocoa-chocolate tea by boiling a piece of the cocoa stick with bay leaves and a piece of cinnamon stick. I swear to you, you've never had a cocoa tea like this before. And when it comes time to drink it, don't worry with fancy cups, get a nice big enamel cup like they used to have long ago. Trust me, you'll need it.

Despite the years of learning the laws of tea from the women in my family, I rarely make my own tea these days. My friend makes the tea the way I like it - strong with some good brown sugar and milk; warm, never hot. The other morning she brought me a cup of tea that was looking a little dark. I was shocked to hear myself say, "Wait, de cow dead?!"

I have become my mother!

▶ Lemongrass Tea, 248–249
▶ Bay Leaf and Cinnamon Tea, 226–227
▶ Cocoa–stick Tea, 240–241

Feasting at Festivals

When we celebrate Eid-ul-Fitr (marking the end of Ramadan), Diwali (festival of lights) and when we have Eid-ul-Adha (commemoration of Abraham's willingness to sacrifice his son) to look forward to, I feel so blessed to come from such a diverse country and family.

Guyana and Trinidad and Tobago are home to the largest populations of Hindus and Muslims in the Caribbean; and Hindu and Muslim religious holidays are, therefore, national holidays. Thus everyone in those countries celebrates in their own way. Those who are not Hindu or Muslim spend part, if not the entire day, with family and friends who observe the religious occasion.

Growing up I was predominantly surrounded by my mother's family, especially my Auntie Betty who was Hindu (she's since converted to Catholicism) and her family. And it was from Auntie Betty that I learnt a lot about festival foods. I would watch her and my cousin, Shantie, and the other relatives who would come to visit for the holidays, prepping and cooking all day. The house would be full of delicious smells and chattering as the women caught up on what was happening in each other's lives and discussing what their children were up to. As for the men, well...come to think of it, I can't remember where the men folk would be. Hmmm...oh, I think they'd be off somewhere playing dominos and having a good laugh. Every now and then they would be disturbed from the serious business of having fun as their wives called on them to come help them with some task. As a kid, I wished for days like these everyday. Not for the food, but the togetherness.

In our Guyanese national calendar Diwali always seemed to be the biggest Hindu religious festivals, especially because of the message that was being preached: the triumph of good over evil, light over darkness etc.

On holidays like these, my mom never cooked at home, we always went to Auntie Betty's home for a food-fest. It was all-day eating. You would just finish eating something delicious only to spy that another dish had been added to the already over-laden table. We children would run around, play a little to burn off some food, and then return to sample the new fare on the table. Vegetarian dishes ruled the day: dhal, rice, potatoes, a variety of sautéed vegetables and an endless array of pickles and chutneys with snacks to go with them.

At festival times, I suddenly developed a sweet tooth and there were two things I was most interested in – parsad and roat. Parsad is made with flour, ghee, sugar, cardamom milk and water. I like it with raisins; some people also add cherries and nuts. It's like a pudding, the flour is toasted with the ghee and the sweetened liquid that's added is gradually cooked with the flour-ghee mixture all the while increasing the volume of the flour making it fluffy and sweet.

Roat is made with a dough made up of flour, ghee, sugar, milk, cinnamon that quickly comes together, flattened into round quarter-inch-thick disks and pan fried.

These two sweets in particular, the parsad and roat, were always served at jhandi(s) (some of you may refer to it as a pooja). So you can imagine my joy whenever festivals such as Diwali come around. Sure I can have these all year round but having it on specific occasions is what makes them special.

A few months ago, I got my cousin, Doris, who lives in Canada to guide me by email through the process of making the parsad and what can I tell you, she is a fantastic guide; I got it right the first time I made it and received high marks from my guide when I emailed her the photographs. This July when I went to Guyana for a visit, I was boasting to my mom and aunt that I knew how to make parsad and all I got was that polite smile saying, "Yeah right, sure honey."

While on the same trip in July, I had Auntie Betty teach me how to make roat.

I especially liked the Diwali evenings, that's when all the action seemed to take place, at least to me. All the children in the family would gather to help fill the diyas with ghee or oil but we were never allowed to light the diyas. I think the adults sensed the excitement we'd have in striking the matches. What is it about children and fire eh? Once the diyas were lit, we'd be instructed where and how to place the diyas around the yard, fence and house. I'd stand enveloped in the warmth and glow of the lit diyas and feel a pang of sadness that I'd have to wait all year to be able to enjoy this again.

As an adult and a broadcaster, I spent many Diwali evenings driving around the city and countryside in the then Guyana Broadcasting Corporation's Outside Broadcast vehicle along with a co-commentator, commenting on the sights and sounds of Diwali. There was always a motorcade, even those who were not Hindus would have their home decorated with fairy lights, people would throng the streets, cars bumper to bumper as they made their way around the city admiring the artistry and colourful lighting. It's times like these that I miss Guyana dearly.

It would be remiss of me to end and not say how very much I enjoy the Eid holidays. While we weren't as involved in activities as we were at Phagwah and Diwali, the joyous atmosphere was very much the same and, again, food played a big part in the celebration. It was through friends, rather than family, that I experienced the Eid holidays. My dear friend Zalaika always treated me like a member of her family. I remember one Eid-ul-Fitr visiting her home and telling her about a mitai (kurma) I had eaten a very long time ago but have never been able to put my hands on since, she quickly recognised it from my description. Later in the afternoon, after a nap, I went downstairs and...excuse me while I savour this memory... Zalaika and her mom were there making the mitai, one rolling and cutting the dough as the other one assembled it for frying. And this was after slaving all day in front of the stove preparing the umpteen number of dishes we had earlier in the day. Thank you, Zalaika.

Another treat I enjoy at Eid is vermicelli cake. My cousin-in-law, Shrieen, makes a vermicelli cake that always makes you ask for seconds. Each slice is perfection with the noodles compact with cherries and raisins populating every bite while the cinnamon and clove perfumes the dish. I'm getting homesick here so I need to stop.

▶ Parsad, 294–295

▶ Roat, 304–305

▶ Vermicelli Cake, 318

Time for Conkies

It's hard work, all that grating, mixing, spooning and folding. But the end result is almost indescribable. You gently but urgently unwrap the parcel and let the aroma waft over your entire face as you take a deep breath. The scent of cinnamon and nutmeg tingle your nose; you gaze longingly at that smooth, thick, warm, square of condensed pumpkin, corn meal, coconut.... Take a bite and immediately your mouth is full of sweet deliciousness. You rub some of it against the roof of your mouth with your tongue all the while savouring the smooth texture of the perfectly cooked ingredients. You chew and smile as you bite into a raisin, a little surprise that is sweet and a little tart at the same time. You take another bite, then another and before you know it, it's all gone. You've just eaten your first conkie of the season.

Conkies are a sweet treat made primarily with corn meal, pumpkin, sugar and spices; they are wrapped and steamed in banana leaves. The dish is African in origin According to the *A-Z of Barbadian Heritage*, the Ghanaian "kenkey" is probably the origin of the local word, conkie.

In Ghana, kenkey refers to similarly prepared corn meal dishes. Throughout the Caribbean each country has its own version of this dish. Back in Guyana, I have only vague memories of my Auntie Betty making conkies. All I can remember, is unwrapping the banana-leaf parcel, seeing a square-shaped orange pudding and smelling that wonderful aroma.

Although you can find a version of the conkie throughout the Caribbean, Bajans in particular take their conkies and conkie-making skills very seriously. In Barbados conkies used to be associated with November 5th or Guy Fawkes Night. However, these days conkies are particularly associated with Independence. Independence, in other words, is conkie season.

Conkie is a food that is a perfect example of cooking by instinct and personal taste –trusting your inner chef. From varying the quantities of ingredients, to modifying the combination of those ingredients, to adjusting the cooking time and, finally, to deciding what is a perfect conkie, all of these are a matter of personal taste. Most of people I know who make conkies do so from memory and observation – "I try to do it the way my mother did it" they say, or how my aunt, my wife or how some other member of the family did it.

In any dish there's always a star ingredient. For many Bajans the star in the Bajan conkie is the pumpkin, though for others it's the corn meal (also called Indian corn or meal corn), the spices or the raisins. The two main ingredients – pumpkin and cornmeal – vary in quantity because it's based on an individual taste. Still, most people talk about having more pumpkin because of the smooth texture when eating, instead of a gritty one from having too much cornmeal. The other ingredients are: coconut, sweet potatoes, sugar, salt, butter or margarine, lard, flour, essence (mixed, vanilla) milk, water, eggs, cinnamon, nutmeg, all spice, and raisins. Some people use *all* these ingredients and some don't. The *best* recipe is *your own* – the one passed down to you or the one you got from someone and tweaked. The recipe I use is a tweaked one.

Once the ingredients are assembled, the hard work really begins – *grating*. A large box grater is the best tool for the job. In these modern times we think of turning to the food processor – don't. You see, all the ingredients need to be the consistency of a very fine grind and using a food processor will only make a very fine chop, or, you would have to add water when using the food processor to give the desired consistency and that can ruin your recipe because it would mean that there is more liquid than required. It is very important to get the consistency right because all the ingredients have to cook at the same time, evenly.

When all the grating is complete all the ingredients need to be thoroughly mixed together. Clean hands work best. A couple of tips: melt the butter, margarine and lard together before adding it to the mixture. Soak the raisins in some warm water or as a friend suggests, some rum to plump them up. Nice! The completed mixture should be soft and moist *not* runny or watery.

The banana leaves are a *very* important ingredient, even though they are not eaten. The banana leaves are used to wrap the conkies and it is very important that you choose them with great care. What this means is that you cannot choose the old leaves, they would be too hard, brittle, and break easily; don't get the young ones either, the leaves are too tender and will not give the sort of protection needed for proper steaming. You want the leaves that are now maturing. Once the leaves are cut, they are cleaned either by washing or wiping clean with a damp cloth. Turn on the stove and over medium heat briefly pass the leaves. This is referred to as singeing. This process makes the leaves pliable enough to fold.

The banana leaves are then cut into large squares, not just to hold the filling, but also to fold properly and securely.

Place the mixture in the middle of the cut out leaf and fold: left, right, top and bottom or bottom, top, right and left; it really does not matter which side is folded first, the main thing is to fold the leaf securing the conkie mixture.

Create a steamer if you don't have one by using the spine (hard stem) of the banana leaves. Cut, chop or break the spines to create sticks and then criss-cross them at the bottom of a large pot (think lattice work). Pour in enough water to cook the cookies creating the desired steam. With the lid on, bring the water to a boil then arrange the parcels in the pot (make sure that the boiling water cannot touch them). and let the conkies steam until done. For extra protection, some people place a few pieces banana leaves on top of the sticks before adding the parcels of conkies and then a few more on top of them creating an even more condensed steaming environment.

The cooking time will vary. It will depend on the size of the conkies and the quantity. A very good friend of mine says he can tell by the aroma wafting through the house that it's done, but most people usually take out one of the conkies at the top to test it. If it meets their expectations – firm, smooth and cooked through – it's done.

Some of my friends like to eat their conkies hot, but I think the best way to have them is warm or at room temperature, that's how I like mine.

I heard of a woman who took conkies to the United States and had them in the freezer for a year. Whenever she had the cravings for one, she warmed it up in a microwave. She said it was fresh and seemed to be even more flavourful. Ah, there's nothing like the taste of home when you're far away.

Certain foods are *made* to be shared. Conkies are one such food. They come already wrapped like presents and made in large quantities to be shared. No one makes just five conkies, twelve is the minimum and you count yourself lucky to be among those invited to partake in this wonderful expression of love, kindness and generosity.

Happy Independence Barbados!

▶   Conkies, 280–283

Gets Better with Age
Pepperpot & Garlic Pork

There are some things in life that just get better with age – wine, steak, cured meats, black cake, and two of the many must-haves for Guyanese at Christmas time: pepperpot and garlic pork. One we cook and leave on the stovetop for days on end and the other, we set and forget, at least for two weeks.

Pepperpot is the dish we cook and leave on the stove top for days, reheating it daily to intensify its flavour. When the aroma of that roaring pot of meats and spices bubbling fills your nose there is a downright homey feeling. For many of us it is a smell we grew up with at this the "most wonderful time of the year." The smell makes us feel at home, even if we are not physically there.

Pepperpot is one of our proud national dishes that comes to us from the Indigenous peoples. Though we traditionally make and eat it at Christmas time it can also be had throughout the year but trust me, pepperpot in June is not the same as pepperpot in December. I firmly believe that it's the atmosphere that prevails and the other smells around that truly makes this dish festive and treasured.

As a rule, I never eat pepperpot the day it is made; I only start eating it after it has been cooked for at *least* 24 hours. This is not an easy rule. The smells of pepperpot are so tempting that there have been times when I barely made the 24-hour mark. You have to think of this dish in terms of a finely aged wine, cheese or cured meat. In the case of the pepperpot, it is all about the aged sauce and bones that have completely absorbed the flavourings of the dish. You see, the more mature the dish gets, through the constant boiling/reheating, the flavour intensifies as the sauce reduces, making it richer and velvety-smooth.... Seriously, talk about flavour to the bone!

In terms of the actual taste of the dish, it strikes a chord between sweet and salt, erring a little more on the side of sweet – but not sweet in a way that's like dessert sweet. More like notes of sweetness that are tempered with spicy ginger and cinnamon, fruity orange oils from the peel, the heat from the pepper and the warmth of the cloves.

Let me back up a little bit and tell you how we come to the flavours and the all-important bones.

For great pepperpot, you've got to start with good ingredients and the key ingredient here is the cassareep – a thick, dark sauce that is made with the juice extracted from grated cassava. The juice is boiled for a very long time until it becomes thick, black and syrupy. It is the natural preservative elements in cassareep that enables pepperpot to stand at room temperature and be eaten for days, sometimes weeks, without refrigeration.

The popular meats for pepperpot are pig trotters, cow-heel, beef, pork and some people add a piece of salt-meat to impart the salt necessary for the dish. Those who don't eat beef or pork for religious reasons make chicken pepperpot ensuring that they add the chicken feet to the dish as it gives that gelatinous component that is key and aids in the slight thickening of the sauce.

So we've got our casareep and meat, now we need the flavourings – cinnamon sticks, whole cloves, fresh root ginger, orange peel and a scotch bonnet pepper with salt and sugar to taste. I know that there are some people that like to "season" the meat before adding it to the pot with herbs etc. that is a mighty big no-no! The herbs, onions and other things added would spoil the pepperpot, I mean that the pepperpot would "turn" or get "sour" because don't forget, it is a dish that is kept unrefrigerated and on the stove top for days on end.

To preserve its long life, pepperpot is reheated twice a day. The entire pot is brought to a boil for a few minutes and then the heat turned off.

Many people, including myself grew up eating pepperpot with home-made bread. I stress *home-made* bread because the sliced bread just does not cut it when it comes to eating pepperpot. Such a hearty dish requires a homemade, rustic, hunk of bread to sop up the pepperpot juice-gravy-sauce. So keep away those dainty, see-through sliced breads. Traditionally, pepperpot is eaten with cassava bread given to us also by the Indigenous peoples. While cassava bread is still available, most people, however, use wheat-flour bread.

A couple of tips for preserving the life of your pepperpot: always use clean utensils whenever dipping into it; always keep it covered; reheat the pepperpot daily bringing it to a boil; if your oven comes with a pilot (you know that little flame that's always on and keeps the oven warm), place the covered pot in there.

Garlic pork, that other aged dish with the other white meat is not as fussy to make and maintain as pepperpot. If you're a pork lover, you've got to try some garlic pork. Thanks to our Portuguese ancestors, we have a lip-smacking dish that wakes up the palette, the household and the neighbours! It's highly aromatic.

Garlic pork in the barest sense is a pickle. It's made with thin cuts of pork and soaked in a salted, distilled vinegar and water solution and seasoned with lots of freshly ground garlic and thyme.

This is a dish you have to plan in advance, in other words, if you want to eat garlic pork on Christmas morning, think about setting it at least two weeks or more in advance. This is necessary because that meat has to soak and absorb the pickling ingredients. I'd say that the least amount of time you can leave garlic pork to set is seven days. Me, I like to have it from two weeks onwards when it's more intensely garlicky-thymey-vinegary-salty.

To cook it, remove from the pickling jar, as many pieces as you wish to cook, heat a pan with only a drizzle of oil and pan fry it on both sides until cooked through. Slice thin and serve. Because garlic pork is an intense dish, it is not generally eaten in large quantities, remember it is like a pickle and as with any pickle, moderation is best for the taste buds.

Tis the season for cured and aged things!

▶ Pepperpot, 180–181
▶ Garlic Pork, 156–157
▶ Baked Ham, 128–129

Christmas Rituals
Making the Cake, Breaking up the House, and Decorating

Warning! DON'T EAT AND DRIVE! Yeah, I know that it's different from the familiar Don't Drink and Drive but I tell you, this should be a label attached to all Christmas black cakes. This is a deep, dark and dangerously intoxicating cake that can make you wobbly at the knees just by smelling it.

Black cake, dark cake, rum cake, Christmas cake, call it what you will, the holidays would not be the same without it, just as they would not be without ham, sorrel, pepper-pot or garlic pork.

Throughout the Caribbean, we each have our own versions of black cake. For some it is not only part of the Christmas tradition but also for weddings, christenings and other significant occasions. What makes it "our" black cake is defined by the rum used. In other words, it is Barbadian black cake because it is made with Barbadian rum or Jamaica's because it is made with their rum and so it goes for each country.

All human lives revolve around rituals and in the Caribbean one of our most important rituals is the ritual of the black cake. We start by "setting" the fruits. By "setting" the fruits, we mean blending or chopping them and soaking the mixture in various alcoholic beverages so that they can absorb the flavours of the alcohol and be cured.

The dried fruits, raisins, currants, prunes, dates, cherries, and mixed peel are all ground together and soaked with one or a combination of these alcoholic beverages - rum, port wine, cherry brandy and, for Barbadians, Falernum.

When to set the fruits and for how long? Some of us follow the tradition of our parents and grandparents and others do whatever is convenient for them. Purely by accident (or maybe not), I follow the tradition of my mother by soaking fruits a year in advance. I always buy more fruit than I need and by the time I'm finished blending, soaking and baking, I have an extra bottle of alcohol infused fruits. Every year, I make a new batch to replace the one I am going to use.

I have a friend who always has some left over from baking and whenever she can, she will grind some fruits and add it to the bottle, always topping it up. By the time Christmas rolls around, she has fruits that have been marinating for a long, long time.

A black cake aficionado can tell the difference between a black cake that's had it fruits soaked for a year and one that's been soaking for only a few days or weeks. The cake made with fruits soaking for only a few days or weeks, while delicious, will be a little dry but the cake made with fruits soaking for 9 months or a year is moist and almost pudding-like. Rituals are special, and you know when you serve your black cake someone who fancies them self an expert will ask you, "So how long did you set your fruits?" And woe betides you if you don't have a good answer. Enjoyed traditionally with an ice-cold glass of ginger beer or sorrel, it is truly one of the pleasures of the season.

Setting fruits for cake is only one of the many rituals when it comes to preparing for Christmas. We are known for "breaking up" the house. All the curtains are taken down, every stick of furniture is pushed far to the corners and covered, and rugs are rolled away, all in preparation for the biggest, deepest clean of the year. Each and every child resentfully learns what hard work means for the one to two weeks as walls are wiped, cupboards scrubbed, silver cleaned, china washed, cushions and chairs re-upholstered. For that period it looks like the house has been hit by a bomb. But, in the end, when everything looks clean and new and all the Christmas decorations are up, you can sit back and enjoy the beauty of your home as you munch on your black cake.

Growing up, in our home, my mother insisted that the house be finished decorating by December 15 because we are Roman Catholics and December 15 marks the beginning of Novena – nine consecutive days of devotion and prayer, in this case, leading up to Christmas. It is a tradition I uphold to date. Apart from the significance of the occasion, mom's justification was that she wanted to admire and revel in the delights of her home. There is no way she would find herself stressed out on Christmas Eve still cleaning, decorating and preparing for the big meal the next day. We often learn our rituals from our mothers, so I keep to my mom's schedule. I don't want to be exhausted on Christmas day. I don't want midnight to find me putting up curtains. I want to be curled up in bed fast asleep or in a comfortable chair basking in the warmth of the fairy lights with a glass of sherry to toast the new day.

I'll forever cherish the memories of Christmas Eve night mass at Sacred Heart Church (burnt down on Christmas morning in 2004). Each year there would be a re-enactment of the nativity, complete with elaborate costumes, two choirs, "Kings" that could actually sing, and a real baby to play the part of Jesus!

I enjoy Christmas Eve more than Christmas day itself, there is something electrifying about the day, something magical as the hours and minutes climb to the midnight hour. I never want Christmas Eve to end. When I was younger, early in the evening Mommy would always make a large pot of cook-up rice. That was dinner and also to feed the 2 a.m. hunger we and some of our friends would have coming home from Midnight Mass.

My most enjoyable meal at Christmas used to be breakfast, well, actually brunch given that we never sat down to the table before 10.30 a.m. My Auntie Betty and her family would join us for this meal. I enjoyed the chatter, the laughter, the teasing, and the togetherness. Equally important and significant in this merrymaking was being able to drink coffee, it was the only time we would be grown up enough to drink coffee. Mom never allowed us to have it otherwise, not until we were adults. Oh, and everyone at the table was also served a glass of sherry with their meal. Oh yeah!

As I sit here, there's a pain in my heart, now everyone's grown up and flung far and wide across the globe with their own families making new traditions and maintaining some rituals. It makes me treasure the memories even more. This year, we're blessed to have a new member in our family, my nephew, Ethan. I look forward to the days when I can share our Christmas rituals with him. Yeah, he looks like he's going to be a strong little boy; he'll be a good lil worker when it comes to breaking up the house.

► Christmas Cake, 270–273
► Ginger Beer, 244–245
► Sorrel Drink, 260–261

I Like it Hot! Hot! Hot!

Whether I am eating pepper raw, boiled or in pepper sauce, I like it so hot that I am barely able to breathe through my nose. I even have a technique: inhale through my mouth welcoming the cool air and then exhale through my nose. I can't exhale through my mouth as the warm breath will only burn my tongue more.

In the Caribbean we have been blessed to have the mother of hot peppers – the scotch bonnet; often we simply call them, "the big hot peppers." It's a pepper that's associated with the Caribbean and made popular perhaps by the Jamaicans in their use of it in jerk seasonings. But it's not only in Jamaica that this pepper is widely used, in fact, it's the entire Caribbean. Ask a Trinbigonian making pelau and they'll tell you they must put a pepper in de pot. Ask a Guyanese making cook-up rice, a Bajan making souse, a Grenadian making oil-down, a St Lucian frying salt fish, a Kittian making escoveitched fish, a Dominican serving up some fish co-bouillon or.... It matters not what we are making, as long as it is savoury we got to have some hot pepper.

Those of us who are real chilli-heads dabble with eating pepper raw or boiled, most others opt for the pepper sauce, but please do not take this as an indication that those who prefer the pepper sauce are less adventurous – scotch bonnet pepper sauce is nothing to scoff at. I have seen people weep from the heat, blow their noses uncontrollably as their sinuses cleared, drink way too much water and vow never to eat pepper again – well, until their next meal.

I cannot emphasise enough how terrifyingly hot the scotch bonnet is. I once heard about a woman who was removing the stems off scotch bonnets to prepare them to make pepper sauce. She didn't use any gloves. BIG mistake! For two straight weeks her hands felt like they were on fire.

Once, whilst visiting the USA, my friend Will gave me some scotch bonnets he'd grown. I put them in the fridge at the place where I was staying and went out to engage in my favourite pastime when I'm in America – patrolling the bookstores. When I got back to my home-base I didn't even realise one of my scotch bonnets was missing until my host gave me her tale of fire and woe. Seems my good friend and host had seen the scotch bonnets in the fridge and mistaken these cute bright red and orange peppers for sweet peppers. She took a big bite out of one of them. Suffice it to say, she learned a great deal about scotch bonnets that day.

But I don't want to give the impression that we Caribbean people like the heat of pepper beyond all common sense and sense of taste. We certainly do not want to mask the flavours of our food with heat, what we are about is adding enough heat to elevate the flavours of ingredients and heightening the eating experience. Thus, though, the Caribbean is known for the scotch bonnet pepper, we also have other varieties of peppers that are also really hot and flavourful. The bird peppers, also known as bird eye chillies, are tiny heat bombs waiting to explode - talk about not judging something by its size! We also have the wiri wiri peppers that are also called cherry peppers because they are small and round, and used for their bouquet in seasonings. These pretty little things command respect. Over the last two years I've been finding fresh, locally grown jalapeno peppers in the supermarket in Barbados and at the farmers' market, the standard chillies – red and green. I think that this is a direct result of our expanding food knowledge.

Since I've only used fresh peppers in my cooking, I was a little skeptical about the dried red chillies I bought once at a spice store in Guyana, I wondered if they'd still be as hot and flavour- enhancing. They were, and now I use them in combination with my fresh peppers. Come to think of it, when I was growing up one of our neighbours preferred to use the dried pepper; they said the flavour was more intense. They used to have a large glass bottle filled with dried scotch bonnet peppers sitting on their kitchen counter and whoever was preparing the spice or herb paste for cooking would add a few pieces of the dried pepper to grind with the other ingredients.

My friend Kumi who is from Sri Lanka introduced me to curd chilli (chillies cured in curd and salt and then dried). Kumi sent the chillies with warnings that they are really hot and spicy. I figured that I'd use them cautiously and so I cooked them in dhal, I liked the subtle flavour they imparted and the gentle heat. As I ate my meal, I sucked on the chilli and let the saltiness bathe my tongue. I like this chilli, a lot, but I need more action so I always add a piece of scotch bonnet whenever I use it. Actually, I like these curd chillies so much that I find myself sucking on them right out of the bag! Oh, I am careful not to bite and get into the seeds, but I am totally hooked on the taste. I try not to have more than two at a go though because the heat can be dangerous. I am sucking on

my second curd chilie as I write and right now I have the sniffles.

When I am cooking for others I always adjust the pepper to suit their palates and even if someone says that they eat pepper, I am never sure what that really means in terms of degree of heat so I add some pepper but not enough to cause discomfort. Depending on what I am cooking, I use different peppers. For example, if I am seasoning meat for chicken and making a paste, I grind up some wiri wiri peppers, but if I'm making a marinade, I opt for the pepper sauce. If I am cooking cook up rice, I put a big scotch bonnet pepper in the pot, being careful not to let it burst, If I am sautéing vegetables, I use the regular chillies, when I am making dhal or curry, I use scotch bonnets, seeds and all.

In every Caribbean home you can find bottles of hot pepper sauce. Even if no pepper sauce is around, there's bound to be some condiment that's as fiery as the pepper sauce, such as an achar or chutney. When we travel overseas we travel with pepper sauce, not only as hostess gifts, but also for ourselves. My mom always packs 2 gallon-size zip bags of wiri wiri peppers for her friend Carol to take back to the US whenever she visits. You see, Carol knows, my mom knows, in fact we all know that it just don't taste like home unless de food got a lil' heat.

▶   Pepper Sauce, 216–217
▶   Fried Fish, 206–207

The Essence of Choka

Choka is one of the most pleasurable foods I have ever eaten. It's one of those things that you crave but don't necessarily make often. This is because making choka involves quite a bit of time and effort. Nevertheless, when all you hear from a roomful of people as they eat is, "uummmm" you realise that time making choka is time well spent it

Choka refers to a method of preparing particular ingredients. It is about fire roasting, pounding and grinding. The fire roasting is absolutely necessary to impart the highly-desired smokiness. The pounding and grinding are to obtain the right consistency and texture. Failure to meet these standards – smokiness, consistency and texture, results in you being dismissed by choka aficionados as merely creating a wannabe choka. Yes my friends there are exacting standards when it comes to making choka.

In Guyana, and I'm sure the same can be said for Trinidad and Tobago, we essentially make six chokas – coconut choka, eggplant choka, tomato choka, potato choka, salt fish choka and smoked herring choka. After the ingredients are roasted, pounded or ground, they are seasoned lightly, some with garlic, onions, green onions, lemon or lime juice and always, always, with hot pepper. Chokas are often made and served in small quantities, they're more a side dish than a main dish, and they're mostly eaten with dhal and rice or roti.

Chokas can be easily divided into the 3 mealtime categories, breakfast, lunch and dinner. Eggplant, tomato and potato are the preferred chokas for breakfast and dinner served with roti while coconut, salt fish and smoked herring chokas are lunchtime favourites with dhal and rice.

In a previous article, I had mentioned coconut choka and how my sister and I always resented making it. It was not because we did not like coconut choka; it was because of all grinding that had to be done. The roasted and grated coconut had to be to ground so fine, releasing the oils and moisture that resulted in the mixture being able to be rolled easily into the shape of a ball! So Pat and I always cringed whenever mom would say that *she* was making coconut choka because that *really* meant that Pat or I were making the choka.

One fine Sunday morning, many years ago, my sister and I thought we'd surprise Mommy by getting up early and making eggplant choka and roti. You see, my mom thought that we were not interested in learning to make such kinds of food. She was wrong. It's not that we weren't interested; rather, it was that, because of the exacting roti and choka-making standards, we often felt inadequate, not up to the task. Still, one morning we decided to try a lil' something.

The household woke up that morning to the aroma of roasting eggplant stuffed with slivers of garlic. Mommy was truly surprised though all she could muster was, "Which pillow did you all put your heads on last night?" In other words, what had gotten into us that resulted in our making such an elaborate breakfast? Her surprise was two-fold, one that we were actually making breakfast (my sister, like me is not a breakfast person) and two, that we had gone to such lengths. We were so proud of our efforts and we were both on our way to mastering the art of choka making.

For me, choka is soul-food, and though growing up I disliked having to make it because there was always something "wrong" with it (it's those exacting standards again), it is a skill and food knowledge that I treasure.

These days, I like making choka and I enjoy the thrill of making it for friends who know about choka, and I like introducing people to chokas. This week, I set about making six chokas and a few other dishes to treat some friends. In the process of my cooking marathon, I confirmed a notion, that is, that the modern day food processor is a choka-making-girl's best friend! Sure enough there's the cleaning and prepping of the ingredients after the roasting but the grinding and pounding, which is what really takes up the time, can be done in minute in the food processor.

The biggest triumph was the coconut choka. After grating it with the box grater (hand grater) I added it to the food processor with the garlic, pepper, salt and lemon juice (I didn't have any green mango which is what we traditionally use) and let me tell you, when it was done, all I had to do was mould it into a ball. The salt fish and smoked herring chokas were perfectly frizzed, fluffy, and light. The pulse button on the processor helped me achieve the right texture for the eggplant and tomato choka. Oh and a potato ricer makes fast work of mashing the potatoes for potato choka.

I should probably clarify something here about making potato choka, especially since one of the tenets of choka is fire roasting. What I do is boil the potatoes first and *then* char them on the open flames on the stove top to give them the required smoke-factor. Most people, however, simply boil the potatoes and mash them, adding onions, green onions, salt, pepper and a drizzle of oil.

Choka is a great way to introduce people to new tastes and flavours, so if you've never had a choka today is the right time to try your hand at making some.

Who knows, soon you too can have a choka lime. Just don't forget to send my invitation!

▶ Coconut Choka, 204–205
▶ Eggplant Choka, 108–109
▶ Salt fish Choka, 218–219
▶ Smoked-herring Choka, 220–221
▶ Tomato Choka, 121–122
▶ Potato Choka, 114–115

A Golden Love for the Golden apple

I owe Barbados for my love of the golden apple.

In Guyana I had seen and eaten a couple of golden apples, but I never got the lure of this fruit with its prickly seed. I didn't get what the fuss was all about, gimme a mango instead. Fast forward about five years after being in Barbados and being given a large bag of green golden apples by George, one of my colleagues. George encouraged me to make some golden apple juice. I heard another of my colleague's remark, "I like golden apple juice but it's a lot of work." Later, I was to truly understand that statement.

I peeled about three-dozen golden apples using a paring knife and then sliced them into small pieces to put into the blender to make the juice. By the time I had finished peeling and slicing, my right hand was hurting and added to that, the next day I saw the blisters on my index finger where the knife rested. It was the kind of blister where the skin puffs up with liquid. The peeling was not that bad, it was the slicing, here's why. A golden apple has a seed and radiating from that seed are fibrous strands that one has to cut through when slicing. The closer you get to the core, the more difficult it becomes to cut the fruit. But I have to tell you, the juice was worth it, blisters and all, I had never had golden apple juice before and it tasted soooo good. I was hooked. It was fruity, aromatic, refreshing and packed with good vitamins.

I shared the juice among my colleagues, since that was the deal, but I was wise enough not to volunteer to make golden apple juice for everyone again. Let someone else take on the job. Now that is not to say that I foreswore making golden apple juice ever again. No way! The next time I planned to use different methods and they worked. Instead of the paring knife, I used a vegetable peeler, and instead of slicing and then chipping the flesh by hand without a cutting board, I decided to stabilise the golden apple with one hand on my cutting board. With my chef's knife in the other hand I just cut any which way – slices, chunks, slivers – and I let the blender do the rest of the work.

Here's another way I owe Barbados for this golden apple love. One fine morning, I went for a swim at the beach. Early, I'm talking about 6 to 6.30 a.m. That early in the morning one sees a lot of retirees and other folks getting in their daily exercise. Well, on this particular morning, as I made my way up from the beach, there was a woman (whom I recognised from seeing often at the beach) holding a plastic bag of ripe golden apples in a liquid that looked just like plain water. She smiled in greeting and offered me a golden apple from the bag. I held onto one of the apples which was dripping with its watery solution and I bit into it. Oh-my-goodness! My eyes opened wide in amazement and my taste buds were immediately shocked into pleasure. The flesh was soft, sweet and juicy, the salty liquid in which the golden apple marinated had permeated the flesh which resulted in two things happening simultaneously – contrasting with the natural sweetness of the fruit and at the same time, heightening the flavour of the fruit. The woman saw my reaction and smiled knowingly. Without my saying a word she explained that the liquid was the sea water. She brought the peeled golden apples from home and then filled the bag with sea water. Gosh, just writing about this has me salivating. I had never tasted anything like that before and am forever grateful for the introduction.

At the beginning of this week I sat pondering what to write about and then yesterday at our beginning-of-the-semester staff meeting I saw my colleague George and he asked if I wanted some golden apples as they are in season.

Well, I think you know what my answer was. George's tree is laden with golden apples so much so that many have fallen and carpeted the lawn. As I drove home with my two bags of golden apple in the back seat, enveloped in the perfume of the fruit, thoughts began to whirl around my head as to the other things I can make with my golden apples. Earlier in the week, I had made stewed guavas so I was excited to try stewing the golden apples. It was just as good as the guavas in its own right. Meaty, soft and kissed with the flavours of cinnamon, cloves and all spice, this is a dish that can be eaten on its own or with ice cream. I've found that the half-ripe golden apple is the best to be stewed, the ripe ones are too soft and I found the green ones just a little too tart. The half-ripe golden apple brings the best of both – sweet from the ripened version and the tart from the green version. The syrup from the stew can also be drizzled over pancakes, over toast with cheese or it can be used in any other creative ways you can dream of.

I'm off now to experiment by making a golden apple crumble. I'm excited at the prospect but am unsure as to how it will turn out.

▶ Golden apple tree pictured at page 1
▶ Golden Apple Crumble, 286–287
▶ Golden Apple Drink, 246–247
▶ Stewed Golden Apple, 310–311

Hard at Work

Making Chinese Cake

In life one should never say "never," so I won't say it; what I will say is that it will be a very, very long time before I ever make Chinese cake again even though I love it so much. There's just too much work involved. Of course, there is always the reward after that hard work of eating one or four of those delectable pastries.

A Chinese cake is a baked pastry filled with sweetened black-eyed peas, and it's one of those things that I've always wanted to learn how to make. So when a Guyanese friend of Chinese heritage visited over the holidays, I eagerly sought an audience with her to get the recipe and have her talk me through the process. Before she even gave me the recipe she warned that it was a lot of work. But I thought I was up to the challenge, after all, I had stirred a pot of cornmeal cou cou for 90 minutes and the pulp to make guava cheese even longer; I had spent the better part of a day making conkies from cutting the branches to steaming the packages, I thought I was ready for Chinese cake. I was wrong.

It all started with the cooking of the black-eyed peas. The actual cooking of the peas was easy, but pressing and mashing them through the sieve can get tiresome. You see, the peas immediately begin to dry off as soon as they are out of the water-cooked solution. So you have to put a little more effort into rubbing, mashing and pressing them through the sieve and you have to be sure to scrape the bottom of the sieve so that there's a clean passage as you continue to mash and press the peas.

Whew, alright that was done; the peas were smooth and creamy, time to cook the mixture for the filling. I had been told that I would have to add equal amounts of sugar to the mashed peas and set it to cook until the mixture came away cleanly from the sides of the pot. I groaned at this prospect. This meant that it was going to take ages and that the heat had to be regulated to avoid scorching and burning. This also meant that I would have to stir the mixture constantly. By the time the filling reached the right consistency and came away easily from the sides of the pot, any chance of making the cakes was shot because the filling had to be cooled completely before being handled. Given the thick, soft, fudge-like nature of the filling, that meant it would be hours before it cooled completely, so I made a decision there and then that I'd complete the Chinese-cake-making process, the following day.

Actually, later in the evening when the filling cooled, it became solid and I started to panic, was it supposed to get like this? But I kept saying to myself all the time, "Nora said break off a piece of the filling." So certainly, it meant that the filling would be solid once cooled. I wasn't convinced though; I worried all night and wondered if I should cook another set of peas. I calmed down enough to overcome that urge.

The next day, it was time to make the pastry dough. You would think that it is one dough to make right? Wrong! There are two different doughs to make this cake/pastry; Nora calls the first one a cheap pastry and the second one a rich pastry. The cheap pastry is one part shortening to three parts flour and the rich pastry is one part shortening to one part flour. The cheap pastry is made first and set aside as the rich pastry is made. The dough of the rich

pastry is divided equally into say, 1 oz pieces and here's where it gets tricky, one now has to divide the rich pastry, which is considerably less than the cheap pastry, into the same number of parts as the cheap pastry! For example, I got 20 1-oz pieces from my cheap pastry and so I needed to get 20 pieces of the rich pastry, the weight of course was different, all you really need is a little more than a pinch but it's important that it is equally divided.

Okay so now the pastries were all divided equally. I then had to flatten each piece of cheap pastry, insert a piece of the rich pastry, enclose it by pinching the edges together then flatten it again and roll it thin with a rolling pin. Once rolled, I had to roll up the dough from one end to another, to form like a thick cigarette, once that's rolled; I twisted it into a swirl. These are necessary and important steps as they provide the necessary layers that are highly desired in a proper Chinese cake.

When I finished filling, flattening, rolling and twisting, I had to fill the dough, *again*, this time with the black-eye peas filling. This was simple, though it took some time. I made a disk of the dough, broke off a piece of the hard filling and then enclosed it, again by pinching the edges together. It is absolutely necessary that the edges are secured if not the filling will burst through the pastry and burn.

Once I'd finish filling the dough, adding a light egg-wash and a dot of red food colouring for decoration, into the oven went the Chinese cakes for 30–40 minutes.

The true test was yet to come; will the hard filling have melted? Is it going to taste like I remembered it? I broke one of the cakes in half and smiled as the pastry broke gently to reveal the layers and the dark, rich, sweet, paste-like filling. I ate it braced up against the cupboard in the kitchen and cast my mind back to my first taste of Chinese cake and one of my fondest memories.

My late Uncle Freddy used to be the head barman at one of the then posh hotels in Guyana, Tower. Some afternoons, when he worked the shift that would end at 7 p.m. my Aunt Betty would take my cousin Keshwar and me for a walk so we could all meet Uncle Freddy as he was coming off his shift. We'd always leave home just as the sun would set and with enough time to stop at Faraj's which used to be at the corner of Main and Quamina streets (now Arapaima). There, Auntie Betty would buy us Chinese cakes and peanut punch. We'd sit on the bench in the avenue and enjoy our treat. I liked biting into my cake and looking up at the bright lights that lit up the hotel outside, all the while waiting for my dear Uncle Freddy.

Nora thanks for the recipe that's helped me to recreate a taste and a memory that's very dear to my heart. Thank you.

▶ Chinese Cake, 266–269
▶ Peanut Punch, 257

Two Ingredients: One Love

On my plate this week is Jamaica's national dish, ackee and salt fish.

The first time I had ackee and salt fish was 10 years ago while on a trip to Jamaica. I had it at the University of the West Indies Mona Campus one morning. Prior to visiting Jamaica I had heard so much about ackee. Everyone that spoke about it described it lovingly. So of course whilst in Jamaica when I saw it on the breakfast menu, there was no doubt what I was going to order.

Sitting on my plate were chunks of bright yellow flesh and there were bits of salt fish strewn all over mingling with onions, tomatoes and sweet peppers. I ignored the fried dumplings served with them and dove right in. I honestly cannot say what I was expecting from the taste but here's what I found – the ackee was soft and creamy, almost melting in the mouth, and there was a hint of sweetness to it which contrasted tastefully with the saltiness of salt fish. The delicate crunch of the onions along with the tomatoes, sweet peppers and herbs made for a complex, interesting and new taste. I know you're probably wondering if after using words like complex, interesting and new taste, whether or not I liked it. The answer is yes! I'd never tasted anything like it before and it was even better when I had it with the fried dumplings.

A few years later having settled in Barbados, I had ackee and salt fish again, this time at a work function and it was served with boiled green bananas. Well, just in case you don't know by now, I love green bananas and when I saw it being served with the ackee and salt fish, I turned a blind eye to the other dishes on offer as I had eyes only for my love that was being served up with ackee and salt fish. In a word: bliss!

This past week, my friend Paula, who has an ackee tree, brought me a bag full, it weighed almost three pounds! I know I'm lucky; all you ackee-loving people please don't be envious! Shame on me though, I had no salt fish in the house and had to delay my enjoyment for a whole

24 hours before I could head out to the supermarket.

I knew there and then that ackee and salt fish was going to be the subject of an article, so I set about doing some homework and talking to a Jamaican friend, Yanique.

Here's what I found out: the ackee tree is an evergreen tree that's native to West Africa and it thrives in tropical and sub-tropical environments. The tree was first brought to Jamaica in the 1700s probably on a slave trip. Today ackee trees can be found all over the island and the fruit is touted as the second largest agricultural export. In 2006, revenue from exports are believed to have been around US$50-million.

Referred to as the national fruit of Jamaica, the ackee when it begins to ripen makes a colour transition from green to bright red to yellow-orange and splits open. When it splits open that's when you know that the ackee is ripe and ready for the picking. The split outer shell reveals three large shiny black seeds attached at the bottom to a soft white to cream-coloured flesh. To clean the ackee, you remove the black seeds and the membrane which would be a pink soft tissue.

Like many fruits and vegetables, ackee is seasonal and peaks from December to March and then again from June to August, however, some people have staggered their planting of

the ackee tree to facilitate fresh ackees being available all-year round.

Cooking ackee is fast and quick work, it takes just about 5 minutes to cook through and it's very important to not stir the ackees too much if not they will disintegrate and turn to mush. Therefore, when you're cooking ackee whether it is fresh or out of a can, you always want to add it last to the pot and to stir it only once. The ackees turn a bright yellow when cooked, hence the resemblance to scrambled eggs; the texture is similar as well.

Apart from being the national dish, ackee and salt fish is also traditional Jamaican breakfast meal and it's served with boiled green bananas, fried dumplings (similar to bakes) or fried plantains. When it's served on the weekends, like Saturday for example, it's eaten with boiled ground provisions such as yams and dasheens; if the ackee and salt fish are served with ground provisions however, the accompanying dumplings are boiled instead of fried. It's a real treat to have with roast breadfruit and at morning weddings it is the meal of choice.

At Christmas time, ackee is served with smoked ham and sometimes, bacon. Yum! Actually, ackee and salt fish have spread beyond the realm of breakfast; it is now enjoyed at any meal throughout the day. This meal has even moved into party-mode of cocktail appetizer not just because of its taste but also because it makes a striking presence. A riot of yellow, red and green sits atop small bammies (Jamaican cassava bread). My friend's (Yanique) mom serves them in phyllo cups, that's such a neat idea and definitely elevates the humble ackee and salt fish.

Although ackee is grown in other parts of the world and other Caribbean countries such as Haiti, Barbados, Cuba and Puerto Rico, it is Jamaica that this fruit and dish is mostly associated with. Those looking for a taste of home abroad or out of season can quickly satisfy that desire by reaching for a can of ackees. If you haven't tried a plate of ackee and salt fish yet, don't wait. Make it a priority.

▶ Ackee and Salt fish, 94–96

My True Love – Curry

Valentine's Day is fast approaching and we all know that romance is often spelled f-o-o-d: from the heart-shaped box of chocolates to the candlelight dinner for two in a fancy restaurant. But what about love *and* food, can we spare a few minutes to think about the foods we love? What is you're favourite dish?

No matter how fancy the food I eat, no matter how sophisticated my palate becomes, curry, will always be my first love. You see, curry is many things at one time, something no other dish I know can claim to be. It is simple, yet exotic; easy to prepare yet difficult to master; it can be spicy, and hot, or it can be mild. Curry is versatile. Vegetables, poultry, meat, seafood, eggs, fruit and ground provision can all be curried. Every time I look at an ingredient, especially if it's new to me, the first thing that comes to mind is, can I curry this? I wonder how this would taste curried?

Admitting to myself, and now publicly, that curry is my favourite dish was no easy feat. Cook-up rice, Chinese food and dhal were serious contenders. Like curry, they are foods that I can eat everyday and never get bored or tired of consuming. Nevertheless, curry was the clear winner once I started to list the things

that can be curried, the variety was staggering. Nostalgia played a part too – the first dish I ever cooked was curried pork.

When did my love affair with curry begin? I do not know. Like love, I think that it is one of those things that just happens. It creeps up on you, catches you unaware. You're confronted by certain situations and then it dawns on you – how much you miss it, how you long for it, how you crave the taste, hunt for the ingredients, and engage people in conversations about it. You have this intense feeling about it that cannot be satisfied until you consume it. That's the kind of hold that curry has over me, it's my love food.

Growing up my mom would ask us what we'd like to eat and my answer was always curry, until one day she said, "Girl, you ain't tired eating curry? Everyday you want curry. Well *I'm* tired of eating curry and I'm not cooking any for 2 weeks." Ouch!

When I arrived in Barbados, of all the foods of home, I missed curry the most. When my mom called to find out if I needed anything, I told her, "Send me some curry powder and garam masala."

My neighbours who live opposite my home are from India, when they make curry, the aroma stops me in my tracks as I make my way from the car to the house. I stand there sniffing the air trying to figure out if it is a meat or seafood curry. It is hard to describe but I can usually tell the difference just by smelling. When it is seafood, there is a lightness of the curry aroma, if it is vegetables, the natural scent of the vegetable is evident amidst the spicy mix. Curried meat and poultry tend to have a more robust, full-bodied aroma.

While I love all curry, my favourite type is seafood curry, specifically fish curry. Catfish, gilbaka and hassar are my favourites. I like my fish curry cooked with hot pepper, and some green mango, saijan or okras. Serve it with a plate of hot white rice and a little achar and I am in curry heaven. I am not big on the meaty part of the fish, give me the head where I can suck the bones! Don't even bother with cutlery, fingers it is! It is the only tool to do the job properly.

I love curry so much that I've often let my desire lead me astray, disappoint me. I've had restaurant servers recommend and encourage me to have the curry on their menus only to leave vowing to cook curry the very next day so that I can block out the awful taste of their curry. I've deliberately gone to establishments touting curry as their prized offering only to be let down.

Over the years, I've come to learn that there is curry and then there is curry. In other words, there is the curry that we eat here in the Caribbean and then there are the curries from other parts of the world. Our curry in the Caribbean is influenced by the curries of North and South India. The North Indian cuisine is considered to be mild while the South, spicier – we prepare both. The South Indian cuisine influenced our use of coconut milk in curries, an ingredient rarely seen in the North. Southerners like rice, the Northerners, wheat, and we know how we love rice *and* roti here in the Caribbean.

In the book *Curry: Fragrant dishes from India, Thailand, Malaysia and Indonesia,* Executive Chef, Vivek Singh best defines curry. "Essentially, any fish, meat or vegetables cooked in and with spices and liquid is a curry. The spices and liquid form a sauce that becomes a part of the dish. It is the spices or spice combinations that make each curry different."

Before my trip home last Christmas, my mom asked me what she should cook for me on the day of my arrival. I said, "Mommy, yuh asking answers?! I want curry!"

▶ Chicken Curry, 132–133

▶ Gilbaka Curry, 158–159

▶ Hassar Curry, 160–161

A New National Dish?

If the criteria for a national dish are that it must be the most popular and represent a nation's heritage, then I think that we need to elevate Chinese Fried Rice to the status it deserves – as a Guyanese national dish.

Here are the reasons:

- Of the three countries in the Caribbean with the largest Chinese population, Guyana boasts the most Chinese restaurants. Sheriff Street alone has 20, central Georgetown, a *conservative* estimate of 50 and in most communities, there are at least two Chinese restaurants.
- Many Guyanese eat fried rice everyday, sometimes more than once a day.
- The cuisine of choice when dining out is often Chinese, with fried rice being one of the most ordered dishes.
- A must-have dish at many family gatherings in homes is fried rice.
- Of the two restaurants to be housed at Guyana's first five-star hotel one is Chinese.

In Guyana, this land of six races and many waters, Chinese food is where we all find common ground, it transcends race and colour and creed. It is the one thing we can all agree on – we love Chinese food, we love fried rice. It is evident in the way we have incorporated it into our culinary offerings in the most intimate and private setting – our homes. It is not just something we consume when we haven't cooked at home.

We just can't seem get enough Chinese food; we can't get enough fried rice. Home cooks have honed and crafted their fried rice-making skills to an art; my cousin's wife, Shireen is one of them. There continues to be debate and discussion on how best to cook the rice: steamed, boiled, parched then boiled etc. Everyone in my family boasts of making good fried rice, even my brother, Eon. At family gatherings, it is an opportunity to your showcase skill.

Our Chinese food influence is predominantly Cantonese. The Chinese came to the Caribbean from the province of Guangdong during the period of indentureship. The city, Guangzhou, known to us as Canton is a major seaport located on the Pearl River. The area also flourishes with rice paddies. It is the

Chinese and the Indians that introduced rice to Guyana. Like many migrant populations, the Chinese found inventive ways of using the ingredients they found here all the while staying true to their culinary heritage. Perhaps that is why they have adjusted so well in the Caribbean.

My earliest memory of eating Chinese food – chicken fried rice, would have been when I was about nine or 10, I can't remember clearly. What I do remember is this: every Saturday afternoon, my Auntie Betty and Uncle Freddy would take me to a Chinese restaurant called National. It was located on Robb Street, sort of obliquely opposite Stabroek News. All week I used to look forward to going with them on Saturdays, it was my weekend outing. We would arrive just as dusk was setting in.

The restaurant was located on the second floor of the building. We'd reach the doorway, and I would stand there flanked on either side by my aunt and uncle, my hands clasped firmly in theirs. Tilting my head up, I'd inhale deeply, I loved the smell. A wonderful world awaited me at the top of those stairs. With my eyes fixed on the top of the stairs, we'd begin our climb.

As we got closer, I would hear voices of the cooks shouting and chatting among themselves, the woks sizzling and laughter. A little out of breath, I'd tug my aunt and uncle's hands as I'd lead them to our usual table. Yup, we had a table. The waiter would

arrive with the menus and I'd bury myself in mine, pretending to read the menu and trying make serious decisions about what to order. When Auntie Betty and Uncle Freddy finished discussing what they would order, they'd turn to me and my uncle would ask, "The usual, baby?" and baby would nod. The usual was chicken fried rice.

As young adults, my sister, Pat, and I would go often to the then Orient Restaurant. At one time it was considered to be the best Chinese restaurant in Guyana. It was located at Camp and Middle streets. The restaurant was on the top floor. We had the same thing every time we visited: corn and chicken soup or cellophane noodle soup; mixed or chicken fried rice, chow mein or low mein. We'd always order different things so that we could share and taste each other's food.

I loved the roast chicken made with peppercorns, ginger and soy sauce, cut up into bite-size pieces and served with your food. You always want a piece that had some bone. The roast pork thinly sliced, the ginger beef - tender, hot, fresh and spicy with smoke rising from the platter; stir fried vegetables, a medley of colours and textures played deliciously with ginger, garlic and oyster sauce; roast duck with its crispy skin that crunches, rice noodles that are silky and succulent. And to top it all off, the pepper sauce; what is in Chinese pepper sauce that makes it so delicious? I just love it.

I say it's time we recognise the contribution that Chinese food has made to our culture and our way of life in Guyana. Food is important to our identity as a people and as a people we cannot live without Chinese food, we do not know what life is like without Chinese food especially the ubiquitous, all-important fried rice. So, let's honour it as one of our national dishes.

▶ Vegetable Fried Rice, 196–197
▶ Chow Mein, 134–136

Holi Hai!

Living in a multi-cultural society is exciting. Those of us living side by side with people from different races and religions gain insights that some people go a lifetime without glimpsing. We get to learn each others ways, customs, and traditions.

For me, growing up in a bi-racial home often meant that I had a front row seat to the cultural heritage of my parents. Phagwah or Holi (a Hindu festival that celebrates Spring) was one of my favourite holidays. As a kid I could not believe that there was a festival that allowed you to drench people with water, and not just plain water, but coloured water! You could also shower them in white and abir or coloured powder.

I loved that everyone participated in the playing of Phagwah. It was always a neighbourhood or village affair. I remember on one occasion some of my mom's friends who were Portuguese came all the way to our home to play Phagwah with us and we are Roman Catholic. Looking back now, I am amazed because that moment spoke volumes. Here were people of different races and religions coming together in celebration. Occasions like these show how much alike we are and how it is possible to get along even if we do not look the same or come from different backgrounds.

I think boys enjoyed Phagwah the most, (I'm sure they still do) as they got to chase the girls around threatening to soak them. I always warned friends and family not to rub any abir on my face. One year I had on a really nice expensive outfit I had gotten from the States. Silly I know. I thought if I gave people "the look" that they would not dare throw anything on me. Wrong! I was soaked in coloured water. Fortunately, three cycles of washing with hot water did the trick – I had my outfit back again.

I remember seeing people at the market all powdered up the afternoon before the holiday, laughing in a joyful carefree manner. And that is what I liked best about Phagwah; it was really a time of letting down the guard. Children could play with adults, adults actually came out to play and there was gaiety all around. It was as if we were all kids without a worry in the world.

My only regret about Phagwah was that at around mid-morning the water throwing would stop and your parents called you inside to get out of the wet clothes lest you caught a cold!

With the morning fun over, it was time to get down to cooking. My mum never cooked on Phagwah day, she would say "I shining me pot and turning it down" because we were always invited to Auntie Betty's home – she lived nearby. Apart from that, it was also guaranteed that the adopted aunties (you know who I mean. We all have adopted aunties, the women who, though not related by blood, are family in spirit and love), Sattie, Shirley and Amy would send over various containers and packages of food and other goodies.

I watched intently as the women in my extended family busied themselves about the kitchen: peeling potatoes, chopping vegetables, roasting spices, grinding spices and boiling split peas. In those days grinding was done by a mill, no food processor. My cousin, Shantie, would have a bowl of cooked split peas that were as yellow as a sunflower, whole cloves of garlic and what seemed to me like a giant big red pepper. She'd grind it all together as that was to be the filling for the dhal puri. No meat was cooked on that day, it was strictly vegetarian.

Eating on that day was never an all together, sit-down at a table affair. It was like an all-day cooking fest so you would eat whenever you were hungry. On that day, I was never really interested in the food-food things, like the aloo and channa curry, dhal, rice etc. We younger ones were eager to get our hands on the snack-like goodies such as biganee – thinly sliced eggplant that's dipped in a phulourie batter and fried; phulourie – a seasoned split peas batter that's formed into balls and fried; aloo-pie – a dough stuffed with seasoned mashed potatoes. These would all be served with freshly made sour with the zing of pepper. Auntie Betty also used to make an oh so delicious sweet rice (rice pudding) with raisins. Gosh I want some now!

My siblings and I used to do our own taste test. We would spread out all the snack food, the ones made by our Auntie Betty as well as the ones from the other aunts. We'd go through them item by item, tasting them with their individual sours and we'd make up our minds about which ones we liked best. Although each household made the same thing, they all tasted different and we loved them all.

When I was a child I wished every day could be Phagwah so that we could keep on playing with the water and the powder. Now, as an adult, I'm more aware of the ways in which this beautiful celebration brought together all the people in my life – no matter their race or faith. That was a real blessing. I pray that we can all cherish the times when we have blessings like that.

Happy Phagwah everybody!

► Mango Chutney, 212–213
► Phulourie, 258–259
► Potato Roti, 116–118

It's All About the Bakes

I say bake, you say float. I say muffin, you say fried dumpling. I say saltfish and bake, you say shark and bake. And the truth is we could go on. The bottom line is – they are fried dough of deliciousness. And we could travel the entire Caribbean seeking to discover what it means in each territory when someone says, "Gimme ah bake."

My first encounter with Bajan bakes was in 1998 while attending a regional media workshop here (in Barbados). One morning, those of us from Guyana sat together for breakfast in the restaurant of our hotel. Most of us ordered something with toast, but one of our colleagues ordered saltfish and bakes. The food arrived. We all saw our colleague's mouth-watering saltfish cooked with onions and tomatoes arrive. Out of politeness we decided to wait for her bakes to arrive before we started eating.

Five minutes passed and we grew impatient, we were hungry. My colleague called the server over and enquired about the bakes. The young lady looked a little taken aback. She said, "Mam, your bakes are right there on the plate with the saltfish." We looked at the plate with dropped jaws.

"Oh my gosh, those are bakes?!"

Neatly arranged on the plate with the saltfish were 4 tiny bakes, each no larger than the size of a phulourie. We did not recognise them as bakes, because they did not look like the bakes we are accustomed to in Guyana. I remembered someone whipping out their camera to take a picture of the bakes. Those media people!

In retrospect, I can suggest, that the chef was trying to save my colleague. Here's why: Bajan bakes might be small but they are dangerously delicious, you can be tricked into eating too many! It's like over snacking. You keep returning to the plate of bakes because they are so handy and you can pop a whole one into your mouth. My friends, Gwen and Marie, shared their recipe with me – an unleavened batter that is pan fried – and now I'm a big fan of Bajan bakes. The only drawback I find is, unlike our Guyanese bakes, you can't stuff anything into a Bajan bake.

I was introduced to Vincentian bakes while making Guyanese bakes, looking for a taste of home. My helper asked me what I was making, and when I told her bakes she looked a little skeptical. She was not accustomed to bakes

being anything at all like what I was making. She began to tell me how different the bakes are that they make in her homeland, St Vincent and the Grenadines. The following week, she turned up with bakes she had made. They were indeed different : they were thick, round, solid, and compact. When you bit into each one, there was a satisfying feel of a mouthful.

Vincentian bakes are really hearty by themselves. They can be eaten just by biting

into them or slicing and spreading with butter or jam. But the Vincy bake also isn't a bake to be stuffed.

Trin-bagonians make two kinds of bake. One is called coconut bake. This bake is made by kneading the dough with coconut milk and then cooking the dough by actually *baking* it in an oven. It's like a quick bread. This means that the Trini coconut bake is the only bake that is actually... well, *baked*. The other Trini bake is sometimes called a float or a fry bake and it's similar to the bake we make in Guyana. Trini bakes, or floats as they call them, are often eaten with fried shark.

Guyanese bakes and Trini floats are great for stuffing with anything! Be it saltfish, shark, eggs, cheese, ham, vegetables, whatever you like. I know some people like theirs with fried mackerel or sardines. In Guyana and many other Caribbean countries, bakes are popularly eaten with saltfish. The thing is if you put bakes on a table among other dishes, the first thing to go would be the bakes! Some people can't wait to sit down to the table for their meal of bakes, like some of my cousins. I remember one evening when my cousin Shantie, was making bakes for dinner. She was busy with the rolling and the frying. Her brothers, Dave and Keshwar, would carefully time when each bake would finish cooking, would sneak by and stealthily grab them one at a time. She got so frustrated and chased them around the house with the pot spoon.

Leaving out texture and appearance, the difference between the bakes has to do with how they feel in my mouth. Bajan bakes are firm and chewy because there is no leavening agent (baking powder or yeast); Vincy bakes are soft and have a really satisfying feel; Guyanese bakes and Trini floats range from feeling soft to chewy because they are often filled with something – you get a combination of textures and flavours.

When my mind calls for bakes, I like to eat them warm with some butter that melts between all the nooks and crannies. Chase it down with a cup of tea and I'm good to go.

Bake time is anytime. It is one of those foods that work well for breakfast, lunch, dinner or as a snack. Bake vendors are found throughout the region. On Friday afternoons, St Lucian women can be seen at some corners frying bakes to sell with the barbeque chicken; in Barbados on Saturdays, vendors can be found outside supermarkets plying their trade. In Trinidad and Tobago, the Breakfast Shed is the place to be for floats and bakes. At Cheapside Market here in Barbados, there is a Guyanese woman, Suzanne that sells bake and saltfish every Saturday morning.

So while they come in various shapes, sizes and textures, and are called many things – bake, float, dumpling, fried dumpling, or muffin – the truth is, we love them. For some of us, bakes are the perfect food, satisfying in their own right and even better with that lil' extra something. Let's be honest, fried dough rules!

▶　Bajan Bakes, 97–98

▶　Coconut Bake, 106–107

▶　Guyanese Bakes, 112–113

▶　Vincy Bakes, 123–124

An Acquired Taste

As a child, I had a love-hate relationship with karaila. I loved it because it was delicious sautéed by itself or with lots of shrimp. I hated it because it meant that I'd have to drink bitters. My siblings and I could not stand karaila bitters, which was extracted by squeezing the liquid from the cut-up vegetable that had been marinated in salt.

When we drank the bitters my mother would stand there watching, to ensure each of us swallowed it all. It was like being led to the gallows, Mommy being the executioner and the bitters, the noose. Pat, Eon and I would stand there side by side. Mommy would pour the bitters, one glass at a time and hand it to us. Being the oldest I always had to go first. I would see the look of trepidation on Pat and Eon's face as I would hold my nose, close my eyes, contort my face and raise the glass to my lips. I have blocked out the memory of the taste so I cannot describe it to you.

A friend of mine, Caroline, whilst on one of her annual trips to Barbados ate some fried karaila I had cooked. I warned her that it would be a little bitter. She tried it, seemed to think it was ok and then promptly pronounced some good ol' Caribbean wisdom: "Something that bitter must be good for you." And that is indeed what a lot of us believe, that karaila, because it is bitter contains certain vitamins and properties that are good for you.

It's a vegetable that has been used for ages as a part of traditional Asian medicine and is said to stimulate digestion. Research is continuing about its use to aid in the control of blood sugar in diabetics. In parts of Latin America it is believed that karaila is useful

in preventing and treating malaria but that has yet to be proven through human testing. In Guyana, the dried karaila leaves are used as part of an ensemble we call "bush" that's usually boiled and dispensed as traditional medicine.

Karaila (karela), the name we know it as, no doubt because of our East Indian heritage, is also known as bitter melon, bitter squash, bitter gourd, bitter cucumber and caraili. It is grown widely in India, South Asia, The Philippines, Southeast Asia, China, Africa and right here in the Caribbean, it thrives well in the tropics.

I am sure that there are lots of ways to cook karaila but I'm only familiar with two.

The first is sautéed with onions, garlic, herbs and tomatoes. It can be cooked by itself or you can add shrimp, chicken or meat. My mom always cooked it with shrimp. She'd start by removing the top and bottom tips and then running her knife along the vegetable slicing it open, on both sides. She'd take out the seeds and discard them and then thinly slice the karaila into little half-moons. With the sliced karaila in a large bowl, she'd liberally sprinkle it with salt and let it stand for a little while, maybe 15–20 minutes or more. This process was used to extract the bitterness from the vegetable. You know when you put salt on cucumbers how they just spring water? Well it's the same thing here.

When she thought enough time had passed, mom would then, in batches, squeeze as much moisture out of the karaila as possible.

Some people would add a little water to aid in the process and to take away some of the saltiness but it is not necessary because the saltiness is taken away with the squeezing of the juice. Whatever salt is still trapped in the karaila is enough for taste so you would not need to add more salt to it.

Once this is done, prep your seasonings – onions, tomatoes etc and whatever else you are putting in and cook.

Here's a tip from my Aunt Golin: when you're finished squeezing out the water/juice from the karaila, place it on a flat surface, like a baking sheet or platter and put it in the sun to dry, extracting whatever moisture is still there. By doing this, you will notice that when you sauté the vegetable, it will not be soggy but dry and you can clearly see each sliver of karaila.

The other way I know Karaila is prepared is stuffed, sautéed and simmered – kalounji (callonjie). My mom has made it this way for us before, stuffed with shrimp but I'd never made it before I came to Barbados.

Off I went to the market on Saturday to get my karaila and shrimp. I was so nervous about making this dish. No matter how competent a cook you think you are, when you're going to be making something for the first time, there are always jitters. If you love karaila, you've got to try this dish.

▶ Kalounjie, 162–164
▶ Sautéed Karaila, 190–191

Part 2

Recipes

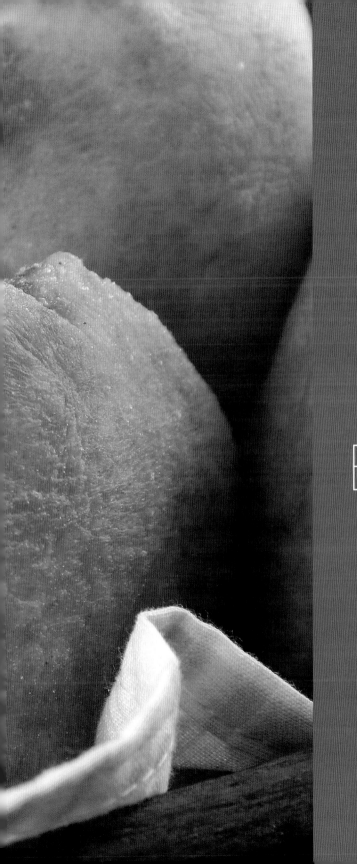

Good at Breakfast

Ackee & Salt Fish

This is the national dish of Jamaica and the first time I had it was in July of 1998; I immediately fell in love with it and I am sure that you will too. Ackees become very delicate once heated so be sure to not toss or turn them too much once added to the pot or pan. If you're using canned ackees, be even gentler with them.

Yield: 10 (½ cup) servings

Ingredients

3 tablespoons oil

1 cup thinly sliced onions

3 sprigs fresh thyme

½ cup diced tomatoes

Hot pepper to taste, finely minced

1 pound boneless salt fish, de-salted and flaked into bits (see page 324)

2 pounds shelled ackees

¼ cup diced green sweet peppers

Black pepper and salt to taste

2 tablespoons green onions sliced thinly (green and white parts)

Equipment

1 large frying pan with cover

1 large spoon

Directions

▶ Heat oil in pan over medium high heat.

▶ Add onions and sauté until translucent, about 3–4 minutes.

- ▶ Add thyme, tomatoes and hot peppers and continue to sauté for about 1 to 2 minutes.
- ▶ Add salt fish, toss, and cook covered for about 2–3 minutes.
- ▶ Add ackees, sweet peppers and salt to taste tossing lightly so as not to break up the ackees. Cook with pan partially covered for 5 minutes or until the ackees turn bright yellow.
- ▶ Serve hot with freshly ground black pepper and green onions sprinkled on top.

Cynthia's Tip

〜〜〜〜〜〜〜〜〜〜〜〜〜〜〜〜〜〜〜〜〜〜

If using canned ackees, drain completely before using.

Bajan Bakes

Don't let the word bake fool you. This is fried dough. Fried delicious dough. Traditionally, it is eaten with salt fish as a breakfast meal.

Yield: 14

Ingredients

1 cup all-purpose flour

1 tablespoon sugar

A pinch of salt

¼ teaspoon ground cinnamon

1 cup water

Oil for shallow frying

Equipment

1 medium-sized bowl

1 tablespoon

1 medium or large frying pan

Paper towels

Directions

► Mix flour, sugar, salt and cinnamon together in the bowl.

► Add water to make a thick batter of dropping consistency.

► Rest batter for 5 minutes.

► Heat oil in frying pan or skillet over medium heat.

► Spoon batter in tablespoon measurements into the pan. Do not overcrowd the pan as this will cause them to stick together.

► Let bakes brown on one side. Flip and cook until the other side turns brown too.

► Drain on paper towels.

► Serve with fried salt fish (recipe on page110), smoked herring or whatever you wish to have them with, or eat as is.

Cynthia's Tip

Shallow fry for flat, disk-like bakes or deep fry for slightly puffed round ones.

Plantains are another of those ingredients that automatically come to mind when people think of the Caribbean. A plantain is *not* a banana. Plantains are sturdier and go through a variety to stages from green to fully ripe and can be used at each stage to make particular dishes. For this particular dish of boil and fry, you want to get very green plantains. The frying process here refers to a sauté. We use the word fry often to refer to a sauté, as in the case here.

Yield: 4 cups

Ingredients

3 large green plantains, peeled and cut into bite-size chunks

Water to cook plantains

2 tablespoons oil

1 cup diced onions

½ cup diced tomatoes

2 tablespoons freshly chopped herbs (thyme, cilantro, celery)

Hot pepper to taste, minced

Salt

Equipment

1 medium pot with cover
1 colander
1 frying pan with cover
1 large spoon

Directions

▶ Add plantains to pot, cover with water and bring to a boil, covered.

▶ Add salt to taste when it comes to a boil.

▶ Cook until soft (test with fork).

▶ Strain in colander.

▶ Heat oil in pan.

▶ Add onions and sauté for 2–3 minutes.

▶ Add tomatoes, herbs and hot pepper, season with salt to taste.

▶ Let cook for 2 minutes.

▶ Add plantains and stir, mixing all the ingredients together.

▶ Cover partially and let cook for 5 minutes on medium-low heat.

▶ Stir and remove from heat.

▶ Serve alone or with fried eggs or any breakfast meat such as sausages or ham.

▶ Can be served as a main meal or as a side dish.

Buljol

Popular in Trinidad & Tobago and Barbados, this is a sort of a mild pickle that's very popular at breakfast time and is traditionally served with bakes. Some people add diced cucumbers to their buljol, but doing so results in the cucumbers yielding a lot of water – diluting the flavour of everything and leaving the buljol sitting in a pool of liquid. Not attractive, not tasty. Serve the sliced cucumbers separately on a dish so that people can add them to their plate if they so desire.

Yield: 2 cups

Ingredients

8 oz de-boned salt fish

Water to boil salt fish

½ cup finely chopped tomatoes

2 tablespoons finely chopped red onions

¼ cup thinly sliced green onions

⅓ cup finely chopped sweet peppers (yellow, red & green)

Hot pepper to taste, finely minced

2 tablespoons oil

Equipment

1 medium saucepot
1 medium bowl
1 wooden spoon

Directions

▶ Add salt fish and water to saucepot and bring to a boil. Boil salt fish twice, each time for 15–20 minutes, discarding the water after each boil.

▶ Let cool to handle.

▶ Flake/shred fish into very tiny bits – rub the pieces of fish between your thumb and index finger.

▶ Add tomatoes, red onions, green onions, sweet peppers, oil, hot pepper and shredded salt fish to medium bowl. Stir with spoon, mixing thoroughly. Let stand for 10 minutes (the longer the mixture stands, the more the flavours develop).

▶ Serve with bread, roti, rice or bakes.

You've had toast with butter I am sure but have you ever had a butterflap? A butter flap is soft white-bread dough that's slathered with an excellent-quality butter that's baked right into the dough! And just in case you're wondering if that's not enough, the butterflap is lightly kissed all over as it comes out of the oven with melted butter!

Butterflaps are popular in Guyana. The name butterflap is made up as a result of butter, the main flavour ingredient and the flap part is due to the shape of the dough.

Yield: 12

Ingredients

1 + ½ cups warm water (110–115°F)

2 tablespoons white granulated sugar

1 tablespoon dry active yeast

4 cups all purpose flour, plus extra for work surface

¾ teaspoon salt

2 tablespoons canola or vegetable oil

1 cup plus 2 tablespoons high quality salted butter

Equipment

1 medium-sized bowl

Plastic wrap

1 dinner fork

1 large bowl, oiled

Damp kitchen towels

1 tablespoon

2 baking sheet-pans

2 wire racks

1 small pastry brush

Directions

► Add sugar to medium bowl, pour in water and stir to dissolve sugar. Stir in yeast. Cover bowl with plastic wrap and put in warm place to proof for 10 minutes.

► Add flour to large bowl along with salt and mix thoroughly.

► Make a well in the centre of the flour; pour in the yeast mixture (scrape the bowl) along with oil.

► Using the fork, stir, mixing the flour and yeast mixture until combined. Turn dough and remnants onto work surface and knead for 3–4 minutes, dusting lightly with flour to avoid stickiness.

► Place dough in oiled bowl and dab a little more oil on top of the dough to avoid a skin, cover with a kitchen towel or plastic wrap and leave to rise in a warm place for an hour and 15 minutes or until dough bulks up.

► Punch down dough, knead for 1–2 minutes, cut into half, and shape into logs then cut each log into 6 equal pieces.

► Working as quickly as you can, form each piece of dough into a solid round ball and then roll into a round disk on a lightly floured work surface. Disk should be about 3–3½ inches in diameter.

► Take 1 tablespoon of butter (or more if you like) and smear the butter all over the insides but not close to the edges.

► Fold over dough to make like a half moon; now fold across to form a triangle. Press down the edges. Place dough on baking sheet; repeat until all the balls have been shaped, rolled, buttered and folded.

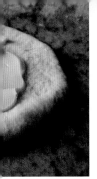

- ▶ Cover with kitchen towel and leave to proof for 1 hour in a warm place.
- ▶ 20 minutes before the hour is up, preheat oven to 400°F. You will need to use both oven racks.
- ▶ Add pans to the oven and bake for 18–20 minutes or until the butter-flaps are nicely browned (not dark brown).
- ▶ Meanwhile, melt 2 tablespoons of butter and brush the butter-flaps as soon as they come out of the oven. Let cool on wire racks.
- ▶ Serve warm or at room temperature.

Cynthia's Tips

As soon as the pans are removed from the oven you can turn the butter-flaps upside down so that the melted butter inside trickles down to the top. This can be done before basting it.

The basting with melted butter *must* be done when the butter-flaps are hot!

Do not grease the baking sheet-pans.

To make cheese-flaps, use a cheese paste instead of butter as the filling (see recipe on page 239).

Coconut Bake

This bake is very popular in Trinidad & Tobago, and is the only "bake" that is actually *baked* in an oven. The bake is best eaten warm with slices of sharp cheddar cheese and it is traditionally eaten at breakfast. If you can, always opt to make it with fresh coconut.

Yield: 1 (9" x 2 ½" thick bake)

Ingredients

3½ cups all-purpose flour

4 teaspoons baking powder

1 teaspoon salt

1 cup whole milk, plus extra if needed

½ cup unsalted butter, room temperature

1 tablespoon sugar

2 cups freshly grated coconut

½ tablespoon oil

Equipment

2 large bowls

1 small saucepan

1 dining fork

Plastic wrap

1 large parchment-lined baking sheet

Parchment paper

Directions

- ► Mix flour, baking powder and salt in bowl.
- ► Warm milk, sugar and butter in saucepan on low heat; stir until sugar is dissolved and butter is melted.
- ► Remove milk-butter-sugar mixture from stove top and cool slightly (approximately 5–8 minutes).
- ► Add coconut to flour mixture and mix.

- ► Make a well in the centre of the flour-coconut mixture, gradually pour milk-butter-sugar mixture, use fork and stir to mix until a dough-like consistency is formed.
- ► Turn dough out on a lightly floured surface and knead for 3 minutes or until dough is silky and smooth.
- ► Transfer dough to a lightly oiled bowl. Cover and rest for 30 minutes.
- ► Preheat oven to 375°F (heat the oven 10 minutes into the resting time).
- ► Roll rested dough into a 7 inch circle, with 1½ inch thickness, transfer to baking sheet.
- ► Bake for 30–40 minutes or until the Coconut Bake is brown; It will have a firm crust and sound hollow when the base is tapped.
- ► Transfer to wire rack and cool for 10–15 minutes before slicing.
- ► Best served with sharp cheddar cheese and butter; can also be had with jam, fried salt fish or smoked herring (see recipe, page 220).

Eggplant (Baigan) Choka

Whenever I smell the eggplant studded with garlic roasting, I always think of the countryside in Guyana. The smokiness from the fire roasting is the star of this dish: roasting it in the oven will give the texture but not the flavour. Eggplant choka is usually eaten with sada or paratha roti at breakfast or dinner time.

Yield: 1½ cups

Ingredients

1½ pounds eggplant

4 large cloves of garlic, sliced (average 1 clove garlic per eggplant)

Hot pepper to taste, minced

Salt to taste

1–2 tablespoons oil

3 green onions sliced thinly (white and green parts)

1 large tomato, fire roasted (optional)

Equipment

1 pair tongs

1 table knife

1 food processor or mortar and pestle

1 fork

1 medium bowl

Directions

▶ Take a sharp knife and make a number of deep incisions into the eggplants.

▶ Fill each slit with a slice of garlic (be sure to push it right in).

▶ On the open medium-flame of your gas burner or outdoor grill, place the eggplant to roast, turning to ensure that it is roasted and cooked through all over. You can roast all the eggplants at the same time – 1 on each burner. The cooking time and process would vary depending on the size of the eggplant. The skin should be completely charred, blackened. The tongs are very useful in this step.

▶ To roast the tomato, place on an open medium-low flame and let roast slowly; turn it to ensure that it's roasted all around.

▶ Remove the eggplants and tomatoes from the flames and let cool until you can handle.

▶ With the help of a table knife, carefully remove the charred skin of the eggplant and tomato. It's okay if bits of the charred skin are in the mixture, so don't worry if you do not get it absolutely clean.

▶ Repeat the process until all the eggplants have been skinned.

▶ Now this stage you can do this one of three ways: with a food processor, in a mortar with pestle or with a fork. In the food processor, add the flesh of the roasted eggplant and tomato and give a couple of whirls. You can let the food processor go for a little longer if you like your choka smooth, some people like it to have a slight chunky texture.

▶ If you are using a fork, then simply mash the eggplants and tomatoes thoroughly.

▶ With a mortar and pestle, pound/grind both ingredients to your desired texture.

▶ In a bowl, combine the whirled/mashed/ground eggplant-tomato mixture, hot pepper, salt to taste, oil and green onions, mixing thoroughly until incorporated.

▶ Serve with roti or rice.

Fried Salt fish

This is a favourite in almost every household. It can be served at any meal and with many things. It is very popular at breakfast with fried bakes, at lunchtime with rice and dhal or boiled breadfruit or ground provisions, and at dinner with roti or bread.

Yield: 3 cups

Ingredients

8 oz de-boned or boneless salt fish, de-salted (see method on page 324)

2 tablespoons oil

1½ cups thinly sliced onions

2 sprigs fresh thyme

Hot pepper to taste, minced

1 cup chopped tomatoes

Black pepper to taste (optional)

Equipment

1 medium frying pan with cover

1 large spoon

Directions

► Crumble salt fish to bite-size pieces.

► Heat oil in a pan.

► Add onions and cook gently sauté until translucent, about 2–3 minutes.

► Add thyme and hot pepper and continue to sauté for another minute.

► Add tomatoes and cook for a minute.

► Add salt fish and stir, incorporating it into the onion-tomato-thyme-pepper mixture and cook partially covered for 5–7 minutes.

► Serve with bakes, roti, rice, bread, breadfruit or ground provisions.

Guyanese Bakes

Each Caribbean territory has its own bake and we prize these bits of fried dough dearly. Guyanese bakes are similar to one of the bakes made in Trinidad & Tobago. These bakes are hollow inside and can be filled with anything. Sautéed salt fish is often the first choice or as in the case of Trinidad & Tobago, fried shark.

Yield: 12

Ingredients

3 cups all purpose flour

3 teaspoons baking powder

½ teaspoon salt

1 tablespoon sugar

¼ teaspoon ground cinnamon

1 tablespoon butter or margarine

1¾ cups warm water to knead dough

Oil for deep frying

Equipment

2 large bowls

Plastic wrap

1 deep frying pan

1 slotted pot spoon

Paper towels

Directions

▶ Combine flour, baking powder, salt, sugar and cinnamon in a bowl.

▶ Rub butter or margarine into flour mixture .

▶ Add water to the flour mixture to make a dough; Knead for 2–3 minutes.

▶ Place dough in a lightly oiled bowl, cover with plastic wrap and let dough rest for at least 30 minutes.

▶ Cut dough into 12 equal pieces and form into balls .

▶ Heat oil in deep pan (but not smoking).

▶ Roll dough to about 3 inches in diameter and ¼" thickness .

▶ Add one at a time to hot oil and fry until browned on both sides. Once added to the oil, the bake initially sinks, but floats to the surface as it puffs and cooks.

▶ If bakes are browning too quickly before the insides are cooked, reduce heat to medium.

▶ Drain on paper towels.

▶ Cut along the sides of the bake to create a pocket and fill with fried (sautéed) salt fish, smoked herring, cheese, ham or cut open completely and slather with jam, butter anything you'd like to have it with and serve.

Potato Choka

Delicious anytime, but potato choka is usually a breakfast or dinner meal. Think of it as a spicy, kicked-up mashed potato. For the choka flavour, do not miss lightly roasting it over an open flame after boiling the potatoes.

Yield: 1½ cups

Ingredients

1 pound potatoes, peeled

Salt to taste

2 tablespoons vegetable oil

Hot pepper to taste, minced

2 tablespoons thinly sliced green onions (white and green parts)

2 tablespoons sautéed onions – a mixture of red and white onions

Equipment

1 saucepan

1 paid tongs

1 medium bowl

1 potato masher

Directions

► Add potatoes and water to a saucepan and bring to a boil, covered. When the pot comes to a boil, add salt.

► Cook potatoes until fork tender, drain and pat dry.

► Fire-roast the potatoes on the open flames of your gas stove or outdoor grill, using tongs (let the potatoes get a little charred).

► Mash potatoes in a bowl with the oil.

► Add pepper to taste and mix in sautéed and green onions. Taste for salt and adjust if necessary.

► Serve with roti or rice.

Cynthia's Tips

If you have some roasted garlic, you can add it to the choka. I do not recommend adding the fresh garlic as it's usually a little pungent when used raw.

You can skip step # 4 and go straight to mashing the potatoes if you like. Roasting it gives it that rich smoky flavour desired in a choka.

Potato (Aloo) Roti

This is a stuffed roti. The mashed potato is highly seasoned with herbs and spices. Little mounds of the stuffing are encased in pieces of cut dough, rolled and cooked on a tawah or flat iron griddle. Always place a piece of wax paper between each roti so that they do not stick together. This is usually made as a breakfast for dinner item.

With a roti such as this, you don't really need to serve it with anything but little Sour if you so desire, but it's really good as is.

Yield: 12

Ingredients

For dough:

3 cups all-purpose flour, plus extra for dusting

¾ teaspoon baking powder

1 teaspoon salt

1 teaspoon sugar

2 tablespoons oil, plus extra for cooking the roti

Warm water to knead dough

For potato stuffing:

1½ pounds potatoes, peeled, boiled and mashed

1 tablespoon chopped cilantro

1 tablespoon finely chopped red onions

1 tablespoon thinly sliced green onions

1 teaspoon ground cumin

Hot pepper to taste, finely minced

Salt to taste

Equipment

2 medium bowls

Plastic wrap

1 rolling pin

1 baking sheet, lightly oiled

1 tawah (iron griddle)

1 spatula

1 small bowl for oil to brush roti

1 pastry brush

12 (4-inch square) pieces of wax paper

1 plate lined with tea-towel and 1 piece of wax paper

Directions

Filling

▶ Mix all the ingredients together and set aside.

Dough

▶ Mix all the ingredients in a bowl and knead to a soft dough.

▶ Lightly oil dough, cover with plastic wrap and let rest for at least 30 minutes.

▶ Once the dough has rested, cut into golf-sized balls.

▶ Using your hands or with a rolling pin, form/roll the dough into a small circle (about 3 inches).

▶ Place one heaped tablespoon of the potato mixture in the center (do not over stuff the dough).

▶ Close up the dough by bringing the ends together and pinch to seal completely.

▶ Place seam-side down on baking sheet; dab a little oil on top of it to prevent a skin forming.

▶ Repeat until all the dough is filled. Cover with plastic wrap.

▶ Let rest for 10 to 15 minutes.

To cook:

▶ Heat tawah or flat iron griddle pan on medium-low heat.

▶ Flour working surface and rolling pin.

▶ Take one of the stuffed dough, form into a disk using your hands, place on work surface and roll making sure the stuffing spreads throughout, keep turning the dough at a 90-degree angle to get it round (you may have to keep flouring your rolling pin as the dough may tend to stick).

▶ Cook roti on both sides, lightly brushing each cooked side with a little oil (it's almost a light toasting of the roti).

▶ Transfer to lined plate (be sure to put a piece of the wax paper between each roti to prevent them sticking to each other and steaming).

▶ Repeat until all the roti is cooked.

▶ Serve hot or at room temperature as is or with a pickle.

Sada Roti

Another kind of roti, this one resembles a typical flat bread and is more rustic in its appearance. When rolled out flat, a sada roti should be at least about 1-cm thick. It is best cooked over medium heat. To eat this roti, you tear it and then separate it revealing the insides. Remember the roti is used as an eating tool so if you don't separate the layers it would be difficult for you to pick up anything with the roti.

This type of roti is often served with eggplant and tomato chokas. It's also very good cut or torn open and slathered with butter.

Yield: 4–5

Ingredients

4 cups all-purpose flour, plus
     extra for the working surface
4 teaspoons baking powder
2 teaspoons salt
1 teaspoon sugar
1 tablespoon oil
Warm water to knead dough

Equipment

1 large bowl
Plastic wrap
1 rolling pin
1 tawah or flat iron griddle
1 spatula
1 plate lined with tea towel

Directions

- ▶ Add flour, baking powder, salt and sugar to bowl and mix thoroughly.
- ▶ Drizzle oil into flour mixture, incorporating.
- ▶ Add warm water and knead to a soft dough.
- ▶ Lightly oil the top of the dough so that a skin does not form and let rest, covered with plastic wrap for at least half an hour.
- ▶ Knead rested dough for 1 minute then divide equally into 4–5 parts.
- ▶ Heat tawah or flat iron griddle on medium low heat.
- ▶ Lightly flour work surface and rolling pin.
- ▶ Take one piece of dough and form into a round disk with your hands, place on work surface and roll into a 6 inch circle with ¼ inch thickness and cook on tawah.

- ▶ As the roti cooks you will notice it puffs up, flip it over and using a spatula, gently press the ends of the roti at first and then let the roti cook (you may need to regulate the heat to low depending on if the roti is getting brown faster than it is being cooked inside. Also, be sure to dust off any excess flour you see toasted on the tawah/griddle as you complete cooking each roti. If you don't dust it off, it toasts and chars the roti on the outside quickly before the inside is cooked.
- ▶ Both sides should be brown-spotted and crusted.
- ▶ Transfer to lined plate; repeat until all the roti is cooked.
- ▶ Serve hot or at room temperature with eggplant choka (page 108), or any choka of your preference or eaten as is.

I dedicate this dish to my best friend, Susan. Sometime back I asked her what her favourite dish was and she couldn't answer. She said she did not have one... until she tried my tomato choka. The combination of flavouring the oil by gently cooking the garlic in it and then adding the roasted pulp of the tomatoes along with onions and chopped cilantro, salt and hot pepper...it's easy to understand her love for this dish.

Yield: 1½ cups

Ingredients

1 pound ripe tomatoes

3 tablespoons oil, divided

(First use 1 tablespoon to rub on tomatoes)

(Second use 2 tablespoons to sauté choka)

3 tablespoons finely minced onions

Salt to taste

Hot pepper to taste, finely chopped

2 larges cloves garlic, thinly sliced

2 tablespoons chopped cilantro

(First use 1 tablespoon to cook with tomatoes)

(Second use 1 tablespoon to stir in when choka is cooked)

1 teaspoon freshly squeezed lemon or lime juice

Equipment

1 small roasting pan
1 food processor or mortar with pestle
1 frying pan
1 medium bowl
1 large spoon

Directions

▶ Preheat oven to 375°F.

▶ Rub tomatoes with 1 tablespoon oil, sprinkle with salt and roast for about 45 minutes or until the skins of the tomatoes are charred and wrinkled.

▶ Remove skins from tomatoes when cool enough to handle.

▶ Add tomato pulp and drippings from the roasting pan to food processor or mortar and pestle. Mash/pulse the pulp (let the pulp have a bit of texture).

▶ Stir in onions, salt to taste and hot pepper to tomatoes.

▶ Heat the 2 tablespoons oil in a pan.

▶ Add garlic and sauté lightly (just turning golden).

▶ Add tomato mixture and 1 tablespoon of cilantro and let cook gently for about 2–4 minutes.

▶ Taste for salt and adjust if necessary.

▶ Turn off heat and stir in the remaining tablespoon of chopped cilantro and lemon juice.

▶ Serve hot with roti or bread. This choka can also be tossed with hot cooked pasta, rice, or boiled ground provisions.

Vincy Bakes

Vincy is the fondly shortened way we refer to people from St Vincent & The Grenadines. The Vincy bake is solid and compact, unlike the Guyanese bake with the hollow inside that can be filled with anything. Vincy bakes are great cut open and dabbed with butter or even jam. They are totally satisfying, and eating just one will fill you up.

Yield: 9

Ingredients

3½ cups all-purpose flour

1 teaspoon baking powder

1 teaspoon instant yeast

1 tablespoon sugar

¼ teaspoon salt

¼ teaspoon ground cinnamon

⅛ teaspoon grated nutmeg

1 tablespoon unsalted butter or margarine, room temperature

1½ cups warm water

Oil for deep frying

Equipment

2 large bowls

Plastic wrap

1 deep frying pan

1 slotted spoon

Paper towels

Directions

▶ Add flour, baking powder, yeast, sugar, salt and spices to a bowl and mix thoroughly.

▶ Rub in butter or margarine.

▶ Add water and knead to smooth dough.

▶ Transfer dough to lightly oiled bowl, cover with plastic wrap, and let rise in a warm place for at least 30 minutes.

▶ Cut dough into 9 equal pieces.

▶ Form each piece of dough into a compact round ball.

▶ Heat pan with oil on medium heat.

▶ Fry bakes 2–3 at a time (depending on the width of your frying pan) turning to ensure that it is browned and cooked all around.

▶ Each batch should take about 10 minutes (regulate the heat to medium-low if you think that it's browning too quickly, remember the dough is compact and needs to be cooked through).

▶ Drain on paper towels.

▶ Serve with butter, jam, cheese or eat as is.

Entrées &
Special Occasions

Baked Chicken

Baked Chicken is one of those dishes that make a regular appearance on the dining table every Sunday and holiday in homes across the Caribbean. Each household has its own recipe for making this dish. Here is how I make mine.

Yield: 5 servings

Ingredients

3 large cloves garlic, chopped

3 tablespoons chopped onions

2 tablespoons chopped fresh herbs (your choice of combination – sage, basil, thyme, tarragon, marjoram)

1 tablespoon diced ginger

1 whole chicken cut into pieces, cleaned and patted dry

1 teaspoon hot pepper sauce or to taste

2 tablespoons Worcestershire sauce

2 tablespoons soy sauce

2 tablespoons dark rum

4 shakes Angostura® bitters

Salt to taste

Equipment

1 mortar and pestle or whatever tool you use to grind things

1 large bowl

1 large baking pan

Directions

► Add the garlic, onions, herbs and ginger to mortar and grind with pestle to a paste.

► Add chicken to large bowl along with the paste, Worcestershire, soy and pepper sauces along with the rum and Angostura bitters and salt to taste.

► Mix all the ingredients with the chicken ensuring that all over is coated with the mixture.

► Cover and let rest for at least 1 hour.

► Preheat oven to 375°F.

► Add seasoned chicken including the marinade to the baking pan and spread out evenly.

► Bake for 50 minutes to 1 hour or until browned and cooked through.

► The juices remaining from the baked chicken can be served separately in a gravy boat or spooned over the chicken when served.

Cynthia's Tips

An overnight marinate really enhances the flavour of this dish.

You can experiment with any flavour combo for baked chicken using a wet or dry, spice or herb marinade.

Baked Ham

The ham we get in the Caribbean is always fully cooked and cured so it's more a matter of reheating it completely by baking it in the oven and adding a glaze along with cloves and mustard. Some people also add pineapple slices and cherries to their ham when baking.

To be honest, our ham is so excellently flavoured that all I use is a pineapple or guava glaze along with the cloves.

Yield: 12 (6-ounce) servings

Ingredients

1 (5-pound) frozen ham, cured and fully cooked, defrosted

Whole cloves

½ cup pineapple jam or a jam of your choice

¼ cup water

Equipment

1 Knife

1 Roasting pan with rack

1 Small Saucepan

1 Whisk

1 Basting brush

Directions

▶ Preheat oven to 350°F.

▶ Remove the rind (skin) of the ham by running a knife along the edge and peeling it back with your hands.

▶ Remove some of the excess fat leaving at least ¼ inch of fat around it.

▶ Take a sharp knife and cut crossways and then diagonally to create a diamond pattern.

▶ Set ham on rack of roasting pan.

▶ Stud ham with cloves in the centre of each diamond-cut; transfer ham to preheated oven.

▶ Meanwhile, gently warm pineapple jam and water in a small saucepan, whisking to incorporate.

▶ Baste ham with pineapple jam glaze one hour after it has been in the oven, and every ½ hour thereafter until the ham has been baking for 2 hours or until it reaches an internal temperature of 140°F.

▶ Remove from oven and let rest, covered with foil to keep warm, for 10–15 minutes before carving.

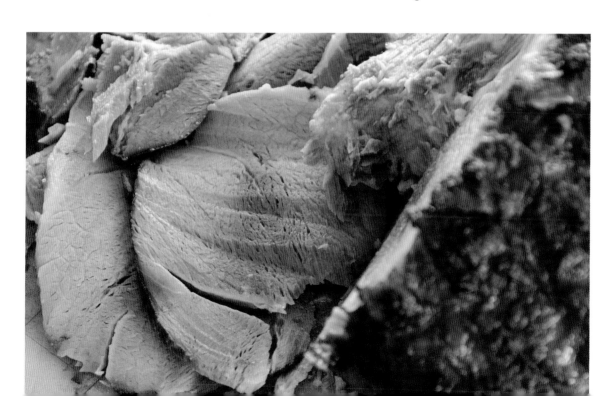

Boiled Breadfruit

Breadfruit is used and cooked very much the same way as potatoes. It is starchy and very filling. When it is boiled as is shown in this recipe, it offers itself as a platform for other highly seasoned accompaniments such as sautéed salt fish. This is a very popular combo in the Caribbean.

Yield: 3 (4 oz) servings

Ingredients

1 pound breadfruit, peeled

Water

Salt to taste

Equipment

1 medium saucepan with cover
1 knife
1 colander

Directions

▶ Cut breadfruit in half, lengthways.
▶ Add breadfruit to water with salt and bring to a boil, covered.
▶ Cook until knife can be inserted easily (approximately 8–10 minutes).
▶ Strain in a colander.
▶ Let cool to handle, and slice thickly or cut into large chunks.
▶ Serve with fried salt fish or smoked herring (recipe on page 220).

Chicken Curry

This is a favourite that's made and eaten often. Just as Cook-up Rice, Cou-cou & Flying Fish or Callaloo are regular weekend dishes, so too is Curried Chicken. In many Indian households, particularly in Guyana and Trinidad & Tobago, it is a must-have dish on Sundays along with dhal and rice or dhal puri.

Yield: 5–6 servings

Ingredients

2 tablespoons oil

3–4 tablespoons curry paste (recipe on page 322)

Salt to taste

1 whole chicken (4–5 lbs) washed, patted dry and cut up into pieces

5–6 cups boiling water

Equipment

1 deep frying pan with cover
1 large spoon

Directions

► Heat oil in pan.

► Chunkay (sauté) curry paste for 1 minute (this is a key step as you are wet-toasting the spiced mixture).

► Add the chicken, salt to taste and stir to coat completely with curry paste (this is another key step. Here you are infusing the chicken with the spices).

► Let sauté until any liquid sprung from the chicken is gone.

► Add enough boiling water to cook the chicken. Scrape the bottom of the pan with your spoon to release any of the spiced mixture that may be stuck to the pan.

► Cover the pot and let curry cook until the liquid is considerably reduced and a nice thick gravy/sauce remains.

► Serve with rice, roti or dhal puri.

Vegetable Chow mein

What is chow mein doing in a book about Caribbean food? Well, our cuisine is heavily influenced by the Chinese particularly in Guyana, Trinidad & Tobago and Jamaica. Dishes such as fried rice and chow mein are very much a part of our everyday eating. While Chinese people are spread throughout the region, the influence in heaviest in the three countries mentioned earlier.

Chow mein is a stir fry so it is important that all the ingredients are prepped before turning on the heat. Do not break the noodles before adding them to the boiling salted water, they are not meant to be broken. Also, the vegetables and meat ingredients should be cut thinly lengthways so they incorporate better with the long noodles. It's about similar shapes. People often complain that all the meat or veggies are left at the bottom of the pan or bowl; this is so because they have been diced so they move through the noodles and rest at the bottom. If they are cut lengthways, then they wrap themselves around and between the noodles.

Yield: 4 servings

Ingredients

Water

1 (16 oz) pack dried chowmein noodles

Salt and pepper to taste

3–4 tablespoons oil

3 cloves garlic, crushed

2 tablespoons finely julienned ginger

2 cups julienned carrots

2 cups bora (yard long bean, snake bean, Chinese long bean) cut into 2-inch pieces (substitute with string beans)

½ cup mixed-coloured bell peppers cut into strips lengthways

½ cup bean sprouts (optional)

½ cup green onions cut lengthways (green and white parts)

1½ teaspoons toasted sesame oil

2 teaspoons five-spice powder

Equipment

1 large pot with cover

1 colander

1 noodle spoon

1 deep frying pan (karahi or wok would be great)

1 large spoon

Directions

▶ Fill pot with lots of water, cover and bring to a boil.

▶ Add salt to water along with chow mein noodles and stir.

▶ Cover pot partially (if the pot is covered fully, it can bubble over).

▶ Cook noodles according to package instructions.

▶ Halfway through the noodles being cooked, heat oil in pan.

▶ Add garlic and ginger and fry for 1 minute or until fragrant (make sure that the garlic does not burn!).

▶ Add carrots and bora and sauté for 2–3 minutes; season with salt and pepper.

▶ Add bell peppers, bean sprouts, and green onions, cooking for just half a minute.

▶ Strain noodles in a colander under running tap water.

▶ Shake the colander getting rid of any excess liquid and add it directly to the vegetables along with sesame oil, five-spice powder and stir, swiftly tossing and mixing the vegetables and noodles moving them around the pan.

▶ Taste for seasoning and adjust for salt and pepper.

▶ Turn off the stove and serve hot.

Variations

- ▶ To make beef, pork or chicken chowmein, slice meat thinly, lengthways, season with soy sauce or salt, pepper, grated ginger and garlic.
- ▶ At step 5, pan fry meat in batches on high heat, constantly moving the meat around.
- ▶ Remove meat and set aside in a warm place.
- ▶ Continue recipe from step 6.
- ▶ Add cooked meat to chowmein at step 10 while tossing all the ingredients together.
- ▶ This same method is used for deveined shrimp, only you do not have to slice the shrimp at all as it naturally cooks up quickly.

Cynthia's Tip

Chow mein, like fried rice is about quick cooking with high heat so ensure that all ingredients are prepped before you turn on your stove.

Cook-Up Rice

The origins of this one-pot dish lie in the use of whatever was remaining at the end of the week, hence the practical name: cook-up. The cooking-up of peas, rice and various pieces of meats cooked in a large pot with coconut milk was traditionally made and eaten on Saturdays. It is common on Old Year's Night (New Year's Eve) in Guyana to make a large pot of cook-up rice. The sentiment remains the same: it is the end of the year so throw everything together and cook-up. The types of meats chosen for this dish are also indicative of the end-of-week theme: tripe, salt beef, pig-tail, chicken wings, backs and necks all get put into the pot. These days, cook-up rice is not only cooked on Saturdays but any day of the week and the meats, though they basically remain the same, have been joined by fresh beef and pork. Some people make a chicken cook-up using the entire chicken. Fried fish and fried ripe plantains are usually served as accompaniments to this dish. Okras can be steamed on top of the rice to go with the cook-up also.

Yield: 8 cups

Ingredients

2 tablespoons oil

1 cup diced onion, divided

(First use – ½ cup to sauté and cook meats)

(Second use – ½ cup to cook rice and peas)

4 sprigs fresh thyme, divided

(First use 2 sprigs to sauté and cook meats)

(Second use 2 springs to cook rice and peas)

½ pound tripe, cleaned and cut up

Salt and pepper to taste

3 ½ cups boiling water

1 pound salt meat (combo of pig tail and salt beef), cut up

1 cup of dried black-eyed peas soaked overnight

4 cups coconut milk (preferably fresh squeezed)

2 cups long grain parboiled rice, washed and drained

⅓ cup diced tomatoes

2 green onions, thinly sliced (white and green parts)

Whole hot pepper

1 sprig basil, leaves torn

Equipment

1 Pressure cooker

1 Large pot

1 saucepot

1 Large spoon

1 Large bowl

Directions

► Heat oil in pressure cooker.

► Add ½ cup onions and thyme and let cook until onions become translucent

► Add tripe, salt and pepper to taste and fry for 2–3 minutes.

► Add water and bring to a boil.

► Close pressure cooker; pressure cook for ½ hour (time starts from the first whistle). Meanwhile, place the salt meat and some water in the sauce pot, bring to a boil and cook on high heat for 20 minutes to remove the excess salt. Drain and set aside.

► Release the valve of the pressure cooker letting out the steam.

► Add the salt meat and peas to the pressure cooker, close and pressure cook for 10–12 minutes.

► Release the valve of the pressure cooker, letting out the steam.

► Place large pot on stove, add coconut milk.

▶ Transfer the peas and meat mixture along with any drippings or remaining liquid to the pot with the coconut milk. Stir, cover and bring to a boil.

▶ Add rice to pot as soon as mixture comes to a boil along with the remaining thyme, onion, tomatoes, green onions, hot pepper and basil.

▶ Stir, taste for salt and pepper and adjust.

▶ Cover and bring to a boil.

▶ Let cook until you begin to see the top of the rice and the liquid has reduced some (do not stir); approximately 6 minutes.

▶ Turn the heat to simmer and let cook for 35–40 minutes or until all the liquid is completely gone.

▶ Stir once and remove pot from heat. Leave the cover slightly off.

▶ The rice should be moist, in separate grains and cooked through.

▶ Let the cook-up rice rest for 10 minutes then serve.

Cynthia's Tips

If you are not using a pressure cooker, then cook the tripe for at least 45 minutes as it is very tough; more water would be needed also. The salt meat and peas should boil for at least 20 minutes.

Long grain white rice would also work well with this dish. Adjust the cooking liquid (coconut milk) accordingly. If using long grain white rice, then use 2 ½ cups coconut milk

If using canned coconut milk, dilute it with at least a 1 to 1 ratio (1 cup coconut milk and 1 cup water)

Any meat or chicken can be used in this dish as well as your favourite peas or beans, fresh or dried.

Cou-cou

Cou-cou and flying fish is the national dish of Barbados. Cou-cou is made with fine cornmeal that's cooked low and slow along with sliced okras until all the cooking liquid is absorbed and it becomes a firm mixture. Cou-cou can also be served with any meat, poultry or seafood where the finished dish has a lot of sauce. The sauce is ladled liberally over the Cou-cou and then eaten. For presentation, be sure not to miss out on moulding the Cou-cou in a buttered dish and then inverting it on to a plate. It is traditionally made on Saturdays.

Yield: 5 cups

Ingredients

2 cups fine-ground cornmeal

2 cups water

1 tablespoon oil

½ cup finely chopped onions

1 tablespoon minced garlic

2 teaspoons finely minced thyme

1+⅓ cups (6) thinly sliced okra

4 cups boiling water

1 teaspoon salt

1 tablespoon butter, plus extra for
    buttering dish

Equipment

1 medium bowl

1 heavy-bottomed pot

1 Slotted pot spoon

2 Small bowls

1 Whisk

1 Wooden spoon

1 Deep bowl for molding, generously buttered

Directions

▶ Soak cornmeal in 2 cups water in medium bowl for 5 minutes.

▶ Heat oil in pot and gently sauté onions, garlic and thyme for 1–2 minutes.

▶ Add sliced okra and sauté for one minute.

▶ Add 4 cups of boiling water, cover pot and let boil for 10–12 minutes.

▶ Using a slotted spoon, remove the okra to a small bowl and set aside; keep warm.

▶ Pour out half of the liquid in the pot in a small bow and reserve for later use.

▶ Turn the heat to very low, add the soaked cornmeal, salt and butter.

▶ Stir constantly using a whisk to avoid lumps and the cornmeal mixture from scorching.

▶ As the cornmeal begins to dry out, add the reserved liquid in stages, stirring with a wooden spoon until the cornmeal is cooked (this takes about 1½ hours but you do not have to stand stirring continuously, just ensure that the heat is very low and stir perhaps at 15-minute intervals).

▶ As the mixture begins to come away clean from the sides of the pot, add back the okra and stir to incorporate fully.

▶ Let cou cou continue to cook until firm (but not stiff). Again, the mixture should come away cleanly from the sides of the pot and when you insert the spoon in the middle of the Cou-cou it should stand and remove easily from the mixture.

▶ Pour mixture into generously buttered bowl and shake it around to form and mold.

▶ Invert bowl with Cou-cou onto a platter.

▶ To serve, create an indentation in the centre and heap with stewed fish or meat or vegetables letting the rich sauce spill over to the sides.

Dhal

Soul food is how I describe this dish. Dhal is a spiced lentil soup that's tempered with whole spices and sliced garlic. Generally, it is eaten with rice and a pickle or with some sort of dry-curry or vegetables. It is a favourite with roti as a breakfast or dinner meal. The peas most often used in these parts to make dhal are the yellow and green split-peas.

Dhal is served as an every-day dish as well as at Hindu and Muslim weddings, functions and festivals.

Yield: 3 cups

Ingredients

1 cup dried split peas (yellow or green)

Water to cook peas

Hot pepper to taste, whole

Salt to taste

3 cups boiling water, reserved

2 tablespoons oil

1 teaspoon black mustard seeds (optional)

½ tablespoon jeera (cumin seeds)

2 large cloves garlic, sliced thinly

Equipment

1 pressure cooker or medium saucepan

1 large spoon

1 metal ladle or small frying pan

1 potato masher or immersion blender if not using a pressure cooker

Directions

Cooking the peas

► Soak split peas with water over night (this is optional, you can cook the peas as is but I have found that hydrating it before helps it to cook faster).

► Wash peas that's been soaking overnight.

► Add peas to pressure cooker along with salt to taste, hot pepper and water that comes about 2 inches above the peas; stir.

► Cover and close the pressure cooker (if using a regular pot, please note split peas at first boil rises to the top of the pot so watch out for that).

- ▶ Pressure cook the peas for about 12–15 minutes, or until it melts completely (time begins at the first whistle).
- ▶ Turn off the stove and relieve the pressure valve. If the melted peas is too thick, add some of the reserved boiling water, return pressure cooker to the stove on low heat resting the cover on top of the pot but not closing it.
- ▶ If you are using a regular saucepan to cook your dhal, add all the ingredients, stir, cover pot partially and bring to a boil.
- ▶ Cook peas until it is melted. Use the potato masher to help get the dhal smooth or puree with an immersion blender.
- ▶ Keep dhal simmering, partially covered as you prepare to chunkay (temper) it.

Chunkay (temper) the dhal - *Using a metal ladle*

- ▶ Heat oil in a ladle on the open flame of a burner.
- ▶ When heated, add the mustard seeds (if using) and let toast in the oil, the seeds will begin to pop; add jeera (cumin seeds).
- ▶ When the mustard seeds and jeera begin to pop, remove ladle from flame and gently add the sliced garlic.
- ▶ Return ladle with garlic and jeera (cumin seeds) and mustard seeds to flame and let continue to toast until the garlic starts to get slightly brown at the edges and fragrant.
- ▶ Turn off the stove.

- Now carefully lift the ladle while simultaneously, partially moving the lid of the pot with the dhal, keep holding the handle of the cover as this is very important.
- *Gently* plunge the hot ladle with oil, garlic, jeera (cumin seeds) and mustard seeds into the dhal, and pull the lid back over the dhal pot to avoid any splatter or the full steam.
- Stir dhal with the ladle, taste for salt, and adjust if needed.
- Turn off the stove, the dhal is done.
- Serve with rice, roti or eat as a soup.

Chunkay (temper) the dhal - *Using a small frying pan*

- Heat oil in pan, add mustard seeds (if using) and when it begins to pop, add jeera (cumin seeds) and toast in oil.
- As jeera (cumin seeds) and mustard seeds continue to pop, add garlic and fry until it starts to get slightly brown and fragrant.
- Turn off the heat and pour the mixture into the dhal and stir in.

Cynthia's Tips

Spinach, pumpkin, okras, tomatoes, even green mangoes can be added to the dhal also. This in turn will make it, spinach dhal, pumpkin dhal etc.

If you are adding any of these ingredients, do so about 5–10 minutes before the cooking process of the peas is complete. The idea is to have the added ingredients cooked in to flavour the dhal and add texture.

Dhal gets very thick when it gets cold (meaning at room temperature), reheat it by adding boiling water and let it heat through by coming back to a boil. Be sure to taste for salt.

I've found that the green split peas cook quicker than the yellow ones.

Dhal Puri

We refer to all the Indian flat breads we make in the Caribbean as roti, so dhal puri is a type of roti. The dough once portioned is then stuffed with a spiced-ground split-peas mixture. It is very popular as a snack when served with sour and as a meal when served with a meat, chicken, seafood or vegetable curry. It's one of those dishes that take practice to perfect.

Yield: 10–12

Ingredients

Dough

4 cups all purpose flour

4 teaspoons baking powder

1 teaspoon sugar

½ teaspoon salt

1 tablespoon oil

1¼ cups warm water to knead a soft dough (a little more water may be needed)

Filling

1 cup yellow split-peas (soaked over night)

Water to cook peas

Salt to taste

4 large cloves garlic, chopped

Hot pepper to taste, chopped

2 teaspoons ground jeera (cumin)

For cooking

Oil to brush both sides of the dhal puri

Additional flour for dusting and rolling

Equipment

1 large bowl

Plastic wrap

1 medium saucepan

1 large spoon

1 colander

1 food processor

1 medium bowl

1 fork

1 baking sheet, lightly oiled

1 rolling pin

1 tawah (flat iron griddle)

1 flat spatula

1 small bowl with oil to brush on dhal puri

1 pastry brush

12 (4-inch square) pieces wax paper

1 large plate lined with tea towel and wax paper

Directions

Dough

► Mix flour, baking powder, salt and sugar in large bowl.

► Drizzle oil into flour mixture and incorporate.

► Add warm water and knead ingredients to make a soft dough.

► Rub dough lightly all over with oil, cover with plastic wrap and let rest for *at least* 30 minutes.

Filling

► Wash soaked peas, add to saucepan with water and salt to taste and bring to a boil.

► Let peas cook until aldenté (with a bite to it). Be sure *not* to cook the peas until soft. The split peas should still be whole and firm but definitely not raw. Check after 5 minutes of boiling.

► Drain in colander; let peas dry somewhat by spreading out in a single layer on paper towels, leave it uncovered for 10–12 minutes (this is to ensure that the peas when pulsed will not paste together due to excess moisture).

► Add the boiled peas, garlic and hot pepper to food processor.

► Pulse until the mixture is of a very fine cornmeal; mixture should *not* be like a paste, it should be able to fluff with a fork.

► Empty the processed peas into medium bowl, add ground jeera (cumin), mixing thoroughly with a fork.

► Taste the mixture but it should not need salt if you adequately salted the peas when it was boiling.

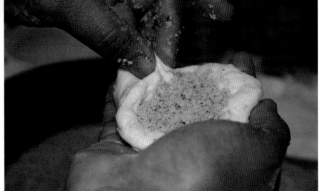

Combining dough and filling

▶ Knead rested dough for 1–2 minutes.

▶ Cut dough into sizes a little larger than golf balls.

▶ Pat each piece of dough into a round disk, about 3 inches.

▶ Now you can do this part 2 ways: place the disk on a flat surface scoop up some of the seasoned split peas, place it in the middle of the flattened dough and bring the ends together, pinching and enclosing the stuffing. Or take the flattened dough and place it in one hand, cupping it. Scoop some of the seasoned filling into the dough-cup. Carefully grab the ends of the dough and pinch it to seal in the stuffing.

▶ Place stuffed dough, seam-side down on baking sheet (or whatever surface you are using).

▶ Pat each stuffed dough-ball with a little bit oil so that a dry skin does not develop.

▶ Continue stuffing the balls of dough with the seasoned split peas until done.

▶ Cover with plastic wrap and let rest for 20–30 minutes.

Cooking the dhal puri

▶ Now it's time to cook the dhal puri. Some people like their dhal puri with tiny, toasted brown spots and some don't, either way it does not matter, it's about personal preference. Personally, I don't mind the little brown spots.

▶ Heat the tawah (flat iron-griddle) on medium-low heat.

▶ Flour work surface and rolling pin.

▶ Using your hands, form a round disk of the stuffed dough-ball; gently and carefully press just off from the centre to the ends, this way you are starting to distribute the filling to the ends.

▶ Place on floured surface and roll dough thinly. You can opt to roll on one side only, constantly turning the dough at a

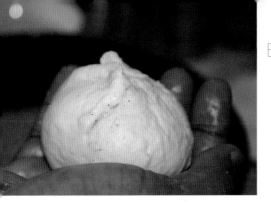

90-degree angle or you can flip the dough over, back and forth and roll.

► Carefully lift rolled dough and place on heated tawah.

► As soon as you start to see the dhal puri puff up with little bubbles, turn the dhal puri on the other side to cook and in the mean time, brush the now cooked side with some oil, be sure to brush the edges also.

► Turn dhal puri and brush the other cooked side.

► Turn one more time ensuring the dhal puri is cooked. Using a spatula, remove dhal puri from tawah and place on lined plate.

► Repeat this process until all the dhal puri is cooked and ensuring that you put a piece of the cut waxed paper between each dhal puri, this will prevent them from sticking to each other and steaming.

► Serve hot or at room temperature with any curry or it can be eaten as is or with a dab of achar or sour.

Egg Curry

Growing up, this was a fast-food dish and it was also one of those things you threw together when you ran out of ideas. Cooking the curry with eddoes or potatoes really makes a difference to the texture of the gravy because you can mash one or two pieces to thicken the gravy.

Yield: 3 servings (2 eggs per serving)

Ingredients

2 tablespoons oil

6 boiled eggs, peeled and patted dry

1½ tablespoons curry paste (recipe on page 322)

Salt to taste

2 large potatoes cut into big chunks

Boiling water to cook the dish

1 tomato, diced

Equipment

1 karahi or deep frying pan

1 slotted spoon

1 splatter cover

Paper towels

Directions

- Heat oil in a karahi, wok or frying pan.
- Slide the eggs, one at a time, into the pan and let them fry, turning to ensure that all around gets fried, this takes about 1 minute in total (this stage is optional but it gives a nice texture to the eggs and helps the curry sauce adhere better to the eggs). Watch out for sputtering from any drops of water that might be on the egg after peeling. Use the splatter cover to prevent being burnt.
- Remove eggs by using a slotted spoon and set aside.
- In the same pan (add a little more oil if needed) add the curry paste and sauté for 1–2 minutes, adding salt to taste.
- Add the potatoes and sauté for 1–2 minutes.
- Add enough boiling water to cook the potatoes.
- Just as potatoes are fork tender, add the tomatoes and eggs.
- Using the back of the pot spoon, mash a couple chunks of the potatoes to thicken the gravy.
- Cover, turn the heat to low and let simmer until the gravy is to your desired thickness.
- Serve with rice or roti.

Roast Eggplant & Potato Curry (dry)

The smoky flavour imparted from the fire roasting of the eggplant is truly the star of this dish. Without the fire-roasting step the desired flavour won't be possible. This dish is one of my favourite and newly discovered ways to eat eggplant. The liquid used to cook the potatoes must be almost gone before adding the pulp of the roasted eggplant.

Yield: 4 cups

Ingredients

2 tablespoons oil

1½ tablespoons masala paste (recipe on page 326)

Salt to taste

2 large potatoes cut into large chunks

Boiling water

2 pounds eggplant, fire roasted, skin removed and flesh lightly mashed

1 cup diced tomatoes

1 tablespoon chopped cilantro

2 teaspoons tamarind pulp

Equipment

1 frying pan

1 large spoon

Directions

► Heat oil in pan.

► Add masala paste with salt to taste and sauté for 1 minute.

► Add potatoes and stir, sauté for a minute or two.

► Add enough boiling water to cook potatoes, cover and bring to a boil.

► Cook until potatoes are fork tender.

► Now add the eggplant, tomatoes, cilantro and tamarind pulp and stir to incorporate.

► Cover, turn to medium low and let cook for 7–9 minutes or until dry, it's okay if it scorches a little at the bottom (this adds more flavour).

► Serve with rice or roti.

Flying Fish in Tomato-Onion Sauce

This is the other half of the Barbadian national dish when served with Cou-cou. It is also made separately and served with root vegetables and ground provisions. The fish are called flying fish because they actually fly and skim the waters they live in.

Yield: 12

Ingredients

12 flying fish, deboned and cleaned

Salt and pepper to taste

2 tablespoons oil

1 cup sliced onions (¼ inch thickness)

2 cloves garlic, crushed

1 cup diced tomatoes

2 sprigs fresh thyme

Hot pepper to taste, minced

2 cups boiling water

2 tablespoons thinly sliced green onions
　　(white & green parts)

Equipment

1 frying pan with cover

1 large spoon

Cynthia's Tips

Any white fish can work with this recipe.

Roll flying fish and secure in place with a toothpick. Remove toothpick before serving.

Directions

▶ Pat fish dry and season lightly with salt and black pepper; set aside.

▶ Heat oil in pan.

▶ Add onions and sauté until translucent (2–3 minutes) with sprinkling of salt.

▶ Add garlic, tomatoes, thyme and hot pepper and sauté for 1–2 minutes; add another sprinkling of salt.

▶ Pour boiling water to pan, reduce heat to medium and let cook uncovered until the liquid has reduced by half (approximately 6–8 minutes).

▶ Check and adjust seasoning.

▶ Add flying fish to sauce, cover and let cook for 5–7 minutes.

▶ Remove from heat and stir in green onions.

▶ Serve with Cou-cou.

▶ This dish can also be eaten with rice, bread or boiled ground provisions.

Garlic Pork

Garlic pork is pickled pork and it is a must-have in most homes at Christmas. This Portuguese influenced dish is highly flavourful and aromatic. As it sizzles in the pan, the kitchen is enveloped with the perfume of thyme and garlic, the main flavourings. Garlic pork should be set at least 2 weeks in advance before use. The longer it cures the more intense the flavour. A mixture of lean and not so lean cuts is best suited for this dish.

Yield: 1¼ pounds

Ingredients

1½ pounds boneless pork

12 large cloves of garlic

5 packed tablespoons fresh thyme

1 cup + 2 tablespoons distilled vinegar

1 cup + 2 tablespoons water

½ tablespoon granulated sugar

Salt to taste, start with 1 tablespoon table-salt

Hot pepper to taste, sliced

Equipment

2 Medium bowls

1 pair Tongs or fork

1 Large glass bottle with plastic cover, clean and dried

1 Wooden spoon

Directions

► Clean meat, pat dry and slice into ½-inch thickness; set aside in bowl.

► In a mortar with pestle (or whatever device you use for grinding things), combine garlic and thyme with 1 teaspoon salt and grind into a paste.

► Add paste to meat in bowl and coat each slice well; clean hands work best.

► Transfer the seasoned pork to the glass jar/bottle using tongs or a fork.

► Mix the vinegar, water and sugar together in a bowl or large measuring cup adding salt to taste. Taste the mixture to ensure that it has the right amount of salt you desire and strength of vinegar; adjust to suit your taste.

► Pour the vinegar-water-salt mixture into bottle with meat, stir gently with wooden spoon to ensure that the liquid surrounds all of the meat.

Cynthia's Tips

Always use clean utensils when taking out meat from the jar.

Garlic pork can last for 3 weeks and more as long as it has not been soiled by unclean utensils.

It is not necessary when pan-frying the garlic pork to add some of the liquid but you can if you'd like.

Discard liquid when all the meat has been used up.

► Add the sliced hot pepper to the mixture.

► Cover the bottle or jar, airtight and set aside on your counter or pantry away from direct heat.

► On day 7 you can begin cooking and eating your garlic pork.

To cook garlic pork

► Rub or drizzle a little oil in a skillet and heat.

► Using clean tongs or a fork take out the amount of meat you need. Shake off any excess juices. Garlic pork is an intense pickle and often 2–3 slices are good to serve 2 people.

► Add pork to pan and cook until golden brown on both sides and the juices in the pan have been absorbed.

Gilbaka (Fish) Curry

I love curry and my favourite is curried fish. In Guyana in particular there is a wide and unusual variety of fish and I love them all. For curry I particularly like the fish that are naturally without scale, such as gilbaka and catfish. Another favourite fish of mine is hassar. For me, fish curry must be cooked with some souring agent such as green mangoes, souree, or tamarind along with a few okras dropped in at the last minute – and of course with lots of hot pepper.

Yield: 5 servings

Ingredients

2 tablespoons oil

1½ tablespoons curry paste (recipe on page 322)

Salt to taste

1 small green mango, cut into large pieces or 1 tablespoon tamarind pulp

2 pounds gilbaka or any firm fish, cut, washed and patted dry

Boiling water to cook fish and make gravy

1 large tomato diced

1 (2-inch) piece fresh ginger, grated and squeezed for juice (just shy of 1 tablespoon)

Equipment

1 deep frying pan

1 large spoon

Directions

▶ Heat oil in pan.

▶ Add curry paste with salt to taste and sauté for 1–2 minutes.

▶ Add fish and stir ensuring that the curry paste coats the fish; Sauté for 2–3 minutes.

▶ Stir in mango (or tamarind if using) .

▶ Add enough boiling water to cook fish and reduce to gravy/sauce.

▶ 3 minutes before the curry is ready to finish cooking, add diced tomatoes and stir in ginger juice.

▶ Check and adjust salt to taste.

▶ Cover and complete cooking.

▶ Serve with white rice, roti or boiled ground provisions.

Cynthia's Tips

I usually add whole okra or drumsticks (saijan) to my fish curries. Add the half-way through the cooking process.

Leave out the green mango or tamarind if you do not have any.

Halibut is a good substitute for Gilbaka.

Hassar Curry

This is one of my favourite fish to have curried. Found in muddy waters and only available during certain times of the year, hassar can be expensive. Cooked in coconut milk with a piece of green mango and a few okras or saijhan (a vegetable also known as drum sticks) the desire to eat hassar curry makes one yearn for home. Eating hassar is all about the bones, once cooked, the outer shell peels off easily so there's a lot of sucking on the bones. The flesh is firm and delicious.

Yield: 6 servings (2 hassar per person)

Ingredients

2 tablespoons oil

2 tablespoons curry paste (recipe on page 322)

Salt to taste

12 medium-sized hassar, cleaned

4–5 cups coconut milk or water

½ cup diced tomatoes

Directions

▶ Heat oil in frying pan or karahi.

▶ Add curry paste and sauté for 1–2 minutes.

▶ Add salt to taste (you are salting the entire dish at this stage).

▶ Add hassar and stir to ensure the curry paste coats the fish. Try to get some of the paste into the slit belly of the fish as well. Sauté for 2–3 minutes, turning the fish a couple of times.

▶ Add coconut milk or to cook hassar and reduce to gravy/sauce.

▶ Cook covered for approximately 10–15 minutes.

▶ About 5 minutes before the curry is going to be finished and gravy/sauce reduced to your desired consistency, stir in the diced tomatoes.

▶ Check and adjust salt to taste.

▶ Cover and complete cooking.

▶ Serve with rice.

Equipment

1 deep frying pan or karahi

1 large spoon

Cynthia's Tips

You can add green mangoes, okras or saijans to this curry half way through the cooking process

If you are using canned coconut milk, thin it out with water using a 1 to 1 ratio.

Kalounjie
(Stuffed Bitter Gourd)

Bitter gourd/bitter melon/karaila is stuffed with minced meat, seafood or masala paste and cooked low and slow with coconut milk or water. Karaila is an acquired taste as the vegetable is bitter. However, once cooked, the bitterness tends to mellow out a little.

Yield: 5 servings (1 Karaila each)

Ingredients

5 large karaila

2½ tablespoons oil, divided

(First usage 1 tablespoon to fry karaila)

(Second usage 1½ tablespoons to sauté masala)

1½ tablespoons curry paste, divided (recipe on page 322)

(First usage ½ tablespoon to cook stuffing)

(Second usage 1 tablespoon to cook the entire dish)

1 cup stuffing (recipe follows)

1 cup diced tomatoes, divided

(First usage ½ cup to cook with curry paste)

(Second usage ½ cup to finish dish)

2 cups fresh coconut milk (water can be substituted or use 1 cup water and 1 cup coconut milk)

Salt to taste

Stuffing

1 cup small shrimp or minced meat

(The original stuffing for this dish is vegetarian, whereby extra curry paste-masala mixture is made and stuffed into the kariala)

Equipment

1 knife

2 teaspoons

1 karahi or deep frying pan

1 large spoon

1 small bowl

Paper towels

Kitchen string

1 pair scissors

Directions

► Cut the bottom and top tips of the karaila.

► Slice the karaila open on one side, start 1 inch away from the top and stop 1 inch from the bottom.

► Gently pry it open the karaila and using your fingers or a teaspoon, scoop out the seeds and the woolly interior and discard. Set aside karaila.

► Heat 1 tablespoon oil in karahi or frying pan.

► Add ½ tablespoon curry paste and sauté for 1 minute; add salt to taste.

► Add shrimp or mince, lightly sauté stuffing until cooked.

► Transfer stuffing to bowl and let cool a little.

► Wipe karahi or pan clean and turn off heat.

► Stuff the karaila with sautéed stuffing, be careful not to over stuff it, but make it compact.

▶ Tie the stuffed karaila snugly with kitchen string. This is to ensure that none of the stuffing comes out in the cooking process.

▶ Heat the remaining 1½ tablespoons oil in karahi or pan and fry karaila in batches until brown all over then remove and set aside (the karaila will get dark brown in various spots). Set aside fried karaila.

▶ In the same karahi with the hot oil, (if there's not enough oil after frying the karaila then add a little more) add the remaining 1 tablespoon curry paste and half of the diced tomatoes and sauté for a minute or two. Season with salt to taste.

▶ Add coconut milk or water, cover and bring to a boil.

▶ As soon as the liquid comes to a boil, add all the fried whole karaila to the pan (the sliced side facing up).

▶ Cover, turn to the heat to medium-low and let cook slowly for 20 minutes.

▶ After 20 minutes, remove cover, turn heat up to high and let the liquid continue to reduce until the coconut milk begins to crack (little curds will form and separate).

▶ 2 minutes before the milk cracks or the liquid reduces, add the remaining diced tomatoes.

▶ There should be no liquid when the kalounjie is finished cooking, just the remnants of the curry paste mixed with the cracked coconut milk, a little oil and tomatoes.

▶ Remove the strings and serve whole, halved or quartered with rice or roti.

Katahar
(Green Breadnut) Curry

This vegetable is also known as breadnut and belongs to the breadfruit family. In Guyana it is called katahar and in Trinidad & Tobago as Chataigne. It is often used when green, curried with coconut milk and sometimes with shrimp. Once peeled, the young seeds and the flesh are cooked together.

The flesh of a ripened katahar is never used, only the nuts (seeds) which are boiled in salted water, peeled and eaten as a snack.

Yield: 4 cups

Ingredients

1 pound peeled and shredded katahar (breadnut)

1½ tablespoons curry paste

Salt to taste

⅓ cup diced tomatoes

4 cups fresh coconut milk (approximately)

Equipment

1 karahi or deep frying pan
1 large spoon

Directions

- ▶ Heat oil in karahi or pan.
- ▶ Add curry paste and sauté for 1–2 minutes.
- ▶ Add tomatoes and salt to taste; stir.
- ▶ Add katahar (breadnut) and stir, mixing it with the curry paste.
- ▶ Let sauté for 2–3 minutes.
- ▶ Add coconut milk and stir.
- ▶ Cover pan, reduce heat to low and let cook until the katahar (bread nut) seeds are soft.
- ▶ Remove cover and let the liquid dry out completely.
- ▶ Serve hot with rice.

Cynthia's Tips

Depending how old the katahar (breadnut) is, it may require more coconut milk and a longer cooking time.

If you are using a pressure cooker, this can be done within 20–30 minutes.

Macaroni & Cheese Pie

Macaroni Pie is another of those dishes that can be found on many tables throughout the Caribbean. In Barbados it's eaten daily and each household has its own recipe for making macaroni pie. Some people like theirs firm, others like it soft, loose. For easy and uniform cutting and serving, let the pie rest for *at least* half an hour after it comes out of the oven. Don't worry about it getting cold as macaroni pie retains its warmth for a long time.

Yield: 1 (8" x 8" x 2" pan)

Ingredients

1 (14.1 oz) packet macaroni (bucatini, elbows)

Water to cook pasta

2 tablespoons unsalted butter, plus extra to butter dish

2 tablespoons all-purpose flour

3 cups whole milk

1 tablespoon grainy mustard

½ teaspoon freshly grated nutmeg

4 heaped cups grated sharp cheddar cheese, divided

(First use 3 cups to make cheese sauce)

(Second use 1 cup to sprinkle on top)

Salt & Pepper to taste

Equipment

1 large pot

1 colander

1 (8 x 8 x 2-inch) baking dish, buttered

1 baking sheet, lined with foil

1 1aucepan

1 wooden spoon

Cynthia's Tips

You can add minced thyme, garlic and dried red-pepper flakes to infuse the sauce.

The longer the macaroni and cheese rests after baking, the easier it is to cut and serve in squares; the cheese sauce solidifies as it rests. However, you can serve it right away but it will not be as firm.

Other tubular-shaped pasta works well too.

Directions

▶ Preheat oven to 350°F.

▶ Bring a large pot of water to a boil; season water with salt.

▶ Add macaroni and cook according to package directions.

▶ Meanwhile, melt butter in saucepan on medium heat.

▶ Add flour and stir letting the flour absorb the butter, *do not* let the mixture develop a colour, reduce heat to low if necessary.

▶ Add milk, mustard and nutmeg and stir until butter-flour mixture is dissolved. Reduce heat to low and let the mixture heat through stirring constantly until the sauce thickens and is smooth.

▶ Drain the pasta and transfer to buttered dish; place dish on baking sheet, this will prevent spillage in the oven itself if the pie bubbles over.

▶ Once the sauce has thickened, remove it from the heat and add in 3 cups of cheese, stirring until its melted.

▶ Taste sauce and adjust seasoning with salt and freshly ground pepper.

▶ Pour cheese sauce all over macaroni and toss thoroughly and gently.

▶ Sprinkle top with remaining cup of cheese.

▶ Bake for 30–40 minutes or until the top is crusty and golden.

▶ Remove from oven and let rest and cool before cutting.

Mettagee
(Tubular & Root Vegetables
Cooked in Coconut Milk)

Many Caribbean countries have their own one-pot dish of ground provisions (root vegetables) cooked with coconut milk, salt fish, meats and dumplings. In Guyana, it is called Mettagee. All the ingredients are cooked together in a large pot with coconut milk until the liquid reduces to a thick sauce.

In Grenada where their version is made and called Oil-Down, all the liquid must be absorbed. When one thinks of dishes such as these, we think of them as soul-food.

Yield: 1 (5-quart) pot

Ingredients

For Dumplings

2 cups all-purpose flour

1 teaspoon baking powder

¼ teaspoon ground cinnamon

¼ teaspoon grated nutmeg

1 teaspoon sugar

A pinch of salt

Water to knead dough

For Fried Salt Fish

1 tablespoon oil

¼ cup diced onions

Hot pepper to taste, chopped

8 ounces Salt fish, de-salted and broken into little
     pieces (see page 324)

3 green onions, thinly sliced white and green parts

Mettagee

4 pounds root vegetables (a combination of any
     of the following: eddoes, yams, sweet potatoes,
     tannia, green plantains, ripe plantains, and
     cassava)

4 sprigs fresh thyme

1 cup diced onions

4 cups coconut milk (preferably fresh)

1 tablespoon oil

10 okras (more or less if you like); tops and bottoms
     removed

1 cup water

Salt and pepper to taste

Equipment

1 frying pan

1 large spoon

1 large pot

1 large bowl

Directions

Dumplings

▶ Place all the dry ingredients in a
    bowl and mix together.

▶ Add water and knead to a soft
    dough.

▶ Cover and set aside letting dough
    rest.

▶ After resting for about 30 minutes,
    gently knead the dough and cut it
    into 8 large pieces (smaller pieces
    can be cut if you like).

▶ Roll dough into balls or oblong and
    set aside, covered.

Salt fish

▶ Heat oil in pan.

▶ Lightly   sauté   onions   until
    translucent.

▶ Add pepper to taste.

▶ Add salt fish and continue to sauté
    for 3–4 minutes.

▶ Stir in green onions.

▶ Set aside.

Mettagee

- ▶ Peel and cut root vegetables and green plantains into large pieces.
- ▶ Cut and reserve ripe plantains separately.
- ▶ In a large pot, heat oil.
- ▶ Add onions and thyme and sauté for 1–2 minutes (thyme will start to pop once added to the hot oil.
- ▶ Add salt and pepper to taste.
- ▶ Add cut root vegetables to pot cover with enough coconut milk and water and stir (*do not* add the ripe plantains and okras).
- ▶ Cover pot and let come to a boil; cook vegetables over medium heat until they are fork tender.

- ▶ Add ripe plantains and okras when the root veggies are tender, and cook covered for 5 minutes.
- ▶ Add dumplings to the pot, *do not stir*; cover and let cook for about 8 minutes.
- ▶ Taste for salt and pepper.
- ▶ In the finished dish, the liquid should be reduced considerably into a thick creamy sauce.
- ▶ Serve with sautéed salt fish sprinkled on top.

Cynthia's Tips

You can add the salt fish or a piece of salt-meat directly to the pot to salt the entire dish

Some people also serve mettagee with fried fish

Fried Okra with Salt Fish

Okra is one of my favourite vegetables. Many people shy away from okra because they complain about them getting slimy, but they aren't when cooked in this recipe. Once the okra is cut I put them into the sun to dry out some of the moisture and I only add salt to the dish just before I remove it from the heat.

Yield: 4 cups

Ingredients

2 pounds okra, sliced into ¼ inch rounds

3 tablespoons oil

1 cup diced onions

3 sprigs fresh thyme

1 cup diced tomatoes

2 large cloves garlic, minced

Hot pepper to taste, finely minced

½ pound boneless salt fish, de-salted and crumbled into pieces (see page 324)

Salt to taste

Equipment

1 baking sheet or platter
1 karahi or frying pan
1 large spoon

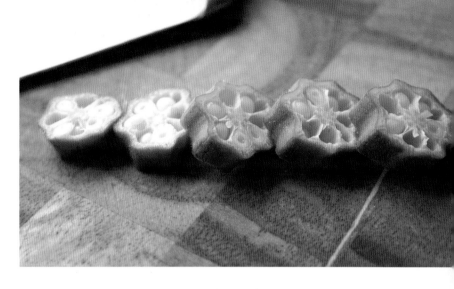

Directions

Okra

► Spread the sliced okras on a large baking sheet or platter and put outside in the sun for at least 30 minutes to draw out the moisture from the okras and prevent it being slimy when cooked. If there is no sun where you are then leave it on the counter top to air out for 45–60 minutes.

► Heat oil in pan.

► Add onions and sauté for 2 minutes.

► Add thyme, tomatoes, garlic and pepper and continue to sauté for another minute or two.

► Add salt fish and cook for 3 minutes.

► Add okras and stir to thoroughly mix.

► Turn the heat to medium-low and let cook, uncovered until okra is cooked through, turning periodically (approximately 12–15 minutes).

► Add salt to taste just before turning off the stove and stir (adding the salt at the end prevents the okra from yielding any moisture or getting slimy).

► Serve with dhal and rice or roti.

Variations

Vegetarian:

► Eliminate the salt-fish

With Shrimp:

► Fry shrimp on high heat for 1 minute, remove from pan and set aside.

► Proceed with cooking the okras as per instructions.

► Just as the okras are about to finish cooking, add the shrimp and stir. Adding the shrimp at this stage prevents it from getting hard, chewy and overcooked.

Okra in Tomato-onion Sauce

In order for the sauce not to get too silky, add the okras to it with just enough time for the okras to cook through and get tender. If you add it too early, then the sauce will become very slimy.

Yield: 2 cups

Ingredients

2 tablespoons oil

1 ½ cups thinly sliced onions

2 sprigs fresh thyme

1 large clove garlic, crushed

1 cup diced tomatoes

Salt and pepper to taste

1 cup boiling water

1 pound okra, tops and bottoms removed

Directions

► Heat oil in pan.

► Add onions and sauté for 2 minutes.

► Add thyme, garlic and tomatoes, sauté for 2 minutes.

► Add salt and pepper to taste.

► Add boiling water and let cook for 3 minutes.

► Add whole okra and cook uncovered on medium heat for 8–10 minutes or until a knife can easily be inserted.

► Adjust salt if necessary.

► Serve as a side dish or as an entrée for a vegetarian meal.

Equipment

1 Frying pan with cover
1 Pot spoon

Paratha (Oil Roti)

In Guyana this is also called oil-roti; in Trinidad, buss-up-shot. The key to making a good Guyanese paratha roti is letting the dough rest adequately between each stage. The ratio of baking powder to flour is also important. For the roti to become fluffy you must clap it almost immediately as it is removed from the tawah (flat iron griddle) If you are afraid to do this with your bare hands, then use a tea towel. All-purpose flour works best in this recipe.

Roti is made daily and eaten with any meal but it is mostly served at breakfast and dinner.

Yield: 10

Ingredients

5 cups all-purpose flour

1¼ teaspoons baking powder

½ teaspoon salt

1 teaspoon sugar

1½ tablespoons oil plus additional oil for oiling and cooking roti

Warm Water to knead dough (approximately 1½ cups)

Equipment

1 large bowl

Plastic wrap

1 table knife

1 small bowl for oil to brush roti

1 pastry brush

1 rolling pin

1 tawah (flat iron griddle)

1 spatula

1 large bowl or basket, lined with tea towel

Directions

▶ Add flour, baking powder, salt and sugar and mix thoroughly.

▶ Drizzle oil into flour and incorporate.

▶ Add warm water and knead to a soft pliable dough about 2–3 minutes.

▶ Lightly rub the dough with oil so as not to form a dry film.

▶ Cover with plastic wrap and let rest for at least 30 minutes (letting the dough rest is important to the end product and texture of the roti, the longer it rests, the better).

▶ Knead rested dough for about a minute or two and then cut into 10 equal pieces.

▶ Form each piece of dough one at a time into a round disk. Roll dough thin on a floured surface, don't worry if at this stage your rolled dough is not perfectly round.

▶ Brush the rolled dough with oil.

▶ Using a table knife or spoon, cut the dough from the center to an end. Roll the dough from the cut end all the way round forming a cone-cup shape.

▶ Insert the loose end of the dough into the bottom where all the layers are visible.

▶ Placing the dough on a flat surface, use your index finger and push on the pointed top of the dough and then press the entire dough with the palm of your hand; the dough will spring back up, that is fine.

- ▶ Rub a little bit of oil on the dough to prevent it drying out and forming a skin.
- ▶ Set oiled dough aside and repeat until all the cut dough are rolled and oiled.
- ▶ Cover with plastic wrap or foil.
- ▶ Let oiled dough rest for at least 30 minutes.
- ▶ Heat tawah on medium low.
- ▶ Taking one of the oiled pieces of dough, form a round disk, the ends should be thin and the center, thick.
- ▶ Place dough on a floured surface and roll into a round circle – turning at 90-degree angles and flipping the dough over, back and forth as you roll (rolling into a circle will take practice so if you can't get it that way, just concentrate rolling the dough in order to cook the roti).
- ▶ Place rolled dough on to the tawah and cook roti (it's almost like toasting).
- ▶ When the first side is cooked, (it should puff up with little bubbles) turn it and brush the cooked side with oil, do the same for the other side when it is cooked remove roti from tawah and clap it. Three quick claps will do (you can use a tea towel to protect your hands as you clap the roti because if you are not accustomed to doing this with your bare hands, you will feel the hot roti sting your hands). The purpose of clapping the roti is to release the steam that reveals the layers and make the roti fluffy.
- ▶ Fold roti and place in lined bowl or basked cover partially and continue making the other roti until done.
- ▶ Serve hot or at room temperature with your favourite curry or vegetables or with just a dab of butter.

Pepperpot

Yet another of Guyana's national dishes, this one from our Indigenous Peoples. Good cassareep (a cassava extract) is necessary for this dish. Pepperpot is cooked for a long time over high heat, breaking down the meats, infusing them with spices and creating a delicious dark sauce to be sopped up with bread. It is called Pepperpot because it was originally made with very little meat but lots of pepper.

This dish is usually served at Christmas, particularly on Christmas morning.

The longer this dish stands the richer and more flavourful it gets.

Yield: 10–12 servings

Ingredients

2 pounds stew, round or rump beef, cleaned and cut into large pieces

1½ pounds pig-trotters (feet), cleaned (they are sold pre cut)

1½ pounds cow-heel (feet), cleaned (sold pre cut)

1 large scotch bonnet pepper

4 (3-inch) cinnamon sticks

2 teaspoons whole cloves

1 (4-inch) piece of fresh ginger, peeled and sliced in half

1 (3-inch) piece dried orange peel (optional)

¾ cup cassava cassareep

1 cup sugar

2 teaspoons salt

Water to cook meats

Equipment

1 large pot with cover

1 wooden spoon

Directions

► Add all the ingredients along with water 4-inches above the ingredients.

► Transfer pot to stove on high heat, stir to dissolve sugar, salt and cassareep.

► Cover pot and let it come to a roaring boil. You will notice some scum/impurities from the meat rise to the top of the pot, skim and discard

► Reduce heat to medium and let it cook for 3 hours.

► Taste the sauce for the right balance of sugar and salt; it should err more on the side of sweet.

► Adjust to taste if necessary.

► Remove from heat.

► This dish is best served the following day after reheating but you can certainly eat it as soon as it's done.

► Serve with hearty bread.

Cynthia's Tips

Pepperpot tastes best the day(s) after it is made as the flavour develops more.

Each day, after it has been made, the pepperpot should be reheated to a boil, morning and evening.

This dish can be made as an all-beef dish or use your own combo of meats

Always use clean utensils when dipping into the Pepperpot.

Plantain Foo-Foo

This is an African inspired and influenced dish. It is another example of what is great about our cuisine - you can get a little bit of everything. Foo-Foo is the name of the dish and any starchy root vegetable can be used to make it. In this case, I used plantains. The boiled ground provision is pounded and mashed with a pat of butter, salt and black pepper and rolled into balls. It can be added to soups but it is usually eaten with some meat, chicken or seafood stew that's cooked with a lot of sauce.

Yield: 12 balls

Ingredients

3 large green plantains, peeled and cut
   into chunks
2 large half-ripe plantains, peeled and
   cut into chunks
Salt and pepper to taste
1 tablespoon unsalted butter, room
   temperature

Equipment

1 medium pot
1 colander
1 mortar and pestle
1 medium bowl

Directions

- ▶ Add plantains to pot with enough water just shy of covering the plantains.
- ▶ Cover pot and bring to a boil. When it starts to boil, add salt to taste.
- ▶ Cook covered until plantains are very soft (test with a fork).
- ▶ When cooked, strain in a colander.
- ▶ Using a mortar and pestle, in batches, pound-grind the plantains to a paste.

- ▶ Transfer ground plantains to bowl.
- ▶ Season with black pepper, check to see if it has enough salt and adjust if necessary.
- ▶ Rub butter into plantain mixture.
- ▶ With clean hands, divide mixture equally and form into balls.
- ▶ Serve with a meat, poultry, seafood or vegetable dish that has lots of sauce, this way, the Foo-Foo soaks up the sauce.

Cynthia's Rice & Peas

Rice and peas is the order of the name in Barbados but in other parts of the Caribbean it is called Peas and Rice and in each place, it is prepared differently with various types of peas. This recipe speaks to the Barbadian Rice & Peas. It is an everyday staple and the peas are always pigeon peas – dried or fresh. If using fresh peas, they will cook in the same amount of time as the rice, but if you are using dried peas that have been hydrated, then you need to cook the peas for at least 30 minutes before adding the rice.

Yield: 5 cups

Ingredients

1 cup dried pigeon peas, soaked overnight and drained

4–5 cups water

2 tablespoons oil

¾ cup diced onions

4 sprigs fresh thyme, divided

(First use 2 sprigs to cook peas and salt meat)

(Second use 2 sprigs to cook rice and entire dish)

Black pepper to taste

2 (2-inch) piece salt meat, (salt beef or pig-tail)

2 cups long grain parboiled rice, washed

4 cups boiling water

Equipment

1 large pot

1 large spoon

Directions

- ▶ Heat oil in pot.
- ▶ Add onions and sauté for 2 minutes.
- ▶ Add 2 sprigs of thyme, salt meat and black pepper and continue to sauté for about 3 minutes.
- ▶ Add the drained peas to onion-salt meat mixture and stir, cooking for 3 minutes.
- ▶ Add water to cook the peas until it is fork-tender (if using a pressure cooker, pressure for 15–20 minutes).
- ▶ When peas are fork-tender and the liquid almost reduced, add the washed rice, the remaining sprigs of thyme, a pinch of black pepper and 4 cups boiling water to cook the rice and peas.
- ▶ Cover pot and let continue to boil.
- ▶ When you begin to see the surface of the rice (5–7 minutes later), turn heat to simmer and let cook for 30–35 minutes or until all the liquid is gone.
- ▶ Serve as a side dish with a meat, poultry or seafood entrée or just as is.

Cynthia's Tips

The salt for this dish usually comes from the salt meat, however, if you are not using salt meat, add salt to taste.

Add a small bay leaf to the peas when cooking if you like

Using canned or fresh peas will reduce the cooking time.

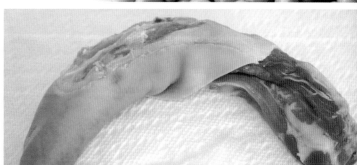

Spiced Roast Chicken

Yield: 6 servings

Ingredients

1 (5-pound) whole chicken cleaned
   and patted dry

2 tablespoons mixed spice rub (recipe
   follows)

1 tablespoon butter, cut into small bits

Mixed Spice rub

Salt to taste

1 teaspoon five-spice powder

⅛ teaspoon ground cinnamon

⅛ teaspoon ground cloves

2 teaspoons red pepper flakes

½ teaspoon chili powder

1 tablespoon garlic powder

Add all the ingredients to a bowl and mix
   thoroughly; set aside

Equipment

Kitchen string

1 roasting pan with rack

1 baster

1 small bowl

1 scissors

Directions

▶ Preheat oven to 400°F.

▶ With your fingers, gently lift as much of the skin away from the breast and thigh areas creating room to sprinkle the spice rub.

▶ Liberally sprinkle the spice rub in the cavity of the chicken, under the skin – thighs, and breast area. Additionally, sprinkle liberally all over the outside of the chicken including the back and under the wings.

▶ Place small pieces of butter under the breast skin of the chicken.

▶ Tie chicken legs together using kitchen string.

▶ Transfer chicken to roasting pan with rack.

▶ Tuck wing tips under the back of chicken so they do not burn.

▶ Bake for 1 hour at 400°F. At the end of the hour, reduce heat to 350°F and continue cooking for another hour and 15 minutes or until juices run clear after piercing the inner thigh with knife.

▶ If chicken is getting too brown after the hour, loosely place aluminum foil on top of chicken and continue to cook.

▶ Remove chicken from oven and let rest for 10–15 minutes before carving; remember to remove string.

Fried (Sautéed) Bora and Shrimps

While pork is the first meat I cooked, and curry the first dish I made, bora was the first vegetable I cooked. This dish is a true favourite of mine. It was one of the dishes I missed most being away from home. Today, I often refer to it as my "home on a plate dish."

Yield: 3 cups

Ingredients

2 tablespoons oil

1 cup shrimp

½ cup diced onions

2 cloves garlic, crushed

2 sprigs thyme

Hot pepper to taste, finely minced

½ cup diced tomatoes

4 cups cut bora (yard long beans, snake beans)

Equipment

1 medium frying pan with cover
1 large spoon
1 small bowl

Directions

► Heat oil in pan until almost smoking.

► Add shrimps and quickly stir-fry for 1 minute *only*.

► Remove shrimp, add to bowl and set aside.

► Add onions to pan and sauté for 1–2 minutes (if pan needs more oil, add a drizzle).

► Add garlic, thyme, pepper and tomatoes and continue to sauté for about a minute.

► Season with salt.

► Add bora and mix all ingredients thoroughly, cover, reduce heat to simmer and let cook for 15–20 minutes or until bora is cooked through.

► 2 minutes before the bora is finished cooking, stir in shrimp and finish cooking with pot uncovered.

► Serve with rice or roti.

Sautéed Bitter Gourd (Fried Karaila)

In addition to being stuffed and cooked with coconut milk, bitter melon/bitter gourd/karaila is also sautéed. It is a favourite with dhal and rice. The recipe outlines how to get rid of a lot of the bitterness.

Yield: 2 cups

Ingredients

5 medium-sized bitter gourds (Karaila) (approximately 4 cups when cut up)

Salt

2 tablespoons oil

½ cup diced onions

½ cup diced tomatoes

1 large clove garlic, minced

1 sprig fresh thyme

Hot pepper to taste, minced

Equipment

1 knife and cutting board

1 medium bowl

1 baking sheet

1 karahi or frying pan

1 pot spoon

Directions

Preparing the bitter gourd (karaila)

► Remove the tips (top and bottom) of the bitter gourd (karaila), slice in half and remove the seeds (use a tea spoon to scrape it out).

► Thinly slice the bitter gourd (into half-moon shapes).

► Transfer to a bowl and sprinkle liberally with salt to taste.

► Let rest for at least 1 hour (this process helps to release the bitterness. Think cucumber when salt is added to it).

► After the resting, in handfuls, squeeze all the liquid from the bitter gourd (karaila). If you like, you can add some fresh water and squeeze again.

► If it's sunny where you are, spread the squeezed bitter gourd (karaila) on to a baking sheet and place in the sun for half an hour (this way, the extra moisture will be extracted and the cooked bitter gourd will not be mushy). If there's no sun where you are, then just leave it on the countertop to air dry for 15–20 minutes.

Cooking

► Heat oil in karahi for frying pan.

► Add onions and sauté for a minute or two.

► Add tomatoes, garlic, thyme and hot pepper; continue to sauté for another minute.

► Add bitter gourd; stir, mixing with sautéed aromatics.

► Cook uncovered on medium to low heat until cooked, turning intermittently.

► Taste bitter gourd for salt (if you'd put enough to taste at the onset, you should not need to add more, but test just in case).

► Serve with dhal and rice or with roti.

Cynthia's Tip

You can skip sun or air-drying the karaila altogether and just move straight to cooking it.

Sautéed
Pumpkin & Shrimps

Pumpkin & shrimps are a favourite to have with paratha roti. Be sure to look for a fully ripe pumpkin with a deep orange colour. And to add a little balance and sweetness to the pumpkin, about a minute or two before it is done, add a little sugar you will be amazed how it enhances the flavour of the pumpkin.

Yield: 2 cups

Ingredients

3 tablespoons oil, divided

(First usage 1 tablespoon to fry shrimp)

(Second usage 2 tablespoons to cook pumpkin)

½ pound small shrimp, peeled, cleaned and patted dry

1 cup diced onions

2 sprigs fresh thyme

1 clove garlic, crushed

1 pound orange pumpkin cut into large chunks

Salt and pepper to taste

½ tablespoon sugar

Equipment

1 frying pan with cover

1 large spoon

1 small bowl

Directions

▶ Heat 1 tablespoon oil a pan or karahi.

▶ Add shrimp and quickly stir-fry for 1 minute only.

▶ Remove shrimp and set aside in a bowl.

▶ Add the remaining 2 tablespoons oil in pan/karahi.

▶ Add onions and sauté for 2–3 minutes.

▶ Add thyme and garlic and continue to cook for another minute.

▶ Add pumpkin plus salt and pepper to taste and cook covered on medium low heat.

▶ Let cook for 8–10 minutes then remove cover and with the back of your spoon, mash the pumpkin, it should melt easily. If it does not, cover and let cook for a few more minutes, then mash.

▶ Stir in sugar.

▶ Let cook for another minute or two, covered.

▶ Add cooked shrimps and stir.

▶ Cook uncovered for two minutes and remove from heat.

▶ Remove sprig of thyme before serving.

▶ Serve with roti or rice.

Variations

▶ This dish can be made vegetarian from step 4

▶ This dish can also be made with chicken or other meats, all you have to do is cut the meat into small chunks, cook fully at step 2 and then continue the recipe as described.

Sautéed Squash
(Bottle Gourd)

This is a very popular way in which vegetables are cooked in Guyana and Trinidad & Tobago, which is appealing to both adults and children. When cooked this way, vegetables are eaten as main dishes with rice at lunch time and as breakfast or dinner when served with roti.

This long squash is the variety of squash we get often in these parts; it's like a huge cucumber really. Some people cook it with the seeds but I remove them.

Yield: 3½ cups

Ingredients

2 tablespoons oil

1 cup diced onions

3 cloves garlic, crushed

1 cup diced tomatoes

¼ cup herbs finely chopped (thyme, marjoram, cilantro)

Salt to taste

Hot pepper to taste, minced

4 (12-inch) long squash (white-fleshed), de-seeded and cut into ¾ inch pieces (approximately 6–8 cups)

Equipment

1 frying pan with cover

1 pot spoon

Directions

▶ Heat oil in pan.

▶ Add onions and sauté until translucent.

▶ Add garlic, tomatoes and herbs along with salt and hot pepper to taste and sauté for 2 minutes.

▶ Add squash and stir to incorporate with onion-tomato-herb mixture.

▶ Cover, reduce heat to medium and cook until the squash becomes translucent and cooked through.

▶ Check for seasoning (salt) adjust if necessary.

▶ Remove from heat and serve with rice or roti.

Cynthia's Tip

If squash springs any water, remove lid and let squash cook until all the liquid has evaporated.

Vegetable Fried Rice

On every table in Guyana and some other Caribbean countries, especially on the weekends, you can find a platter of fried rice; whether it is vegetable fried rice, chicken, pork, beef or shrimp fried rice. Like the chow mein, this dish is a stir fry and therefore all the ingredients should be prepped beforehand. The rice should always be completely cool. If you know that you plan to make fried rice that day, then cook the rice very early in the morning. When entertaining, my mom would cook the rice at around midnight so by the morning it was completely cool.

The trickiest part of making fried rice is the cooking of the rice. Carefully measuring the water to rice ratio and steaming or cooking by absorption is your best option. Remember to cook the rice with salt to taste also.

We are big on fried rice having some colour and so people add cassareep, browning or burnt sugar to the rice when frying it. If you insist on colouring the rice, I'd suggest seasoning it with some soy sauce when preparing to cook the rice.

Yield: 10 cups

Ingredients

4 tablespoons oil

1 tablespoon minced ginger

2 cloves garlic, crushed

½ cup finely diced carrots

1 cup thinly cut bora (yard long beans, snake beans); or 1 cup frozen sweet green peas, thawed

½ cup diced sweet peppers (combination of colours)

6 cups cooked and cooled long grain white rice, (recipe on page 321)

1 tablespoon grated ginger

2 tablespoons dark soy sauce

2 teaspoons toasted sesame oil

½ tablespoon fish sauce

2 teaspoons 5-spice powder

Salt and pepper to taste

1/3 cup thinly sliced green onions (white and green parts)

Equipment

1 baking sheet

1 wok, karahi or large sauté pan

1 large spoon

Directions

► Heat oil in pan until very hot but not smoking.

► Add minced ginger and garlic and sauté for less than a minute.

► Add the carrots and bora and cook for 1 minute.

► Add sweet peppers to mixture.

► Season with salt and pepper.

► Add rice, grated ginger, 5-spice powder, soy sauce, fish sauce, a few grinds of black pepper and stir, working quickly and constantly moving the rice and vegetables.

► Taste the rice for seasoning and add salt if necessary.

► Serve hot with your choice of baked or roast meat or poultry or as is for a vegetarian dish.

Cynthia's Tip

Leftover rice makes excellent fried rice

Variations

► To have meats, shrimp or chicken cooked into the fried rice, cut them into bite-sized pieces, season with grated ginger, garlic, salt, pepper and a couple dashes of soy sauce and cook thoroughly.

► Add the cooked meat at step 5 and continue with the directions.

Vegetable Rice

Yield: 6–7 cups

Ingredients

2 tablespoons oil

1 cup diced onions

3 sprigs fresh thyme

2 cups of vegetables cut into chunks (tomatoes,
okras, pumpkin or spinach)

Salt and pepper to taste

2 cups Basmati rice, washed and soaked for at
least 30 minutes, drained

2+⅔ cups water

Equipment

1 large saucepan with cover

1 large spoon

Directions

- ▶ Heat oil in pot.
- ▶ Sauté onions and thyme for 2 minutes.
- ▶ Add vegetables and sauté for 2 minutes.
- ▶ Season with salt and pepper to taste.
- ▶ Add rice to vegetables and stir thoroughly; continue to sauté for another minute.
- ▶ Pour in water, stir, check for seasoning – salt and pepper and adjust if necessary.
- ▶ Cover pot and bring to a boil. As soon as it comes to a boil, reduce heat to low and let cook for 25 minutes. Turn off heat at the end of this time and leave untroubled for 10 minutes.
- ▶ Stir and fluff with a fork.
- ▶ Serve as a main or side dish.

Cynthia's Tips

The water can be substituted with chicken or vegetable broth

A combination of vegetables can be used to make a mixed-vegetable rice

Use your rice of preference adjusting the cooking liquid according to package directions

Variation

- ▶ Shrimp or any firm fish, cubed, could be added to this dish for a seafood and vegetable rice

Condiments & Sides

Boiled Ripe Plantains

Firm ripe plantains are a treat when boiled, and make a meal by themselves when eaten with a dab of plain butter or herbed butter. They can be eaten as a breakfast or lunch meal. Boiling ripe plantains in their skins makes peeling easy and looks more attractive when presented.

Yield: 2 cups

Ingredients

1 pound firm ripe plantains
Water to cook plantains
Salt, a pinch

Equipment

1 knife
1 pot with cover
1 colander

Directions

- ▶ Cut the tops and bottoms off of the plantains leaving the skins intact.
- ▶ Add plantains to pot, with water coming half way up the plantains along with a pinch of salt.
- ▶ Cover and bring to a boil until plantains are cooked through about 7 minutes (time starts when it boils); in some cases the skin will naturally split indicating that it's done.
- ▶ Turn off heat and drain in colander.
- ▶ Let cool a little before peeling; skin will remove easily.
- ▶ Slice and serve with butter, eat as is or as a side dish with your meal.

Coconut Choka

Of all the chokas, coconut choka is the most time consuming as it requires a lot of grinding to get it to the desired consistency but the modern-day food processor works well as a substitute for the traditional flat stone grinder (lorha & sil). Fire-roasting the coconut to bring out its natural oils and flavours makes it one of the best-loved chokas. This is not one of those cases where dried coconut can be substituted; fire-roasting is necessary for the flavour.

Yield: ¾ cup

Ingredients

1 large coconut, cracked and the flesh removed (Approximately 2 cups coconut pieces); alternately, just crack the coconut in half and place open side down on the stove to roast as shown

Hot pepper to taste, chopped

1 clove garlic, finely minced

Salt to taste

1½ teaspoon lemon juice (or 1 tablespoon of finely minced green mango or 1 to ½ teaspoon of tamarind pulp)

2–3 tablespoons water

Equipment

1 box grater

1 food processor or mortar and pestle
  or lorha and sil (flat brick grinder)

1 small bowl

Directions

▶ Roast the pieces of coconut on the open flame of your gas stove, turning to ensure that it is roasted all around; you want it charred, blacked in some parts.

▶ When cool enough to handle, take a knife and gently scrape off some of the burnt parts but be sure to leave on some of the brown parts because that is what is going to add flavour to the choka!

▶ On the fine sharp side of a box grater (the side with lots of little holes), grate the coconut.

▶ In a food processor, add the grated coconut, pepper, garlic, salt to taste, lemon juice or mango or tamarind and the water.

▶ Turn on the processor and let it grind/whirl and mix all the ingredients together, do this for 1–2 minutes stopping at intervals, (you don't want to burn the engine of your food processor by letting it run continuously).

▶ Taste for seasoning (salt and pepper), adjust, then remove from food processor, place into a bowl and mould into a ball or simply pat into a dome.

▶ If using a mortar and pestle or lorha and sil, grind the ingredients in batches until the texture is that of a textured paste.

▶ Serve with dhal and rice.

Cynthia's Tip

The souring agent should be to your individual taste, the reason for putting it in is that it contrasts well with the other flavours but it is not necessary to add any if you do not want to.

Fried Fish

Lightly seasoned, dusted in flour and pan fried, this is always a winner. It is generally served as the main protein in some meals or as an accompaniment as in the case of cook-up rice. Fried fish is also a popular thing for people to munch on while knocking back a few drinks. Oh, and don't forget to serve it with some hot pepper sauce!

Yield: 8 pieces

Ingredients

1 tablespoon finely chopped garlic

2 tablespoons diced onions

Hot pepper to taste, finely chopped

1½ tablespoons fresh thyme, finely chopped

2 pounds grey snapper or any white fish of your
   choice, cut, cleaned and patted dry

Salt to taste

Flour to dust fish

Oil for frying

Equipment

1 mortar and pestle

1 frying pan

1 slotted pot spoon

Paper towels

Directions

- ► Add garlic, onions, thyme and hot pepper to mortar and pestle and grind to a paste. If you don't have a mortar and pestle use whatever tool you generally use to grind stuff.
- ► Rub-massage the fish all over with the paste and add salt to taste.
- ► Heat oil in frying pan on medium heat.
- ► Dust fish lightly with flour shaking off the excess.
- ► Fry until browned on both sides. Do not over crowd pan, fry in batches. The time will vary depending on how thick the fish is cut.

Cynthia's Tips

You can experiment with different coatings for the fish such as regular bread crumbs, panko (Japanese bread crumbs), biscuit crumbs, cornmeal or you can try wet & dry coatings.

In order for the fish not to curl up in the pan, score (cut) the skin-side of the fish before seasoning it.

Fried Ripe Plantains

This favourite can be found anywhere that Caribbean food is sold. Very ripe plantains make this a winner. Cook it in a non-stick pan so you'll use less oil and watch it all the time as it can burn easily because of the high sugar content of the plantains at this stage.

Yield: 1½ cups

Ingredients

2 very ripe plantains, peeled and sliced
lengthways, round or diagonally
Oil to pan fry
Salt (optional)

Equipment

1 non-stick frying pan
1 spatula or fork
Paper towels

Directions

▶ Heat a non-stick frying pan with a drizzle of oil. Once heated, turn heat to medium.

▶ Add sliced plantains and let brown on both sides. Cook in batches and each batch should take 2–3 minutes in total depending on how thick the plantains are cut.

▶ Drain on paper towels. You can sprinkle with salt as soon as you take it out of the pan. This gives another layer of flavour.

▶ Repeat until all the plantains are fried. Be sure to lightly oil pan in between batches.

▶ Serve as a snack or as a side dish.

Cynthia's Tip

Remember to not walk away from the stove when frying these as they burn easily because of the high sugar content in the ripe plantains.

Achar

An achar is a spicy Indian pickle made with spices, lots of hot pepper and fruit; it serves as a flavour enhancer and is used as a condiment. Some achar are cooked and some are not, dependent on the desire of the person making it. Cooking the achar makes it ripe and available for eating almost as soon as it done, uncooked, it takes anywhere from 2 weeks to a month to be ready, in which time the spices would have infused the main ingredient and cured it at the same time. If prepared raw, achar ripens more quickly when placed in the sun but you can certainly leave it on your countertop to ripen, it will just take a little longer.

Achar is eaten in small quantities as a condiment with meals. It is also served with savoury snacks like phulourie, biganee and black pudding.

Yield: 3 cups

Ingredients

6 large green mangoes, grated, pounded or finely minced (Average 6 cups pulp)

6 large cloves garlic, minced

Hot pepper to taste, minced

2 heaped tablespoons amchar or garam masala

A few drops of water

6 tablespoons mustard oil or canola oil

Salt to taste

Equipment

1 deep frying pan

1 mortar and pestle or whatever tool you use to grind stuff

1 wooden or large plastic spoon

1 (3-cup capacity) sterilized jar with airtight cover

Variations:

► Ripe tamarind is shelled before cooking or can be mixed raw and cured in the sun for 2–3 weeks.

► Sourees (bilimbi), green tomatoes, & five-finger (star fruit) are sliced before cooking.

Directions

► Squeeze and discard any excess juice from the grated or pounded green mango.

► Grind the garlic and pepper together, to a paste.

► Add the garlic-pepper mixture to the ground masala along with a few drops of water to make a paste.

► Heat oil in pan.

► Add paste and sauté gently for 1–2 minutes.

► Add salt to taste.

► Add mangoes and mix until it is fully incorporated with the masala mixture

► Turn heat to low and let cook for 30–35 minutes or until the mangoes are cooked through.

► Check for taste and if needed, add some more salt to suit your taste.

► Remove from heat and let the achaar cool completely in the pan you cooked it in.

► Overnight cooling is best.

► Fill sterilised jar and store in your pantry or refrigerator. *You can opt to drizzle a little film of oil on the surface but this is not necessary.*

► Only use clean cutlery when dipping into achar to avoid spoilage.

Cynthia's Tips

The sliced mangoes can be pulsed in a food processor but do not add water.

Any vegetable oil will work well but mustard oil is traditionally used to make achar.

Green Mango Chutney

This chutney is uncooked and generally prepared and consumed the same day. It is important to ensure that this chutney is finely grated or pureed in a food processor to get a very fine texture.

If kept in an airtight glass bottle in the fridge, it can last for 2 weeks or more.

Yield: 1½ cups

Ingredients

4 large green mangoes, peeled and
   sliced

1 large clove garlic, minced

Hot pepper to taste, minced

Salt to taste

Equipment

1 food processor or box grater

1 wooden or plastic spoon

1 (2-cup capacity) sterilised jar with airtight cover

Directions

(Food Processor)

▶ Add mangoes, garlic, hot pepper
and salt to food processer.

▶ Pulse to a smooth consistency.

▶ Check for seasoning – salt; add
more if desired.

▶ Transfer to sterilized jar and store in
refrigerator.

(Box Grater)

▶ Grate mangoes on the fine side of the grater
(the side with many little holes).

▶ Discard excess juice (do not squeeze pulp).

▶ Grind garlic and pepper to a paste.

▶ Add garlic-pepper paste to grated mango
and stir until fully incorporated.

▶ Add salt to taste.

▶ Transfer to sterilised jar and store in refrigerator.

Sour

This is a cooked chutney made mostly of un-ripe, tart fruits such as mango, star fruit, tamarind or souree (bilimbi). Salt and hot pepper are usually added to the fruit, which is cooked slowly with a little water. A sour is eaten with savoury snacks such as biganee, phulourie, egg balls etc.

Yield: 3 cups

Ingredients

4 large green mangoes

Approximately 1 ½ cups water

1 large hot pepper

Salt to taste

1 teaspoon sugar

Equipment

1 knife

1 cutting board

1 sauce pan

1 wooden spoon

1 (3-cup) capacity glass jar

Directions

- ▶ Peel and slice mangoes getting as much flesh as you can; keep the seeds as well with a little flesh on it
- ▶ Transfer cut mangoes with seeds to saucepan
- ▶ Add hot pepper and just enough water to come half-way up the ingredients
- ▶ Cover and bring to a boil; reduce heat to medium and let the mangoes cook until they become soft, and almost all the water is gone
- ▶ Using the back of the wooden spoon, mash the flesh of the mango and the pepper
- ▶ Remove from the heat, add salt to taste, sugar, and stir
- ▶ Let cool completely then transfer to sterilized jar and refrigerate
- ▶ Serve with savoury snacks such as fish cakes, phulourie, biganee, vegetable fritters; tastes great with dhal puri (split-pea-filled roti)

Note:

- ▶ This sour can be made with a combination of green and not so green mangoes

Variations

- ▶ Replace cut mangoes with whole souree (bilimbi), tamarind or green carambola (star fruit)

Pepper Sauce

We really love our pepper sauce here in the Caribbean. Sit down to a meal at home or invited out and one of the first things you ask for is the pepper sauce, that is, if it is not clearly visible on the table. And the hotter, the better. Scotch bonnet peppers rule the day in these parts. When purchasing peppers in the Caribbean, they are simply labelled as "hot peppers."

If you are looking for a smooth texture for your pepper sauce use a blender, but if you desire a very fine texture, a food processor is your tool.

Chunks of peeled green mangoes, cucumbers or cut lemons or limes can be stirred into the pepper sauce. Add a little more salt if adding any of these items as it will assist in the curing process.

Yield: 2 cups

Ingredients

4 cups of scotch bonnet peppers (or your choice of hot pepper)

4 large cloves garlic, minced

Salt to taste

Distilled vinegar to moisten the sauce; start with ⅓ cup

Equipment

1 pair kitchen gloves

1 colander

1 food processor

1 wooden spoon

1 medium bowl

1 (2–3 cup capacity) sterilized glass jar

Cynthia's Tips

Oil can be used in combination with the vinegar or instead of vinegar; water is also an option.

Wash your blender or food processor in lots of hot soapy water. You can even consider soaking it in the hot soapy water for a while before washing it.

Directions

▶ **Wear the gloves for the entire process as this pepper is extremely hot**

▶ Wash the pepper in a colander over running water. Remove stems.

▶ Add pepper, garlic and salt in a food processor and pulse until very finely minced (scrape down the sides of the bowl).

▶ Add vinegar to moisten the mixture and pulse a few more times.

▶ Pour into a bowl first and then transfer to sterilised jar.

▶ Store in pantry or refrigerate (my mom likes to put hers in the sun for a few days to cure before using).

▶ Always use clean utensils to avoid spoilage.

Salt Fish Choka

This is yet another interesting and delicious way in which we use salt fish. Do not ignore the fire roasting that is necessary, it is the part of the essence of a good choka. Dhal and rice are the favourite accompaniments of this choka; it works well with fried bakes also.

Yield: 1½ cups

Ingredients

8 ounces boneless salt fish

Hot pepper to taste, chopped

1 large clove garlic, finely minced

1 tablespoon fresh lemon or lime juice

2 tablespoons oil

¼ cup thinly sliced green onions (white and green parts)

¼ cup finely diced onions

Equipment

1 medium saucepan

1 baking sheet

1 pair tongs

1 food processor

1 medium bowl

Cynthia's Tip

There's no need to add salt to the fish as it should still have enough salt to taste after boiling. You can check it to be sure though that it has enough for your taste.

Directions

▶ Add salt fish to saucepan with enough water to cover it by 1 inch, bring to a boil.

▶ Let salt fish boil for 25 minutes, drain and pat dry.

▶ If there's sun where you are, let it dry out in the sun a little for 10–15 minutes. If there's no sun where you are then leave it on the countertop uncovered to air dry, you want to ensure that there's no moisture.

▶ On the open gas flame of your stove or outdoor grill, using tongs, place the salt fish directly on the flames and roast it. Flip it over getting it charred and blackened in some parts. This is the essence of choka, fire roasting it to impart a smokey flavour.

▶ Let cool enough for you to handle and then with your fingers, break up the fish into little pieces.

▶ Add salt fish, pepper and garlic to food processor and pulse for 1–2 minutes (salt fish will be completely shredded).

▶ Add lemon juice and oil to mixture and pulse 3–4 times.

▶ Remove mixture from the food processor and transfer to a bowl.

▶ Stir in sliced green onions and diced onions, mixing thoroughly.

▶ Serve with dhal and rice, roti, bakes or ground provisions.

Smoked Herring Choka

Ingredients

Everyone knows (in a good way) when you are cooking smoked herring! The aroma permeates the air and brings your hunger to the forefront.

If you cannot get fillets to make the choka, roast the whole herring over an open flame, it will open up easily for you to remove the bones and skin. Smoked herring is great sautéed too with lots of onions and tomatoes.

Yield: 1½ cups

½ lb smoked herring fillets

Water

Fresh hot pepper to taste, minced

1 large clove garlic, finely minced

1 tablespoon lemon or lime juice

2 teaspoons vegetable oil

¼ cup thinly sliced green onions (white and green parts)

¼ cup finely diced onions (red or white)

Equipment

1 saucepan
1 pair tongs
1 baking sheet
1 food processor or mortar and pestle
1 medium bowl
1 fork

Directions

► Add smoked herring fillets to saucepan with water to cover it by an inch and bring to a boil.

► Boil fillets for 15 minutes; strain off water.

► Pat dry and if there's sun where you are, spread on a baking sheet and let it dry out in the sun a little, 10–15 minutes is enough. If there's no sun where you are then just leave it on the countertop uncovered, you want to ensure that there's no liquid.

► On the open gas flame of your stove, using tongs, place the fillets 1–2 at a time and roast them all over getting them a little charred and blackened in some parts.

► Let cool enough for you to handle and then with your fingers, break up the herring fillets into little pieces.

Cynthia's Tip

There's no need to add salt to the fish as the smoked herring should still have enough salt to taste after the boiling. You can check it to be sure though that it has enough for your taste.

► In the food processor, add the smoked herring, pepper, garlic, lemon juice and oil. Pulse for 1–2 minutes.

► Turn the smoked herring mixture into a bowl, add green onions and regular onions and mix thoroughly.

► If using a mortar and pestle, pound-grind fish with garlic and hot pepper. Stir in lemon juice, oil and the onions.

► Fluff with a fork and serve with dhal and rice or roti, bakes or bread or ground provisions.

Snacks & Drinks

Bajan Fish Cakes

In essence this is a salt fish fritter. It is delicious when served hot and with the addition of some Pepper Sauce or Sour on the side – i's an unbeatable combo. When making these fish cakes to be served in Barbadian Rum Shops in particular, lots of hot pepper is added to the mixture.

Long ago, instead of boiling and then frizzing the salt fish, it used to just be pounded and then be added to flour and seasonings to create a batter.

Yield: 20

Ingredients

8 ounces salt fish

Water to boil salt fish

Hot pepper to taste, finely minced

Freshly ground black pepper to taste

1 tablespoon thinly sliced green onions
    (white & green parts)

½ teaspoon minced thyme

1 teaspoon minced garlic

1 cup all-purpose flour

1 teaspoon baking powder

1 cup water (approximately), for batter

Oil for deep frying

Equipment

1 saucepot

2 medium bowls

1 slotted pot spoon

Paper towels

1 deep frying pan

2 tablespoons

Directions

► Add salt fish and water to saucepot and bring to a boil. Boil salt fish twice, each time for 15–20 minutes, discarding the water after each boil.

► Set aside until cool enough to handle.

► Finely shred the salt fish; you can do this with your fingers or pound it in a mortar with pestle or give it few whirls in a food processor.

► Add the salt fish, hot pepper, black pepper, green onions, thyme and garlic to a bowl and mix thoroughly.

► In a separate bowl, mix together the flour and baking powder.

► Add the flour-baking powder to the salt fish mixture and enough water to make a batter of dropping consistency.

► Heat oil in pan until very hot but not smoking; deep fry in batches using tablespoons to measure and drop the batter (do not overcrowd the pan).

► Fry until browned on both sides.

► Drain on paper towels.

► Serve hot or very warm or at room temperature.

► Serving the fish cakes with pepper sauce or some sour really gives it an extra kick.

Bay Leaf &
Cinnamon
Tea

This tea is highly fragrant and aromatic and is very popular in some rural parts of the Caribbean. It is best made with fresh bay leaves.

Yield: 3 cups

Ingredients

4 large fresh bay leaves

1 (2-inch) piece cinnamon stick

3½ cups water

Sugar and milk to taste

Equipment

1 large saucepan

1 sieve

Directions

► Add bay leaves and cinnamon stick with water and bring to boil in saucepan.

► Reduce heat to low and let simmer, covered, for 5 minutes.

► Remove from heat and let steep for 3 minutes.

► Strain into mugs, sweeten with sugar and milk and serve (do not over power with milk, all you need is a little splash).

Cynthia's Tip

Add more bay leaves if you would like your tea stronger.

Biganee

This is one of the snacks made during the Hindu spring festival of Holi (Phagwah). It is best eaten with a sour or pickle. It's a sneaky way to introduce people to eggplant, since the eggplant is sliced thinly and bathed in batter before frying.

Yield: 1½ lbs

Ingredients

1 pound eggplant, sliced thinly
1 cup seasoned split-pea batter (recipe follows)
Oil for deep frying

Split-pea batter
½ cup split-pea flour
1 cup all-purpose flour
1 teaspoon baking powder
¼ teaspoon ground turmeric
1 teaspoon minced garlic
1 teaspoon finely minced hot pepper or to taste
Salt to taste
1 cup water (a little less or more depending)

Equipment

1 medium bowl

1 whisk or wooden spoon

1 deep frying pan

1 slotted spoon

Paper towels

Cynthia's Tips

If you find the batter is too thick and is not adhering easily to the eggplant, thin it out with a little water.

The batter can also be made with ½ cup of yellow split peas soaked overnight which will yield 1 cup peas. Add the drained peas to a blender then pour into a bowl and mix with flour and other ingredients.

Directions

Split-pea batter

▶ Mix all the ingredients together in medium bowl with enough water to make a smooth batter of dropping consistency.

▶ Rest batter for 15–20 minutes.

Assembling

▶ Heat oil in pan.

▶ Dip eggplant slices into batter one at a time ensuring that it is coated on both sides.

▶ Add as many of the battered-slices to the pan without overcrowding it.

▶ Fry until golden brown on both sides.

▶ Drain on paper towels.

▶ Serve with your favourite sour or fresh mango chutney.

Breadfruit Chips

You've probably heard of or eaten plantain chips or cassava chips – well, breadfruit chips are just as delicious. Use a slicer to get thin long slices and they cook up in no time and are not greasy at all.

Yield: 8 ounces

Ingredients

1 pound breadfruit, peeled
Oil for shallow frying
Salt to taste

Equipment

1 slicer or knife
1 frying pan
Paper towels

Directions

► Slice breadfruit thinly.
► Heat oil in pan on medium heat.
► Fry in batches.
► Drain on paper towels and immediately season with salt.
► Serve as is.

Five-finger (Star-Fruit) Drink

This fruit is popularly known as five-finger and star fruit. In Guyana, it is also sliced, stewed, dried and used just as raisins and other fruits in baked goods.

Yield: 8–9 cups

Ingredients

1 pound five-finger (mixture of ripe and green),
   sliced
8 cups water
1 teaspoon lemon essence or ½ teaspoon lemon
   extract
Sugar to taste

Equipment

1 blender
1 sieve
1 large bowl
1 glass jar or container

Directions

▶ Blend fruit and water in batches.

▶ Strain into bowl.

▶ Stir in essence/extract.

▶ Sweeten to taste.

▶ Pour into jar or container and refrigerate.

▶ Serve well-chilled or with ice.

Cassava Balls

Texture is very important to a good cassava (yucca) ball. It should be creamy. Therefore, it is important to spend some time mashing it. Do not use a food processor or mill; the results will not be the same and you could wreck your appliance.

Yield: 7–8 balls

Ingredients

For batter

⅓ cup all-purpose flour

¼ teaspoon ground turmeric

⅛ teaspoon salt

Water

For cassava ball

1 pound peeled cassava, quartered

Water to boil cassava

1 tablespoon vegetable oil

¼ cup diced onions

½ teaspoon minced thyme

Hot pepper to taste, finely minced

2 tablespoons thinly sliced green onions

Salt to taste

1 tablespoon salted butter, room temperature

Oil for deep frying

Equipment

1 whisk

1 small bowl

1 saucepan

1 colander

1 large bowl

1 potato masher

1 pan for deep frying

1 slotted spoon

Paper towels

Directions

For batter

▶ Mix all the ingredients together using a whisk or your hand, adding enough water to make a thin batter (the consistency of crepe batter).

▶ Set aside.

For cassava ball

▶ Add cassava to pot with water and bring to a boil covered. When the pot comes to a boil, add salt to taste.

▶ Boil cassava until it's soft and begins to fall apart by splitting open.

▶ Meanwhile, heat the 1 tablespoon of oil in a pan.

▶ Add onions and thyme and sauté gently until translucent; season with salt.

▶ Stir in hot pepper and let cook for a minute.

▶ Remove pan from heat and immediately stir in sliced green onions.

▶ Strain boiled cassava using a colander; *do not* wash off the starch.

▶ Discard the stems found in the middle of the cassava.

▶ Add the hot, cooked cassava to a bowl along with the butter and mash until it becomes creamy (this requires some elbow-grease as the mashed cassava thickens).

▶ Once the cassava is creamy, scrape off the bits from the masher and set the masher aside.

▶ Add the sautéed onion mixture to the mashed-creamed cassava and with clean hands gently combine the two; taste for salt and adjust if necessary.

▶ Divide the cassava mixture evenly and roll into balls; set aside.

▶ Heat oil for deep frying in pan.

▶ Dip the cassava balls one at a time into the batter to coat completely, shake off the excess and fry; depending on the width of your pan, you can fry 3–4 cassava balls at a time; be careful that they do not stick to each other.

▶ Fry until golden brown all over and drain on paper towels.

▶ Serve warm or at room temperature. Cassava balls can be eaten as is or with your favourite sour or pickle.

Channa

There are two stars in this dish - the freshly ground cumin and the peas. For the best results in taste and texture, use dried chick peas (garbanzo beans) that have been hydrated and cooked in salted water. Using canned peas will give the channa a bland flavour, no matter how aggressively you season it.

Yield: 3 cups

Ingredients

1½ cups dried chick peas

3 tablespoons oil

½ cup finely diced onions

½ teaspoon minced hot pepper or to taste

1 tablespoon chopped cilantro (optional)

1¼ teaspoon ground cumin

¼ cup thinly sliced green onions

Salt and black pepper to taste

Water

Equipment

1 saucepan with cover or pressure cooker

1 colander

1 frying pan

1 pot spoon

Directions

► Soak peas over night to hydrate.

► Wash peas and add to saucepan along and enough water to cook and bring to a boil covered. When the pot comes to a boil, add salt to tastes. Cook peas for 45 minutes or until they are soft.

► If using a pressure cooker, add peas and 5 cups of water, salt to taste, cover and let pressure for 15–20 minutes or until peas are soft (time begins from the first whistle).

► Strain in colander.

► Heat oil in pan.

► Sauté onions until translucent.

► Stir in hot pepper and salt and black pepper to taste along with cilantro, if using.

► Add chick peas and cumin, stir and coat thoroughly.

► Let cook uncovered for 5–7 minutes.

► Sprinkle green onions, stir and remove from heat.

► Serve hot, warm or at room temperature.

Cheese Rolls

These were such a treat at the tea parties I'd go to as a child. The short crust pastry melts in your mouth to reveal the spiced cheese mixture within.

Yield: 8

Ingredients

1 ¼ pound short crust pastry (recipe on page 320)

8 ounces cheese paste (recipe follows)

All purpose flour for dusting

2 egg yolks

2 tablespoons water

Cheese paste filling

8 ounces sharp cheddar cheese, finely grated

1 teaspoon mustard

2 tablespoons unsalted butter, room temperature

Hot pepper sauce to taste

Salt to taste

Equipment

3 forks

1 rolling pin

1 tablespoon

1 knife

1 parchment-lined baking sheet

1 pastry brush

2 small bowls

1 wire rack

Directions

Filling

▶ Add all the ingredients to a bowl and mash to a paste with the back of a fork.

▶ Set aside.

Assembling

▶ Preheat oven to 350°F.

▶ Beat egg yolks and water in a bowl to make egg wash; set aside.

▶ Divide dough into 8 equal pieces.

▶ Flour working surface and rolling pin.

▶ Roll and cut each piece into 4-inch squares with 1mm (a little less than ¼-inch) thickness.

▶ Take a heaped tablespoon of cheese paste and spread along 1-inch away from the opposite edge.

▶ Fold over the edge to cover the paste and keep rolling towards the other end (in case your shape is not a perfect square, always keep in mind that you are rolling lengthways).

▶ Dip the prongs of a fork in flour and use it to seal the top and bottom edges of the pastry by pressing down; trim the edges to make them uniform.

▶ Transfer the cheese roll, seam-side down on the baking sheet.

▶ Repeat until all the cheese rolls are made.

▶ Brush with egg wash and bake in heated oven for 20–25 minutes.

▶ Cool on a rack.

▶ Serve warm or at room temperature.

Cocoa-Stick Tea

Organic, local cocoa sticks are grown and produced in Guyana, St Vincent & The Grenadines, St Lucia and Grenada. The raw cocoa is ground with bay leaves and other spices and rolled into sticks. Because it is natural cocoa, it is bitter. It can be used in savoury and sweet dishes. The coca stick can be placed whole into the pot to boil where it will disintegrate naturally. For a true taste of chocolate, you must try this tea.

Yield: 3 cups

Ingredients

1 (5-inch) rolled cocoa stick
1 (3-inch) cinnamon stick
1 large bay leaf (preferably fresh)
6 cups water
Sugar and milk to taste

Equipment

1 large saucepan
1 fine sieve

Directions

- ► Add the cocoa stick, cinnamon stick and bay leaf to saucepan with the water, cover partially and bring to a boil.
- ► When liquid has reduced to half, remove from heat.
- ► Strain into mugs, sweeten with sugar and milk and serve.

Egg Balls

Apart from being sold by the snack-vendors at schools, these are treats that used to be sold outside of the cinemas in Guyana long ago. Back then, a show at the cinema consisted of two movies, not just one, so a snack such as an egg ball along with a drink would hit the spot during intermission.

Yield: 4

Ingredients

1 pound of cassava ball mixture (recipe
   on page 234)
4 hard boiled eggs, peeled
Oil for deep frying
⅓ cup batter (recipe on page 234)

Equipment

1 pan for deep frying
1 slotted spoon
Paper towels

Directions

► Divide cassava ball mixture evenly
into 4 (4 oz each).

► Rub a little oil on your hands
and make each portion of the
cassava ball mixture into a flat disk,
spreading it out a little.

► Take an egg and place it the
middle of the flattened mixture.

► Encase the egg securely in the mixture; roll
into a ball and repeat until all are done; set
aside.

► Heat oil in pan.

► Dip each egg ball in batter and fry until
golden brown all over.

► Drain on paper towels.

► Serve warm or at room temperature; can be
eaten as is or with your favourite sour or pickle.

Ginger Beer

Spicy and fruity, ginger beer can be made all year-round but it is traditionally made at Christmas time in Guyana. It is important to leave it to ripen for the time specified in the recipe; this helps the flavour to develop.

This drink needs 3 days and 2 nights to ripen and develop its flavour.

Yield: 10 – 12 cups

Ingredients

1 pound fresh ginger, washed

16 cups water

1 (4-inch) cinnamon stick

10–12 whole cloves

Brown sugar to taste (start with 2 cups)

Equipment

1 box grater
1 wooden spoon
1 large glass jar with cover **OR** plastic
   container or non-reactive container
   with cover
1 large sieve

Directions

▶ Grate ginger on the large side of box grater.

▶ Add the ginger, water, cinnamon stick, cloves and sugar to glass jar or container. Stir to dissolve the sugar.

▶ Cover tightly and let ripen for 3 days and 2 nights.

▶ Open jar, bottle or container, stir with a wooden spoon and taste. Adjust sugar to suit your taste.

▶ Strain and chill in fridge.

▶ Serve cold with ice.

Golden apple (June plum) Drink

This drink is usually made with green golden-apples but it can also be made with the ripened fruit. Shake or stir the drink before serving as the pulp tends to settle with all the good Vitamin C. Enjoy it ice cold.

Yield: 10–12 cups

Ingredients

2 pounds green golden apples, peeled and
   cut up
10 cups water
Sugar to taste

Equipment

1 blender
1 sieve
1 large bowl
2 (5-cup) glass jars (or any containers you have)

Directions

▶   Blend fruit with water in batches.
▶   Strain into large bowl.
▶   Sweeten to taste.
▶   Refrigerate and serve chilled or with ice.

Lemongrass Tea

My mom refers to this as fever grass tea. Whenever she'd make it for us there never seemed to be enough. You don't need to me tell you how flavourful lemongrass is: you can opt to slice the lemon grass or just crush it and add it whole to the pot.

Yield: Approximately 3 cups

Ingredients

4 tablespoons chopped lemongrass or a handful of
    the lemongrass leaves themselves
3¼ cups water
Sugar and milk to taste

Equipment

1 large saucepan with cover
1 sieve

Directions

- ► Bring water to boil in covered saucepan.
- ► Add lemongrass to boiling water. Boil covered for 2 minutes and remove from heat. Let steep for 3–4 minutes.
- ► Strain into mugs, sweeten with sugar and milk and serve (do not over power with milk, all you need is a little splash).

Cynthia's Tips

Add more lemongrass if you'd like your tea stronger.

You can make this tea with a combination of lemon grass and fresh bay leaves.

Mauby

The syrup for this drink is widely available in parts of the Caribbean, especially Barbados but to truly enjoy and appreciate the unique flavour of mauby, you should, at least once, try having it made brewed directly from the bark concentrate. Some people shy away from mauby complaining that it is too bitter but if it is adequately brewed, ripened, spiced and sweetened, it is one of the most refreshing and tasty drinks you will taste.

It takes two and a half days for the mauby to ripen and develop its flavour.

Yield: 18–20 cups

Ingredients

For concentrate:

1½ cups water

½ ounce mauby bark

3 (3-inch) cinnamon sticks

8 whole cloves

½ nutmeg, cracked or 1 tablespoon mace

For drink:

1 gallon + 2 cups water (18 cups)

1 (3-inch) stick cinnamon

4–5 whole cloves

½ nutmeg, cracked or 1 tablespoon mace

Brown sugar to taste

Equipment

1 small saucepan
1 large plastic container with tight lid
1 wooden spoon
1 large cup

Directions

For concentrate:

► Add all the ingredients to a saucepan and bring to a boil until the liquid is reduced by half (¾ cup).

► Cool mixture completely.

For drink:

► Fill container with the water.

► Strain the cooled mauby concentrate into the water – do not throw away the boiled bark and spices!

► Add the fresh spices for the drink and sweeten to taste. Bear in mind that you will add ice when serving so sweeten adequately.

► Brew using a large cup; dip into the mixture, fill the cup and then pour it back into the container, do this for at least 3 minutes.

► Cover the container and set aside.

► Add 1½ cups of water to the reserved bark and spices. Cover, bring to a boil and immediately remove from the heat.

► The following day, a full 24 hours later, open the container with the mauby and strain the liquid from the reserved bark and spices into the mixture and brew for 3 minutes. At this stage, you will start to smell the ripening of the mauby.

► Cover the container and set aside.

► Add another 1½ cups of water to the reserved bark and spices. Cover, bring to a boil and immediately remove from the heat.

► The next day, 48 hours later, strain and pour the reserved bark and spice mixture into the mauby. You may now discard the bark and spices.

► Brew mauby for 3–4 minutes.

► Cover the container and set aside.

► 4–5 hours later, taste the mauby for desired sweetness and strength. If you feel it is too strong, add some water adjusting to your taste and brew for 3 minutes.

► If the strength and sweetness is to your desired taste, strain the mauby into bottles – plastic or glass and refrigerate.

► Serve chilled with ice.

Mini Quiches

These are great anytime – as a meal or served with a salad. We often serve these at tea parties and brunch.

Yield: 12

Ingredients

1 tablespoon oil

1 pound short-crust pastry dough (recipe on page 320)

8 bacon rashers, chopped

4 tablespoons minced onions

½ cup grated sharp cheddar cheese

3 eggs, room temperature

¾ cup heavy cream

2 tablespoons thinly sliced green onions (white & green parts)

Salt and pepper to taste

All-purpose flour for dusting and work surface

Equipment

1 (12-cup) standard-sized muffin pan

1 pastry brush

1 rolling pin

1 (4-inch) round cutter

1 frying pan

1 slotted spoon

Paper towels

1 medium bowl

1 whisk

1 large baking sheet

Directions

► Brush muffin pan with oil.

► Roll dough to ¼ inch thickness on a lightly floured surface and cut into 4-inch circles using a cookie cutter, bowl or other utensil as a mould.

► Fit each of the cut circles into the muffin pan until all 12 cups are filled.

► Put pan in the fridge to chill until ready to you are ready to fill them.

► Preheat oven to 350°F.

► Heat a frying pan and add bacon.

► Let bacon cook until it's lightly browned and the fat has rendered (separated) from the bacon.

► Using a slotted spoon, remove bacon and let drain on paper towels; set aside.

► Remove the pan from heat and discard all but 1 tablespoon of the bacon fat.

► Return pan to stove; turn on the heat and sauté onions until they are translucent.

► Remove onions from pan and let cool slightly.

► Whisk eggs and cream together in medium bowl, season with salt and pepper to taste.

► Remove chilled muffin pan from fridge and place on baking sheet (this will stabilize the muffin pan in the oven).

► Add some of the sautéed onions to each of the pastry cup.

► Add a little cheese to each of the cups.

► Divide the bacon and add to each of the cups.

► Fill each cup with the egg-cream mixture until it is just shy-short of the top of the pastry cup.

► Sprinkle each filled cup with the sliced green onions.

► Bake in oven for 40 minutes or until the quiche is golden brown.

► Remove pan from oven and let rest for 5–10 minutes before serving.

► Serve as is or with a green salad.

Minced-Meat Patties

Patties can be filled with ground meat, chicken or vegetables. The true star here of course is the pastry. It is the same rich short-crust pastry that's used to make the cheese rolls and pine tarts.

Yield: 12

Ingredients

1¼ pounds short crust pastry dough (recipe on page 320)

1 pound minced meat filling (recipe follows)

All-purpose flour for dusting

2 egg yolks

2 tablespoons water

Filling

2 tablespoons oil

3 tablespoons finely diced onions

1 teaspoon minced garlic

1 tablespoon finely chopped herbs

1¼ pounds ground meat of your choice (beef, pork, chicken; vegetables can be substituted)

Salt and pepper to taste

Equipment

1 frying pan

1 pot spoon

1 small bowl

1 rolling pin

1 (3-inch) round cutter

1 tablespoon

2 parchment-lined baking sheets

2 forks

1 pastry brush

2 wire racks

Directions

Filling

► Heat oil in a frying pan.

► Gently fry (sauté) onions until translucent.

► Add garlic and herbs and continue to sauté.

► Add minced meat, stir to mix with onion-garlic-herb mixture.

► Fry until it starts to get slightly brown.

► Add salt and pepper to taste, stir and remove from heat.

► Let the filling cool completely.

Assembling

► Preheat oven to 350ºF.

► Beat egg yolks and water together to make egg wash; set aside.

► Cut pastry dough equally into 24 pieces.

► Flour work surface and rolling pin.

► Roll one of the pieces into a 3 ½-inch circle with 1mm (a little less than ¼-inch) thickness.

► Place 2 tablespoons of the filling in the middle of the circle, spreading it a little.

► Roll another piece of the dough into a 3 ½-inch circle and spread it over the pastry with the filling.

► Dip the prongs of a fork into some flour; using the fork seal the patty all around the edges gently pressing and stretching the ends of the pastry together to form a seal (this will create a designed edge also).

► Take the 3-inch circle cutter and cut the patty into a round disk.

► Transfer to a lined-baking sheet.

► Repeat until all the patties are made (try to work quickly but carefully).

► Brush the patties with egg wash and bake in oven for 20–25 minutes or until just golden brown.

► Cool on a rack.

► Serve warm or at room temperature.

Cynthia's Tips

I make these in batches of 6

Place the dough not being used in the refrigerator to keep cool until you are ready to use it

Plantain Chips

Green plantains are used to make these chips. A slicer makes quick and fast work here giving you thin, uniform slices. Season chips with salt as soon as they are removed from the frying pan.

This is a snack to be served anytime, and can be found at many food stands outside of schools and packaged in supermarkets.

Yield: 2½ cups

Ingredients

2 large green plantains, peeled and sliced very thinly

Salt to taste

Oil for shallow frying

Equipment

1 frying pan

1 slotted spoon

Paper towels

Directions

► Heat oil in pan on medium heat.

► Add sliced plantains and fry until golden brown (fry in batches and do not overcrowd pan).

► Drain on paper towels and immediately sprinkle with salt to taste.

► Repeat until all the chips are fried.

► Serve hot, warm or at room temperature as is.

Cynthia's Tips

If you do not have a slicer or mandoline gives thin even slices, barring that, use a sharp knife.

You can jazz up your plantain chips by sprinkling it with a flavoured salt such as cumin salt

Peanut Punch

Packed with protein and calcium this drink is a favourite among many. I particularly enjoy having mine with a freshly baked Chinese Cake. In terms of taste, think of a peanut-flavoured crème liqueur.

Yield: 4 cups

Ingredients

⅔ cups of chunky or smooth peanut butter

3 cups whole milk, cold

4 tablespoons sugar

A pinch ground cinnamon

⅛ teaspoon freshly grated nutmeg (extra to garnish if you like)

Equipment

1 blender

1 glass jug

Directions

► Add all the ingredients, milk first, into blender and whiz for 1 minute until smooth

► Serve over ice or as is or pour into a jug and chill some more then serve

Cynthia's Tips

For an adult peanut punch, spike with Baileys or other crème liqueurs, these are added to the ingredients before blending.

Skim milk can also be used but for the real creamy goodness, use whole milk.

Phulourie

This is another snack made at the Hindu festival of Holi (Phagwah) but it is so popular and widely eaten that it's available all year round. It's a seasoned split-peas fritter that's served with a sour.

Yield: 1¾ lbs

Ingredients

1 cup of dried split-peas, soaked overnight

2 teaspoons minced garlic

Hot pepper to suit your taste, finely minced

Salt to taste

1+⅓ cups water (a little less or more, depending)

2 cups all-purpose flour

4 teaspoons baking powder

½ teaspoon ground turmeric

Oil for deep frying

Equipment

1 food processor
1 large bowl
1 wooden spoon
1 deep frying pan
2 teaspoons
1 slotted spoon
Paper towels

Cynthia's Tip

You can add a little more flour if the batter is too peas-rich for your taste. If you are adding more flour, be sure to add ½ teaspoon baking powder for every ½ cup of flour added.

Directions

► Wash and drain soaked split peas.

► Add split peas, garlic, hot pepper, salt, and ⅓ cup of water to the food processor; pulse until the mixture becomes a smooth paste with a fine grainy texture.

► Mix flour, baking powder and turmeric in a large bowl.

► Add the split peas mixture to flour and mix thoroughly, adding enough water as needed to make a batter of dropping consistency.

► Let batter rest for about 20 minutes.

► Heat oil on medium for frying (test if oil is ready by dropping a little batter into the oil, if it sinks and stays at the bottom, it is not hot enough but if it sinks and then floats up right away then the oil is ready).

► Using 2 teaspoons (one to dip the batter and the other to help remove the batter from the spoon when dropping into oil); dip batter and drop as many as can hold into the frying pan. Be careful not to overcrowd the pan.

► Let phulourie fry until golden brown all over and cooked through. I usually taste-test one from the first batch before moving on as this will also inform me if the heat is regulated properly.

► Continue to fry in batches until all the batter is used.

► Drain on paper towels.

► Serve warm with your favourite chutney, sour or pepper sauce.

Sorrel Drink

Christmas in the Caribbean would not be the same without this ruby-red, fruity, spiced drink. The fruit is available from November through to early February. North Americans and Europeans may know this as the hibiscus fruit.

Yield: 8–10 cups

Ingredients

1 pound de-seeded sorrel
1½ (3-inch) cinnamon sticks
6 whole cloves
8 cups water
Sugar to taste

Equipment

1 large pot
1 large bottle or container
1 wooden spoon
1 sieve

Directions

► Add sorrel, cinnamon, cloves and water to pot and bring to a boil covered (water should come up to the same height or slightly over the sorrel).

► Boil for 5 minutes and then turn off heat.
► Remove pot from stove and let drink steep and cool completely (overnight is best).
► When completely cool, strain and sweeten to taste.
► Refrigerate.
► Serve well-chilled or with ice.

Sweet
Treats

Cassava
Pone

Yield: 2 loaves

Ingredients

4 cups (3 lbs) grated cassava

2 cups grated coconut

2 cups brown sugar

1 teaspoon salt

1 teaspoon ground cinnamon

½ teaspoon grated nutmeg

4 oz unsalted butter, melted

4 oz vegetable shortening, melted

1 teaspoon vanilla essence or vanilla extract

2 cups water

Equipment

1 large bowl

1 wooden spoon

2 (9 x 5 x 3-inch) loaf pans, oiled or
buttered

1 metal skewer or knife

1 wire rack

Directions

► Preheat oven to 325°F with oven
rack in the middle.

► Add all the ingredients to a large
bowl and mix thoroughly with
wooden spoon.

► Pour mixture into pans and bake in
preheated oven for 1 hour or until a
skewer or knife inserted comes out
clean.

► Remove pans from oven and
place on wire racks to cool.

► Let the pones cool in pans until
completely firm. Unmold and slice.

Cynthia's TIps

Grate the cassava using the fine side of a
box grater (the side with lots of little holes).

The coconut can be grated on the fine
side of the box grater too or use whatever
tool you would normally for finely grated
coconut.

Chinese Cakes

When I think of peanut punch I also think of Chinese cakes because that's how I've always had them – together. Making these cakes is a little time consuming, since the filling should be cooled completely before the cakes are assembled, I suggest making the filling the day before.

Biting into one of these cakes to taste and reveal the sweet bean-paste is such a treat and is sure to bring a smile to your face. This is a part of the Chinese influence in the Caribbean.

Yield: 20

Ingredients

Pastry # 1

4 ounces vegetable shortening or lard, room temperature

12 ounces all-purpose flour

Water to knead dough

Pastry # 2

2 ounces vegetable shortening or lard, room temperature

2 ounces all-purpose flour

Filling

½ cup dried black-eye peas

Enough water to cook peas

1 cup brown sugar (approximately)

⅛ teaspoon ground cinnamon

¼ cup vegetable oil

Other

2 egg yolks

2 tablespoons water

½ teaspoon red food colouring

Equipment

2 medium-sized saucepots

1 wooden spoon

1 sieve

1 baking sheet, lightly oiled

1 rolling pin

Plastic wrap

2 parchment-lined baking sheets

1 matchstick

2 Wire racks

Directions

▶ Make the filling first before starting the pastries, as the filling must be cooled completely before using. I'd advise making the filling the day before.

Filling

▶ Soak peas overnight.

▶ Wash soaked peas and bring to a boil with enough water; boil peas until soft.

▶ With a sieve, mash and press peas through, including the water it has been cooked in.

▶ Scrape the bottom of the sieve intermittently to ensure the peas can pass through freely.

▶ Measure the mashed peas.

▶ Transfer mashed peas to a medium-sized saucepan. Add sugar (equal amount as the measured peas), cinnamon and oil, and stir until thoroughly mixed. Bring to a boil on high heat.

▶ Turn heat to low and let mixture cook until it comes away cleanly from the sides of the pot. Keep stirring to avoid scorching or burning. This can take as much as 45–60 minutes.

▶ Remove filling and spread on a lightly oiled baking sheet and let cool completely; the filling will harden.

Pastry # 1

▶ Cut in or rub shortening into flour.

▶ Add just enough water to bring the dough together.

▶ Knead lightly for 30 seconds.

▶ Rub a little oil on the dough, cover and set aside.

Pastry # 2

▶ Cut-in or rub shortening into flour.

▶ Bring together into a ball (flour your hands well to handle dough at this stage as the dough becomes moist from the shortening).

▶ Cover and set aside.

- ► Take pastry # 1 and cut it into 20 equal pieces – 1 oz each.
- ► Take pastry # 2 and break off 20 equal pieces – each would be the size of a small glass marble.

- ► Flatten pastry # 1 and place pastry # 2 on top; enclose the second pastry by pulling and pinching the edges of the first pastry forming it into little ball.
- ► Repeat until the two pastries are combined into little balls.

- ► Take one ball of pastry, flour your work surface and with a rolling pin, roll the dough thin.
- ► Using your hands and starting from one end, roll the dough to the other end, it will look like a thick cigarette or cigar when done.
- ► Now starting at one end, roll the dough inwards, just like creating a swirl.
- ► Tuck the loose end underneath the swirl.

- ► Repeat until all the dough balls are rolled and swirled.

- ► Preheat oven to 350°F.
- ► Prepare egg wash and set aside the red food colouring.

- ► Cut/break filling into 20 equal pieces, each piece should be no more than 1½ inches in diameter.
- ► With your hands, flatten the swirled dough and put the filling in the middle.
- ► Enclose the dough by pulling and pinching the ends of the dough, ensure that the filling is securely sealed.
- ► Repeat until all the swirled dough balls are filled; place them seam-side down on the parchment-lined baking sheets.
- ► Brush stuffed Chinese Cakes with egg wash and using a match-stick, dip into food colouring and dot the cake in the middle.
- ► Bake for 30–40 minutes or until pale brown.
- ► Cool on a cooling rack.
- ► Let cool to room temperature before serving, if served hot the filling will burn you.

Christmas Cake

Each Caribbean country has its own recipe, name and nuances when it comes to making this cake. I call it Christmas cake because that is what I associate with the making and eating of this cake. Just as the British feed their Christmas puddings with rum, some people feed their Christmas cake with rum. I don't. Throughout the years that I have made this intoxicatingly delicious cake, I have found that the key is to ensure that the blended fruits have been soaking for at least 12 months. My fruits are usually soaked more than a year in advance. This long soaking gives the alcohol enough time to breakdown the fruits even further and for the flavours to meld – fruits and alcohol. With the fruits this well-cured, the cake is naturally moist, rummy and fruity without having to add extra rum to it after baking.

I have found that if the fruits have not been curing long enough the cake will be dry and does not have enough of the rummy-ness that makes it so appealing. I also do not add any dark colouring to my cake, but rather use more prunes in the fruit mixture and that give the cake the desired "blackness."

This cake can be stored at room temperature for an extended period of time due to the curing properties of the rum.

Yield: 1 (10" x 2¼") cake

Ingredients

For Rum-Cured Mixed Fruit

1 pound raisins

1½ pound pitted prunes

¼ pound preserved cherries

¼ pound mixed peel (if you don't find any, replace with more prunes or currants)

½ cup brown sugar

1 x 750 ml good dark rum, plus more if needed

For cake

8oz unsalted butter, room temperature (plus extra for greasing the baking pan)

1 cup brown sugar

6 eggs, room temperature

2 teaspoons vanilla essence or 1½ teaspoons vanilla extract

4 cups rum-cured mixed fruit (see below for method)

½ teaspoon ground cinnamon

2 teaspoons baking powder

2 cups all-purpose flour, plus extra for dusting the baking pan

Equipment

1 Electrical blender

2 Large bowls

1 Whisk or hand mixer

1 Wooden spoon

1 (10 x 3-inch) round cake pan

1 Wire cooling rack

Directions

For Rum-Cured Mixed Fruit

▶ Make this in batches

▶ Mix together all the fruits in a large bowl.

▶ Add 2 cups of rum and some of the mixed fruits along with ¼ cup sugar and blend until it's like a paste. Add a little more rum if it gets too thick and not blending easily and be sure to scrape down the sides of the blender-jug.

▶ Repeat this process until all the fruits are blended.

▶ Store in an airtight glass jar with a drizzle of rum to cover the surface; no need to refrigerate, this can stay on the countertop until ready to use.

▶ The fruits can stay this way for years, as long as no unclean utensils are used to dip into it.

For Cake

- ▶ Preheat oven to 350°F with the baking rack in the middle of the oven.

- ▶ Grease the cake pan, first by rubbing butter all around and then dusting with flour all around. Tap the pan and turn it over to remove any excess flour.

- ▶ Line the bottom of the pan, only, with a cut-out round piece of greased parchment paper; set aside.

- ▶ Cream butter and sugar until it reaches a pale cream colour; if you are using a hand mixer, 5–6 minutes; set aside.

- ▶ Mix together the flour, baking powder and cinnamon in a large bowl and set aside.

- ▶ Whisk eggs until frothy in a separate bow.

- ▶ Add essence to eggs and continue whisking for a few seconds.

- ▶ Add whisked eggs to creamed butter and sugar and stir gently, incorporating (the mixture will look curdled, that's okay).

- ▶ Add the rum-cured mixed fruit and mix thoroughly until fully incorporated.

- ▶ Add the flour-baking powder-cinnamon mixture and mix thoroughly to incorporate, but do not over mix or beat the batter.

- ▶ Pour batter into baking pan.

- ▶ Bake for 1 hour and 30 minutes or until inserted skewer comes out clean

- ▶ Remove from oven and cool on wire rack in pan for 10 minutes.

- ▶ Carefully, gently and quickly invert pan and remove cake .

- ▶ Cool completely on a wire rack.

- ▶ Cut and serve with a glass of ginger beer, sorrel drink, tea or coffee or just as is.

Cynthia's Tips

This cake can be stored on your countertop wrapped in foil and in an air-tight canister for a long time or store in the fridge.

The longer the cake stays, the more intense the flavour develops as the rum continues to cure the cake.

Coconut Drops

Coconuts are used widely in Caribbean cuisine in savoury and sweet dishes, especially baked goods. These drops are bun-like and are served at breakfast, as a snack or with an afternoon cup of tea.

Yield: 9 large drops

Ingredients

1 cup all-purpose flour

1 teaspoon baking powder

½ teaspoon ground cinnamon

½ teaspoon grated nutmeg

2 ounces unsalted butter, room temperature

½ cup brown sugar

1 lightly beaten egg at room temperature

1 teaspoon vanilla essence or ¾ teaspoon vanilla extract

2 cups grated coconut

¼ cup raisins

Equipment

2 medium bowls

1 hand mixer

1 wooden spoon

1 baking sheet lined with parchment paper

1 ice cream scoop (regular sized)

1 wire rack

Directions

- ▶ Preheat oven to 400°F.
- ▶ Mix flour, baking powder, cinnamon, and nutmeg in large bowl.
- ▶ Cream butter and sugar in separate bowl with hand mixer for 3 minutes.
- ▶ Beat egg and essence into creamed butter and sugar mixing for about half a minute.

Cynthia's Tips

You can use a smaller scoop to yield more drops.

Using an ice cream scoop ensures each drop is even. It also makes the drops perfectly round. However, using a tablespoon or your hands is just fine.

- ▶ Add the dry ingredients (flour, baking powder & spices) to the butter-sugar-egg mixture; stir using wooden spoon.
- ▶ Stir in coconut and raisins.
- ▶ Batter should be stiff.
- ▶ Using the ice cream scoop, add scoops of mixture onto the lined baking sheet.
- ▶ Bake in oven for 15–20 minutes or until lightly brown.
- ▶ Transfer to wire rack and cool.
- ▶ Serve with tea, coffee or your favourite soft drink.

Coconut Ice Cream

The first time I ate this ice cream was in Trinidad & Tobago. I was on my "reward-trip" for having successfully passed my Secondary School's Entrance Examination and the taste memory has stayed with me. Freshly squeezed coconut milk heightens the flavour of this ice cream but canned is a good substitute.

Yield: 5 cups

Ingredients

1½ cups coconut milk, well chilled

¾ cup granulated sugar

1½ cups heavy cream, well chilled

Equipment

1 ice cream maker

1 medium bowl

1 whisk or hand mixer

1 (32 oz) plastic container with cover

Directions

▶ Freeze ice cream bowl overnight in freezer.

▶ Add sugar and coconut milk to bowl and whisk until the sugar is dissolved (about 2 minutes).

▶ Stir in heavy cream to coconut milk-sugar mixture.

▶ Pour mixture into ice cream maker and proceed with churning according to manufacturers instructions (the ice cream will still be soft at this stage).

▶ Scoop out ice cream and fill the container, cover with lid and freeze to harden until ready to serve or cover the ice cream bowl and return to freezer to harden the ice cream.

Coconut Shortbread Cookies

I like these cookies not just because of the coconut flavour but also because they are not overly sweet.

Yield: 46–48

Ingredients

8 oz unsalted butter, room temperature

½ cup granulated sugar

½ teaspoon salt

1½ cups freshly grated coconut

3 cups all-purpose flour

1 egg, room temperature, lightly beaten

1–2 tablespoons granulated sugar for dusting

Equipment

1 fork

1 large bowl

Plastic wrap

1 rolling pin

1 small cookie cutter (shape of your choice)

1 parchment lined-baking sheet

Directions

► Add butter to bowl and stir a few times with a fork to ensure that it is completely at room temperature and soft.

► Stir in sugar and salt.

► Add coconut, flour and egg to butter-sugar mixture and mix well.

► Cover bowl and chill in the refrigerator for 1 hour.

► Preheat oven to 300°F, 20 minutes before the hour is up.

► Remove dough from the fridge, place on work surface and divide dough into three equal parts.

► Roll each piece into ¼" thickness.

► Cut into various shapes and transfer to baking sheet.

► Sprinkle cookies with sugar.

► Bake for 25–30 minutes until the cookies are delicately brown.

► Cool on racks and serve with your favourite hot or cold beverage.

Conkies

Each Caribbean territory has its own version of this dish and it is enjoyed widely. In Barbados, Conkies are made at Independence time. Wrapping and steaming the mixture in bananas leaves is what makes this dish uniquely flavourful. The texture is like that of a steamed pudding. While they are cooking the aroma wafts through the house pulling everyone into the kitchen like a magnet.

The conkies can also be wrapped in wax paper and then foil and be steamed; the texture would be the same but not the flavour.

Yield: 20 conkies (4oz) or 10 conkies (8oz)

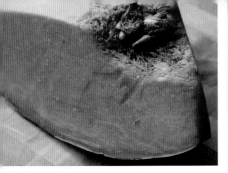

Ingredients

2 cups grated orange pumpkin

1 cup grated sweet potato

2 cups grated coconut

1½ cups sugar

¾ cup raisins

4 ounces unsalted butter, room temperature

1 ounce vegetable shortening, room temperature

1 teaspoon salt

½ teaspoon grated nutmeg

1 teaspoon ground cinnamon

1 teaspoon almond essence

2 cups corn flour

½ cup all-purpose flour

½ cup water or whole milk (on standby)

Equipment

1 large bowl

1 wooden spoon

Banana leaves

1 large pot

1 large steamer

1 large spoon

1 pair tongs

Directions

▶ Mix thoroughly, the pumpkin, sweet potato, coconut, sugar, raisins, butter, shortening, salt, spices and essence in large bowl.

▶ Add the corn flour and all purpose flour to the mixture and continue to mix.

▶ Add the water or milk half at a time to the mixture to attain a dropping consistency (the mixture should be moist but not watery). Depending on the liquid from the pumpkin, it may not be necessary to add all the water or milk.

▶ Set mixture aside.

- ▶ Light stove and warm the banana leaves one at a time (pass each leaf over the open flame to make it pliable). The colour of the leaf gets brighter as the heat touches it.

- ▶ Wipe clean with a damp cloth or paper towels, the leaves that have been singed and made pliable.

- ▶ Cut the leaves into large squares (these will become wrappers for the conkie mixture). Set aside.

- ▶ Cut and arrange the stems of the banana leaves in a criss-cross pattern to create a steamer; now add your regular steamer on top of the stems (that is, if you have one, if you don't that's not a problem).

- ▶ Pour enough water into the pot to steam the conkies, stopping short of the water touching the metal steamer (if using), if not, then stop short of 2 inches from the top of the banana stems (if you have banana leaves remaining, arrange a few pieces on top of the stems).

- ▶ Cover pot, transfer to stove and bring to a boil on high heat.

- ▶ Meanwhile, spoon the conkie mixture into the individually cut wrappers (the leaves) and fold just as you would closing a box; repeat until all the conkies are wrapped.

- ▶ Add the wrapped conkies, seam side down to the pot of boiling water with steamer.

- ▶ Cook covered until done, approximately 40 minutes (cooking time varies depending on the size of the conkies, the quantity, and the size of the pot).

- ▶ Carefully remove the lid of the pot and using tongs, remove the steamed conkies.

- ▶ Serve hot, warm, room temperature or cold.

Cynthia's Tips

The box greater gives the best grating texture to the ingredients for this dish.

You can opt to soak the raisins in rum to plump them up. When adding to the dish, include the liquid from soaking.

You can make strings out of the banana leaves and tie the parcels if you like.

Flutees
(Flavoured ice-blocks)

These frozen fruit-ice blocks were very popular when I was in primary school. The flutee-lady would come with a flask full of these beauties and they would be sold out in no time. We always tried our best not to let the juice drip on our uniforms – some of us succeeded and some of us didn't.They are a sweet, juicy treat that's enjoyed in the hot weather.

Ingredients

1 (0.14 oz) Cherry-flavoured
    unsweetened drink mix
2⅓ cups water
⅛ teaspoon vanilla essence or extract
Sugar to taste

Equipment

Jug
Wooden spoon
2 (16-cubes) ice trays

Directions

► Empty the contents of the drink mix into jug.

► Add water, essence and sugar to taste.

► Stir to dissolve sugar and drink mix.

► Pour mixture into ice-cube trays and freeze.

► To serve, gently wet the bottom of the tray to release the cubes.

Cynthia's Tip

You can use any kind of freezer-proof moulding trays or containers to make this treat.

Golden apple
(June plum) Crumble

This fruit is also called June Plum. I created this dish one day when I still had lots of golden apples left over after making drink and stewing some. If you like apple crumble, you'll love this dessert.

Yield: 1 (8" x 8" x 2") pan

Ingredients

For filling

3 pounds ripe golden apples (June plums) peeled and cut up

3–4 tablespoons granulated sugar

½ tablespoon cornstarch

¼ teaspoon ground cinnamon

⅛ teaspoon ground allspice

For crumble

1 cup all purpose flour

¾ cup brown sugar

¼ teaspoon ground cinnamon

6 oz cold unsalted butter, cubed, plus extra to butter dish

Equipment

1 (8″ x 8″ x 2″) dish, buttered

1 large bowl

1 wooden spoon

1 medium bowl

2 table knives or whatever you use to cut in butter

1 baking sheet lined with parchment paper

1 wire rack

Directions

▶ Preheat oven to 375°F

Filling

▶ Add golden apple (June plum), sugar, cornstarch, cinnamon and allspice to a large bowl and mix well. Set aside.

Crumble

▶ Mix flour, sugar and cinnamon together in a medium bowl.

▶ Cut in butter with knives until it resembles peas.

Assembling the dish

▶ Pour the filling into the buttered dish and spread evenly.

▶ Sprinkle the crumble evenly and liberally on top of filling, be sure to get the edges and corner.

▶ Place dish on lined baking sheet and bake for 45–55 minutes or until the top is brown and crisp.

▶ Remove from oven and cool on wire rack for about 15–20 minutes before serving.

▶ Serve as is or with your favourite ice cream.

Gooseberry Syrup

Sweet and tart at the same time, this makes for a delicious snack and would also be great over your favourite ice cream.

Yield: 1 cup

Ingredients

1 pound gooseberries, stems removed

2½ cups brown sugar

1 (3–4-inch) stick of cinnamon

2 whole cloves

Approximately 6 cups water (more may be needed)

Equipment

1 Large saucepan

1 Wooden spoon

1 Glass jar

Directions

▶ Wash the gooseberries and add to saucepan with sugar, cinnamon and cloves, adding enough water to cover 2 inches above the gooseberries.

▶ Stir to dissolve the sugar over medium-low heat, then cover pot slightly and bring to a boil.

▶ When it comes to a boil, reduce the heat to medium-low and let the mixture cook until the gooseberries are cooked through and have shrunk (this takes about 1 hour or more depending on the size of the gooseberries).

▶ The gooseberries and syrup should turn a deep rich burgundy; the syrup should be thick, not watery.

Cynthia's Tips

The cooking time for this syrup is not exact so it is something you will have to monitor. If you find the liquid has reduced significantly and the gooseberries are still too tart and raw to the taste, then add more water and let it continue to boil.

You can go about doing your other chores as the syrup cooks, you do not have to constantly monitor it.

Some people opt to parboil the gooseberries to cut down on the cooking time.

Guava Cheese

We say guava cheese but it is also known as guava paste. The cooking time is long but well worth it.

Yield: 18–20 squares

Ingredients

4 cups guava pulp (recipe follows)

4 cups granulated sugar plus extra for dusting & sprinkling

A little oil to grease baking sheet and knife

Guava Pulp

2 pounds ripe guavas, peeled and cut into chunks

2 cups water

1 (3-inch) cinnamon stick

Equipment

1 Large saucepan

1 Sieve

1 Large bowl

1 Ladle

2 Wooden spoons

1 Heavy bottomed pot

1 Splatter cover

1 Baking sheet

1 Knife

1 Plate-tray dusted with granulated sugar

Directions

Guava pulp

(Makes approximately 4 cups)

▶ Add guavas, cinnamon stick and water to saucepan.

▶ Cover and bring to a boil until guavas are soft and cooked through.

▶ Turn off stove and remove pot from heat.

▶ Set the sieve over the bowl.

▶ Add 2 ladles at a time of the cooked guavas, juice and all.

▶ Mash and press the guavas through the sieve with the back of the wooden spoon (you will need to constantly scrape the bottom of the sieve so that the pulp can pass through easily.

▶ Repeat until all the guavas have been mashed and pressed through the sieve.

▶ Measure 4 cups pulp to make guava cheese.

Guava Cheese

▶ Combine pulp and sugar in heavy-bottomed pot, stirring to dissolve sugar.

▶ Place on high to medium heat and bring to a boil.

▶ Cover with splatter cover when it begins to boil (you will hear plopping sounds).

▶ Turn heat to low/simmer and let cook until the mixture gets very thick and comes away easily from the sides and bottom of the pot, stirring intermittently.

▶ Lightly grease a baking sheet with oil.

▶ Pour mixture onto baking sheet and spread evenly about ½ inch thick.

▶ Let cool completely. When cooled, put into the fridge to harden further if you like.

▶ Using an oiled knife, cut into squares and serve on a granulated-sugar-dusted tray or plate (sprinkle some of the sugar on top as well).

▶ To store, dust container with granulated sugar and stack one set at the bottom, then sprinkle some sugar on top of that set and stack. Continue until all are in the container.

▶ Store in an airtight container in a fridge.

Nutmeg Ice Cream

The first time I had this ice cream, I was drawn to it because of the aroma. It smelt like my mom's kitchen while she was baking on a Saturday afternoon. Nutmeg ice cream is simply delicious and has a really great homemade taste to it.

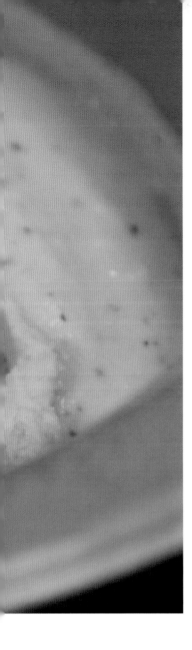

Ingredients

1 cup whole milk, well chilled

¾ cup granulated sugar

2 cups heavy cream, well chilled

2 teaspoons freshly grated nutmeg

Equipment

1 ice cream maker

1 medium bowl

1 whisk or hand mixer

1 (32 oz) plastic container with cover

Directions

► Freeze ice cream bowl overnight in freezer.

► Add milk and sugar to bowl and whisk until sugar is dissolved (about 2 minutes).

► Stir in heavy cream and nutmeg to milk-sugar mixture.

► Pour mixture into ice cream maker and proceed with churning according to manufacturers instructions (the ice cream will still be soft at this stage).

► Scoop out ice cream into container, cover with lid and freeze to harden until ready to serve or cover ice cream bowl and freeze to harden ice cream.

Parsad

Parsad is a sweet dish of flour and clarified butter that's made and shared at various Hindu religious ceremonies such as a Pooja. The dish is flavoured with cardamom and the texture is smooth. The plump raisins are a pleasant surprise as you bite into them.

Yield: 2½ lbs (8 x ½ cup servings)

Ingredients

½ cup ghee

1¾ cups all-purpose flour

1 cup sugar

¼ cup raisins, washed

1 teaspoon ground green cardamom (elaichi)

1 cup whole milk

3 cups boiling water, divided

(First usage: 1 cup to dissolve sugar)

(Second usage: 2 cups to cook mixture)

Equipment

1 karahi (Indian-style wok) OR deep heavy-bottomed pan with sides 4 – 5 inches high

1 whisk

1 wooden spoon

Directions

► Heat ghee in karahi until very hot.

► Add flour to hot ghee and keep whisking until all the ghee is absorbed.

► Turn the heat to low and continue to stir the mixture; the mixture will start to get wet (as if liquid has been added to it) as it continues to cook. This process takes 15–20 minutes.

► Stir in the raisins.

► Dissolve sugar in 1 cup of boiling water and add immediately to the mixture; be careful and watch out for the steam.

Cynthia's Tips

Step 3 is key – if the flour and ghee mixture is not allowed to cook and develop moisture, the parsad when eaten will leave a tacky film on your tongue.

At step 8, I found that it was not necessary to stand in front of the stove stirring all the time. Once the heat is properly regulated so that the mixture does not scorch, you can check on it and give it a proper stir at 5-minute intervals.

► Keep stirring, this time with the wooden spoon; at this stage you will notice the mixture coming together.

► Add milk, the remaining 2 cups of boiling water and cardamom and stir.

► Keep stirring until all the liquid is incorporated and there are no lumps (the heat should still be on low, this is important so that the parsad does not scorch).

► Stir until the mixture comes away cleanly from the pan and attempts to form a ball; this can take any where from 10 to 15 minutes.

► Serve warm or at room temperature in half-cup servings.

Paynoos (Sweetened, Spiced Milk Curds)

This is a sweet treat made from curdled milk – firm pieces of sweet cream with a hint of spice. Originally this treat was made from the milk of the cow just after it had given birth. I imagine that in some rural areas this practice still obtains. Today however, whole milk is used. The milk is curdled with lemon juice or distilled vinegar and then boiled with the spices.

Yield: ¾ cup

Ingredients

1 litre whole milk

2 tablespoons fresh lime juice or 150 ml distilled vinegar

1 (3-inch) cinnamon stick

3 whole cloves

½ cup sugar

Equipment

1 large saucepan

1 wooden spoon

Directions

► Pour milk into pot and bring to a boil.

► Just as the milk boils (it will start to rise), add lime juice or vinegar and stir; immediately, you will see the milk curdle with the whey and curds separating.

► Add cinnamon stick and cloves to curdled milk and let boil for 15 minutes.

► Stir in the sugar dissolving it.

► Let the mixture continue to boil for 30 minutes or until the curds begin to harden and the liquid is almost gone.

► Remove from heat and let cool completely.

► Serve in small portions as a snack.

Pine Tarts

This is my mom's favourite pastry. It's pineapple jam encased in a rich short crust pastry. It's a part of the trio of pastries, the others being patties and cheese rolls.

Yield: 18–20

Ingredients

2½ pounds short crust pastry dough (recipe on page 320)

2 (12-oz) bottles pineapple jam (preferably homemade)

All-purpose flour for dusting

3 egg yolks

3 tablespoons water

Equipment

1 rolling pin
1 (5-inch) round cutter (I used the cover
    of one of my sauce pots)
1 tablespoon
1 fork
2 Parchment-lined baking sheets
1 pastry brush
2 wire racks

Directions

▶ Prepare the Pine Tarts in 2 batches. Keep one batch of pastry-dough balls in the refrigerator while working on the other.

▶ Preheat oven to 350°F.

▶ Beat eggs and water to make egg wash; set aside.

▶ Divide pastry dough into equal amounts that will yield about 18–20 balls.

▶ Flour work surface and rolling pin.

▶ Roll the ball to 5 inches circle with 1mm (a little less than ¼-inch thickness).

▶ Cut into a circle.

▶ Spread 1 heaped tablespoon of jam on pastry dough leaving ½ –¾-inch of the edges free.

▶ Fold together, the left and right side of the top half of the circle letting them over lap each other.

▶ Lift the bottom part of the circle towards the overlapped seam, forming a triangle.

▶ Dip the prongs of the fork in flour and then gently press the 3 points-edge of the triangle to seal the pastry.

▶ Transfer pine tart to parchment-lined baking sheet.

▶ Repeat until baking sheet is full.

▶ Brush with egg wash.

▶ Bake in preheated oven for 20–25 minutes.

▶ Cool on a rack.

▶ Serve warm or at room temperature.

Pound Cake
(aka as sponge cake in Guyana)

We refer to this as a sponge cake and it happens to be my mom's favourite. I like it when it's still warm with a cup of tea. If you can, always ensure that you include orange, lemon or lime zest as these add great flavour to the cake.

Ingredients

1¾ cups all-purpose flour

2 teaspoons baking powder

⅛ teaspoon salt

Zest of one orange or lemon (optional)

1 cup granulated sugar

8 oz unsalted butter at room temperature

4 large eggs at room temperature

2 teaspoons vanilla essence or 1½ teaspoons vanilla extract

Equipment

2 (9 x 5-inch) loaf pans, lined at the bottom with parchment paper, greased and dusted with flour

1 large bowl

1 hand mixer

1 whisk

2 medium bowls

1 spatula

1 wooden spoon

Directions

► Preheat oven to 350°F with baking rack in the middle of the oven.

► Add flour, baking powder, salt and zest to medium bowl and mix; set aside.

► Cream the sugar and butter in a large bowl with a hand mixer for 5–6 minutes. The creamed butter and sugar should be pale cream.

► Whisk eggs in a medium bowl until frothy adding the essence/extract half way through whisking.

► Pour egg mixture into creamed butter and sugar; use a flat spatula to scrap all the egg mixture.

► Stir and mix; the mixture will look curdled (this is normal, don't worry).

► Add the flour mixture to the wet ingredients (sugar-butter-egg) and using a spatula or wooden spoon, mix thoroughly to incorporate but do not overmix.

► To test that the batter has enough flour, the spoon should be able to stand alone in the middle of the mixture.

► Pour equal amounts of batter into 2 loaf pans

.

► Place pan with batter in oven and let bake for 50–60 minutes or until a bamboo skewer inserted in the middle of the cake comes out clean.

► Place cakes on a cooling rack for 10 minutes and then remove cakes from pans and let cook on wire rack.

Variation: Simple Fruit Cake

► ½ cup raisins, dusted in flour

► ½ cup pitted cherries, patted dry and dusted in flour

► Sprinkle the fruits on top of the cake just before adding them to the oven

Cynthia's Tips

For excellent results, it is necessary to ensure that the butter and eggs are at room temperature.

Once the cake is in the oven do not peek! Check it at the 50-minute time mark to see if it's done.

Vanilla-Cardamom Rice Pudding

Rice Pudding, Sweet Rice, Kheer. Call it what you will, this is one of my all-time favourite desserts. Creamy, well-spiced and with some fruity raisins is how I like my rice pudding. It is a celebratory dish made at festivals and holidays.

Yield: 7 cups

Ingredients

1 cup long grain white rice, washed

4 whole cloves

2 green cardamom pods, bruised

1 vanilla bean pod, de-seeded

3 ½ cups water, divided (2½ cups + 1 cup)

3 cups whole milk, divided (2 cups + 1 cup)

Granulated sugar to taste, about ¾ cup

½ cup raisins, soaked in rum, drained

Equipment

1 heavy-bottomed large saucepot with cover

1 wooden spoon

Directions

▶ Add 2½ cups water, 2 cups milk, rice, cloves, cardamom and vanilla bean (pod and seeds) to pot. Stir to mix and bring to a boil on medium high heat (be sure to pay attention to the pot, as it boils, the milk tends to froth and rise).

▶ Cook on medium high heat for 8 minutes then reduce to simmer and cook covered for 20 minutes.

▶ Now add the remaining 1 cup water and 1 cup milk along with raisins and sugar. Stir to dissolve sugar.

▶ Cook on low heat/simmer for another 15–20 minutes. Taste and adjust for sweetness if necessary.

▶ Serve warm or at room temperature or place into individual glass or bowls, chill in refrigerator and serve.

Roat (Roth)

Of all the goodies packed in the paper bag one gets at the end of a Pooja (Jhandi, a Hindu service), roat is my favourite. It's made of clarified butter, flour, sugar and ground cardamom. It's like eating a piece of fried pastry; therefore, it was always served in small pieces.

Yield: 6–7

Ingredients

3 heaping tablespoons sugar

Whole milk to knead dough, start with ¾ cup

2 heaping tablespoons ghee

¼ teaspoon ground cinnamon

1 teaspoon ground cardamom (green or black)

2 cups all purpose flour

1 tablespoon raisins (optional)

Oil for shallow frying

Equipment

1 medium bowl
1 frying pan
1 slotted pot spoon
Paper towels

Directions

- ▶ Dissolve sugar in ¼ cup milk.
- ▶ Stir in ghee to the milk-sugar mixture.

- ▶ Add the spices, flour, raisins (if using) to a bowl. Pour in ghee-milk mixture and add the milk a little at a time to form a dough.
- ▶ Rest dough for 5 minutes.
- ▶ Divide dough in to 2 ounce balls and flatten to ¼ inch round disks; prick all over the top with a fork to prevent puffing up.
- ▶ Heat oil in pan or karahi on medium flame.
- ▶ Fry Roat until brown; drain on paper towels.
- ▶ Serve warm or at room temperature.

Salara (Coconut Roll)

This is also known as coconut roll. If you are using fresh coconut, do not squeeze it for milk or cream first, as the filling will be become dry and husky. If using dried coconut, opt for sweetened and eliminate the sugar called for in the recipe.

Yield: 2 (14-inch) rolls

Ingredients

Filling

2 cups finely grated coconut

1 cup granulated sugar

½ teaspoon ground cinnamon

1 teaspoon vanilla essence or extract

Red food colouring

Dough

1 tablespoon active yeast

¼ cup warm water

1 teaspoon sugar

¼ cup vegetable shortening

3 cups all-purpose flour

1 teaspoon salt

¼ cup sugar

½ cup whole milk

1 egg, room temperature, lightly beaten

1 tablespoon unsalted butter, melted

1 lightly beaten egg white, room temperature

1 teaspoon water

Equipment

2 large bowls (for kneading and proofing dough)

1 medium bowl (for mixing filling)

1 small bowl (for yeast proofing)

1 parchment-lined sheet pan (12 x 18 x 1-inch)

Directions

For Filling:

▶ Mix all the ingredients together in a bowl and set aside for 1 hour (use as many drops of food colouring until it gives you a rich red colour).

For Dough:

▶ Dissolve yeast in water with 1 teaspoon sugar; cover and let proof in a warm place for 10 minutes.

▶ Rub shortening into flour.

▶ Add salt and sugar to flour.

▶ Warm milk.

▶ Add proofed yeast, lightly beaten egg and warm milk to flour mixture and knead to a dough.

▶ Transfer dough to a lightly oiled-bowl, cover dough and let rise for 1 hour or until doubled in size, in a warm place.

▶ Punch down dough after it has risen, knead lightly for a minute and divide equally in half.

▶ On a well floured surface, roll each piece of dough into a 12 x 8 inch rectangle.

▶ Brush each rectangle (the side facing up) with the melted butter.

▶ Divide the filling in half and spread evenly onto both dough rectangles, leaving 1 inch free around the edges.

▶ Roll up the dough with mixture, lengthways, pinching the ends to seal it (do not over stuff the rolls. The seam side should be facing down when it's finished rolling).

▶ Transfer to baking sheet, cover loosely and let rise for 45 minutes or until doubled in size.

▶ Preheat oven to 375°F, 20 minutes before the 45 minutes are up.

▶ Lightly beat egg white and the teaspoon of water.

▶ Brush rolls with egg white egg wash and bake in oven for 20–30 minutes.

▶ Cool on a rack.

▶ Wait until completely cooled before slicing.

▶ Serve with your favourite hot or cold beverage.

Soursop Ice Cream

The fragrance of this fruit is best captured in the expression - "things are coming up roses". The pulp is silky and creamy. Soursop (guanábana) is used widely to make a variety of desserts and drinks in the English- and Spanish-speaking Caribbean.

The seeds must be removed before using the fruit and to do this, you'll need to work with clean hands or latex gloves, gently feeling the pulp and squeezing out the seeds. Some West Indian grocery stores sell the pulp already de-seeded.

Yield: 5 cups

Ingredients

1 cup whole milk

¾ cup granulated sugar

2 cups heavy cream

¾ cup blended soursop pulp

Equipment

1 ice cream maker

1 medium bowl

1 whisk or hand mixer

1 (32 oz) plastic container with cover

Directions

▶ Freeze ice cream bowl overnight in freezer.

▶ Add milk and sugar to bowl and whisk until the sugar is dissolved (about 2 minutes).

▶ Stir in heavy cream and pulp to milk-sugar mixture.

▶ Pour mixture into ice cream maker and proceed with churning according to manufacturers instructions (the ice cream may still be soft at this stage).

▶ Scoop out ice cream into container; freeze to harden until ready to serve or cover ice cream bowl and freeze until ready to serve.

Stewed Golden apples (June plum)

This fruit easily absorbs the flavours of the spices it is cooked with and the low slow cooking ensures that the flavour goes right through. These can be stored in air-tight glass bottles in the fridge for a long time. The syrup is great for pancakes and ice cream too.

Yield: 8

Ingredients

8 half-ripe golden apples
2 (3-inch) cinnamon sticks
4 whole cloves
3 whole allspice berries
Sugar to taste
1 cup water

Equipment

1 vegetable peeler or paring knife
1 large saucepot
1 wooden spoon

Directions

► Peel golden apples.

► Add golden apples to pot along with whole spices, sugar and water.

► Place pot on high heat and stir to dissolve sugar.

► Cover pot and bring to a boil.

► As soon as it starts to boil, with pot still covered, reduce heat to simmer and let cook for approximately 45–50 minutes or until the golden apples are cooked through.

► If the syrup is watery at this stage, remove the golden apples from the pot, turn heat to high and let

the syrup reduce until it thickens to desired consistency. Return golden apples to pot with syrup and turn off heat.

► Let cool completely.

► Serve warm, at room temperature.

► This dessert works well by itself or with ice cream.

Stewed Guavas

Often when people talk about fruits in the Caribbean, coconuts, pineapples and banana come to mind. Allow me to introduce you to guavas: whether they are stewed, juiced, made into a paste, jam, jelly or a crumble, you'll fall in love with this fruit the first time you taste it.

Yield: 1¼ cups

Ingredients

2 pounds ripe guavas

2¼ cups water

Sugar to taste

1 (3-inch) cinnamon stick

2 whole cloves

2 whole allspice berries

½ teaspoon fresh lemon or lime juice

Equipment

1 paring knife
1 teaspoon
2 medium saucepans
1 medium bowl
1 wooden spoon
1 slotted pot spoon

Directions

► Wash, peel and cut guavas into quarters, reserve the skins.

► With a paring knife or teaspoon, cut/scoop out the centre of the guavas which contains all the seeds; set aside scooped out pulp.

► Add reserved skins, pulp, water and sugar to taste in a saucepan, cover and bring to a boil.

► Let the pulp, skin and sugar boil for 10 minutes.

► Strain the liquid along with the skin and pulp through a sieve, mashing and pressing some of the pulp through with a wooden spoon.

► In another saucepan, add the quartered-scooped-out guavas as well as the strained liquid and whole spices.

► Cover the pot and bring the mixture to a boil; when it begins to boil,

reduce the heat to simmer and let cook gently until soft and cooked through (approximately 1 hour and 20 minutes).

► With a slotted pot spoon or spider strainer, remove the guava from the simmering pot and set aside.

► Turn the heat to high with the pot uncovered and let the liquid reduce and thicken to a syrup; stir in the lemon juice.

► Put the guavas back into the syrup, when it has thickened, remove from heat and let cool.

► Serve warm or cold. Can be eaten as is, with ice cream, pancakes, or anything you want to have with a fruit and syrup.

Coconut Sweet Bread

Sometimes these are just labelled at "sweet bread" or "coconut bread". Coconut, ideally freshly grated, is the star of this bread. Any combination of dried fruit can be added as desired. Some people like their coconut to be incorporated throughout the bread and others like the coconut sweetened and layered in the middle so it would be clearly visible when sliced. I prefer it to be incorporated throughout the mixture. It is served at breakfast, as a snack, as part of a dessert or at tea-time. Try it also with a slice of sharp cheddar cheese; the sweet and salty tastes contrast very well.

Yield: 2 loaves

Ingredients

3 ½ cups all purpose flour

2 teaspoons baking powder

1 teaspoon ground cinnamon

4 oz cold unsalted butter plus extra for
greasing pans

1 ½ cups brown sugar

2 cups freshly grated coconut

1 cup raisins

⅓ cup chopped cherries

¼ cup currants (optional)

¼ cup candied mixed peel (optional)

3 eggs at room temperature, lightly
beaten

1 teaspoon vanilla essence or extract

¾ cup whole milk or water

Equipment

1 large bowl

1 wooden spoon

1 small bowl

1 fork

2 (9 x 5 x 3-inch) loaf pans, greased with
butter

Directions

► Preheat oven to 325°F with rack in the middle
of the oven.

► Mix flour, baking powder and cinnamon
together in large bowl.

► Rub butter into flour.

► Add sugar, coconut, raisins, cherries, currants,
mixed peel (If using), and mix thoroughly.

► Add lightly beaten eggs, vanilla and milk
or water to the dry ingredients and mix until
incorporated; do not knead.

► Divide mixture equally between two greased
loaf pans.

► Bake in oven for 45–50 minutes or until tester
comes out clean.

► Cool on rack in pans for 10 minutes then
remove from pans and continue to cool on
rack completely before slicing.

► Serve with tea, coffee or your favourite hot or
cold soft beverage.

Tamarind Balls

Like tamarind? Then pucker up and get ready for the sweet, salt, sour and heat that will hit you in layers and waves. This recipe requires no cooking and the longer the tamarind balls rest, the more the flavour develops. This is another snack that's found at many school stands and in supermarkets.

Yield: 36

Ingredients

4 cups shelled tamarind

4 cups brown sugar

1 tablespoon salt

1 teaspoon hot pepper sauce

1 large clove garlic, ground to a paste

½ cup granulated sugar, plus extra for dusting baking sheet

Equipment

1 large bowl

1 tablespoon

1 large baking sheet, dusted with granulated sugar

Directions

▶ Clean hands are needed for this job!

▶ Break tamarind into segments in a large bowl.

▶ Add brown sugar and mix together by gently rubbing the tamarind with sugar .

▶ You have an option here, you can feel for the seeds and remove them from the mixture as I do or you can leave them in.

▶ Add the salt, pepper and garlic and continue to mix until fully incorporated.

▶ Wash hands but leave them damp as you take mixture, little by little (teaspoon or tablespoon) to roll into smooth round balls.

▶ Roll the balls lightly into the granulated sugar.

▶ Store in an airtight container in a cool place or in the refrigerator.

Vermicelli Cake

This is another of those treats made during Muslim religious holidays – at least that was my first introduction to it. While it will taste really good without the fruits, do not leave them out as they are welcome bites of surprise as you eat. To easily cut the cake into squares and serve, ensure that it is completely cool.

Yield: 18 squares

Ingredients

1 tablespoon unsalted butter, plus extra
    for buttering casserole dish

1 (10 oz) packet of vermicelli

2 cups water

2 cups whole milk

1/3 cup raisins

½ teaspoon ground cinnamon

⅛ teaspoon ground clove

2 teaspoons vanilla essence or 1½
    teaspoons vanilla extract

1 (14 oz) can condensed milk

1 tablespoon custard powder

2 tablespoons water

⅓ cup preserved cherries

Equipment

1 karahi (Indian-style wok) OR a pan with sides 4–5
    inches high

1 slotted spoon

1 (13 x 9 x 2-inch) rectangular casserole dish, buttered

Directions

▶ Heat butter in karahi on medium heat.

▶ Break vermicelli into pieces and add it to the butter; parch until the vermicelli gets light brown.

▶ Turn heat to low and add water in intervals, half-cup at a time to cook the vermicelli as it parches. This will take 15–18 minutes.

▶ Add the whole milk, raisins, cinnamon, clove and essence and bring to a boil on medium heat.

▶ Let liquid reduce to half and then sweeten to taste with condensed milk.

▶ Dissolve the custard powder in 2 tablespoons water and add it to the vermicelli; keep stirring until the mixture becomes thick and creamy.

▶ Stir in cherries.

▶ Remove from heat and turn the entire mixture into the buttered casserole dish, spread out evenly and let cool completely.

▶ When completely cool, cut into squares and serve.

How-to-Guide

All Purpose Pastry Dough

Yields 2 x 9" crusts

Ingredients

4½ cups all-purpose flour, plus extra for
   dusting
1 tablespoon sugar
¼ teaspoon salt
4 oz vegetable shortening, cold
12 oz unsalted butter, cold
6 – 8 tablespoons iced water

Equipment

1 large bowl
1 pastry blender
Plastic wrap

Directions

► Mix together flour sugar and salt in
   a large bowl

► Cut in butter and shortening until the mixture
   resembles coarse grains (use a pastry blender,
   food processor or rub in with your fingers)

► Add 2 - 3 tablespoons of water at a time and
   mix to combine (bring together the dough);
   do not knead. I use a pastry blender and after
   all the water has been added to the dough,
   I turn the contents of the bowl onto a lightly
   floured surface and bring it together, I find I
   have more room to work with this way than in
   the large bowl

► If using a food processor, only pulse, do not let
   mixture whirl for too long as the dough is not
   supposed to be kneaded or mixed too much.
   In the food processor, as soon as the dough
   begins to come together, stop; empty the
   contents onto a lightly floured work surface
   bring it all together with your hands

► Gather dough into a ball

► Divide the dough in half and pat into round
   disks

► Wrap tightly with plastic wrap and refrigerate
   from ½ hour or overnight, depending on
   when you want to use it

► When you take the dough out of the fridge
   it will be cold, let rest and relax for 10 - 12
   minutes so that it does not crack and is easy
   to work with (the time for the dough to relax
   here will depend on the temperature in your
   home/kitchen)

► Flour your work surface and rolling pin and roll
   out and cut as specified by the recipe you
   are making

Cooked Rice (Absorption method)

Yield: 6 cups

Ingredients

2 cups long grain white rice, washed

2 ¾ cups water

Salt to taste

1 tablespoon oil

Equipment

1 large saucepan with cover

1 large spoon

1 fork

Directions

► Bring water to boil in saucepan on high heat

► Add rice, salt and oil. Stir and cover pot

► Bring to boil and cook for 5 – 6 minutes on high heat then reduce heat to low/simmer

► Cook covered for 20 minutes or until all the liquid has been absorbed

► Fluff with a fork and use according to directions in recipe

Cynthia's Tips

For fried rice, spread the cooked hot rice onto a large baking sheet and let cool completely. Toss a few times to ensure all over is cooled

All rice is not created equal and each requires a different rice to water ratio to be cooked and some rice are best cooked using particular methods. The best advice is to follow the instructions on the package

Curry Paste

Our curry is neither North Indian nor South Indian, it is a little of both and then some, so it is most definitely Caribbean. In Guyana we make what is called a curry paste that is the base of our curry. There are three important things to note when making when making curry: first is to ensure that the paste is sautéed well with hot oil - it is like toasting the mixture in oil. If this is not done properly then the spices in the curry will taste raw, they need to be tempered. Secondly, add the salt to taste for the dish when sautéing the curry paste, this way, when the meat or vegetables are added and the paste infuses, so too does the salt. Third, once the meat, potatoes or vegetables are added to the sautéed paste, allow it to cook for at least 3–4 minutes before adding any liquid to cook it. This way, the spices infuse the meat and vegetables.

If using potatoes in your curry, be advised that they absorb a lot of salt so you may have to taste the curry before it is finished cooking.

There is no need for a thickening agent when it comes to making Caribbean curry, once the liquid is reduced and the ingredients cooked, it thickens naturally.

Yield: 8 – 9 tablespoons

Ingredients

4 tablespoons diced onions

2 tablespoons finely chopped garlic

1 tablespoon freshly grated ginger

2 tablespoons chopped cilantro or celery or sweet basil

Hot pepper to taste, chopped

2 tablespoons ground garam masala (see recipe on page 326)

2 tablespoons ground turmeric **OR** 3 tablespoons curry powder

Water to make paste

Equipment

1 mortar and pestle or any brick-like grinder

1 small bowl

1 spoon

Directions

▶ Grind the onions, garlic, ginger, herbs and hot pepper to a paste

▶ Transfer mixture to a bowl and add turmeric (or curry powder) and garam masala

▶ Add just enough water and mix to a thick paste (paste should not be watery)

▶ Average 1 tablespoon curry paste to 1 pound of meat or poultry when making curry

▶ Average ½ tablespoon curry paste to 1 pound seafood or vegetables when making curry

Cynthia's Tip

Curry paste can be stored for up to a week in an airtight glass or plastic container in the refrigerator. Letting is store longer runs the risk of losing the potency of the spices.

De-salting Salt Fish

Ingredients

½ pound (8 ounces) boneless salt fish
8 cups water, divided in 2 (4-cups)

Equipment

1 saucepan
1 colander

Directions

▶ Add salt fish to saucepan with 4 cups water

▶ Bring to a boil on high heat for 15 – 20 minutes

▶ Drain in colander

▶ Add salt fish back to saucepan with the remaining 4 cups water

▶ Bring to boil on high heat for 15 minutes

▶ Drain in colander

▶ Let cool to handle and proceed using salt fish according to recipe

Cynthia's Tips

You can opt to soak the salt fish overnight in boiling water, covered. Drain off the water in the morning and then boil it once with fresh water for 15–20 minutes.

A squeeze of lemon juice when boiling aids in the quick cutting of the salt.

You never want to *completely* de-*salt* the salt fish, just to remove the excess and leave enough to taste.

Fresh Coconut Milk

Ingredients

Freshly grated coconut (average 1 cup
grated coconut for 1½ cups milk)
Lukewarm water according to the
amount of milk required in recipe

Equipment

2 large bowls
1 large sieve

Directions

- ▶ Clean hands are required!
- ▶ Add grated coconut to bowl along
with required amount of water
- ▶ Using both hands or one hand,
squeeze coconut for 1 to 2 minutes
releasing the milk (juice)
- ▶ Place sieve over bowl and strain
coconut milk. Press coconut firmly
against the sieve to extract all the
liquid
- ▶ Use coconut milk according as
instructed by recipe

Cynthia's Tip

You can opt to line the sieve with cheese cloth, pour the
coconut milk through it and then gather the ends of the
cheese cloth and squeeze out the remaining milk.

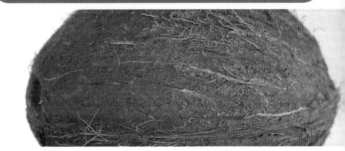

Cynthia's
Garam Masala Mix

Garam masala literally means "hot spices," and it is a mixture of various spices that are roasted and then ground to a powder. There are many variations of this spice blend depending on where you are from and often it is based on an individual's taste. In other words, all garam masalas are not created equal. As I've mentioned before, the curry we make in the Caribbean is neither North Indian nor is it South Indian, it is Caribbean. And even within various parts of the Caribbean the garam masala mix is different. This recipe is *my* garam masala mix made to suit my taste.

I usually mix the spices together and keep them in an air-tight glass bottle and roast and grind a small amount when I am ready to use it. Once I have taken out what I need to use, I store the rest of the ground masala in another glass bottle with a tight lid.

Ingredients

¾ cup coriander seeds

¾ cup cumin seeds

10 green cardamom pods

5 (3-inch) cinnamon sticks, broken into small pieces

2 tablespoons whole cloves

½ nutmeg, crushed

1 tablespoon mace

1 tablespoon fennel seeds

1 tablespoon black pepper corns

1 tablespoon fenugreek seeds

1 tablespoon kalongi seeds (black onion seeds)

1 tablespoon whole allspice

1 tablespoon yellow mustard seeds

2 (3-inch) dried turmeric, broken into tiny pieces

6 whole star anise

Equipment

1 frying pan

1 wooden spoon

1 mortar and pestle, spice or coffee grinder

Directions

▶ Mix all the ingredients together

▶ Heat dry frying pan on medium low heat and add the spices

▶ Stir and shake the pan as the spices begin to toast, crackle and pop

▶ You will know the spices are toasted as they will become fragrant and aromatic, this usually takes anywhere between 10 – 15 minutes

▶ Remove from pan and let to cool

▶ Grind the spices with a mortar and pestle, a spice grinder or a clean coffee grinder

Cynthia's Tips

The spices are not to be roasted on high heat; the aim here is to coax the oils and flavours of the spices.

When ground, your garam masala should be brown not black. If it is black, it means that the spices are burnt and this will be reflected in the taste of your curry with end notes of bitterness

Washing Rice

Ingredients

Rice (based on amount suggested by recipe)
Water

Equipment

1 large bowl

Directions

▶ Add rice to bowl and under a running tap, rub/massage rice. Discard milky water. Repeat the process about 3 – 5 times or until the water runs clear

▶ Drain and use as directed in recipe

Cynthia's Tips

If using a small amount of rice, place it in a sieve and rub/massage it under running water until the water runs clear.

For Basmati rice to really bloom when cooked, soak it after washing for at least ½ hour in water, drain and then cook as per instructions in recipe

Glossary
Ingredients & Terms

Achar – a spicy Indian pickle made with unripe mangoes, the very sour bilimbi (souree) and ripe tamarind. The spice combination for an achar is similar in nature to a garam masla mix that's used to make curries, however the addition of mustard oil to achar is what gives it that unique and distinctive taste. Achar is meant to be eaten in very small quantities. It is a condiment.

Breadfruit – is a starchy fruit that's used in savoury dishes pretty much the same way as a regular potato. It is round in shape, with a green, textured skin. Once cut in half, the stem is removed and the center where tiny little black seeds lie is sliced away before peeling and cooking. The fruit is so versatile that when it's ripe, it is used to make sweets such as puddings and punch.

Carambola – also known as five-finger and star-fruit. Carambola when ripe or green can be eaten raw or made into a juice. It can also be stewed and served as a dessert.

Cassareep – is the juice of grated cassava that has been cooked low and slow for a very long time until it caramelises, thickens and gets a deep dark brown colour, almost black. Cassareep has its origins with the Indigenous Peoples of Guyana. It is used to make the very popular Christmas dish, Pepperpot. Because cassareep has natural preservative properties, Pepperpot is allowed to stand at room temperature for days with gentle reheating twice a day.

Cassareep is also used as a colouring agent in place of browning for various stews, rice dishes, and baked meats.

Choka – refers to a method of preparing a dish which involves fire roasting, pounding and grinding. The essence of a choka has to do with the smoky flavour. Eggplant, potatoes, tomatoes, smoked herring, salt fish and coconut are the chokas made in the Caribbean. A choka is eaten primarily with dhal and rice or roti.

Chunkay – to chunkay means to add meat or fish to a hot pan that already contains aromatics (herbs & spices) that have been toasting in oil. The term is usually used when referring to curries. So you'd hear someone say, "I'm going to chunkay my curry."

Chutney – is a condiment made fresh to be used with a meal, much the same way as an achar is used. No preservative agents are added to a chutney as it is intended to be consumed the same day. The ingredients in a chutney are grind using a mortar and pestle or pureed in a food processor. Hot pepper, garlic and herbs are used to flavour the chutney.

American and European styled chutneys are usually made with fruits. The fruits are cooked to a reduction and preservatives such as oils, vinegars are used to ensure a long shelf life.

Dhal – refers to the dish as well as the legumes used to make it. It is a spicy pea soup that's tempered with whole spices and garlic that's been toasted in oil. Dhal is a daily must-have in some households.

Foo-Foo – refers to a method of preparation of starchy, tubular root vegetables. Plantains, eddoes, cassava etc. are boiled, mashed and formed into balls and eaten with stews, broths and soups.

Gaff – means to have a chat, to catch up on things and to reminisce.

Ghee – is clarified butter. It is not used for everyday cooking in the Caribbean but it is widely used when preparing food for Hindu religious festivals.

Golden apple – also known as June plum. It is a fruit that is eaten ripened and un-ripened. The seed has spikes and fibrous veins running from it. Golden apples are used to make juices, jams, jellies and as shown in this book, they can be stewed and also be made into a crumble.

Gooseberry – is also known as Malay gooseberry, Tahitian gooseberry, and Country gooseberry. It is a round, ribbed acidic fruit that grows in dense clusters close to the branches of the tree. Gooseberries are used to make syrup, drinks, pickles and even used in curries as the souring agent.

Karahi – is a deep heavy flat-bottomed pan that is used in Indian cooking all the time. It has similar properties of a wok. The karahi is used for curries, stews, sautés, stir-fries, deep-frying etc.

Karaila – is also known as bitter gourd or bitter melon. It is a member of the cucumber family. Oblong in shape with a bumpy texture, this vegetable is an acquired taste because of its bitterness. Most of the bitterness can be removed by liberally sprinkling the cut vegetable with salt which will extract the bitter juice.

Katahar – also known as breadnut is family to the breadfruit. Think of it as a seeded breadfruit. Katahar is also round in shape; its skin is green and has dull spikes protruding from it. A green katahar once cut and peeled, the flesh is then shredded by hand and the tender nuts shelled and sliced. A ripe katahar on the other hand is brown on the outside and only the seeds (nuts) are used, often boiled and eaten as a snack. The seeds of a ripe katahar are used by vegetarians as a source of fiber and protein in meals.

Lime – this means to get together and hang out with food and drinks.

Lorha & Sil – a flat version of a mortar and pestle. The lorha is a flat piece of brick stone; the surface being textured, the sil is an oblong-shaped brick stone. Herbs and spices are ground by rocking the sil back and forth on the lorha.

Mauby – refers to the bark of an evergreen tree belonging to the Rhamnaceae family. It also refers to the name of the drink that is made from the bark. Mauby bark is bitter and by extension, the drink has notes of bitterness that's balanced with sweetness as long as the mauby has been brewed properly and allowed to ripen over a period of two to three days.

Roti – the term used to describe a variety of Indian-inspired flat breads.

Salt fish – fish that has been salt cured and dried.

Sorrel – also known as Roselle and Hibiscus fruit, is used to make a drink that's a favourite in the Caribbean at Christmas time.

Sour – is a cooked chutney that's served as a condiment with savoury snacks. It is often made with un-ripe mangoes, souree (bilimbi) or tamarind.

Soursop – known as guanábana in Spanish and graviola in Portuguese, this fruit's flavour is hard to describe because it is complexly aromatic; as you inhale there are notes of pineapple, banana and coconut; there's also a hint of citrus. To eat soursop, the seeds must be removed. Soursop is widely used to make juice, punch, ice cream, sorbet and other desserts.

Tawah – a round, flat, iron-griddle that is used to cook roti.

Index

A

Achar
  Mango, 211
  Souree, 211
  Tamarind, 211
Ackee and salt fish, 94–96
Aloo roti (see potato roti)

B

Bakes
  Bajan, 97–98
  Coconut, 106–107
  Guyanese, 112–113
  Vincy, 123–124
Bajan fish cakes, 224–225
Bay leaf (see tea)
Biganee, 228–229
Bora (see vegetables)
Breadfruit
  Boiled, 130–131
  chips, 231
Buljol, 101–102
Butter-Flaps, 103–105

C

Cake
  Chinese, 266–269
  Christmas, 270–273
  Sponge, 300–301
Carambola, 329
Cassava balls, 234–235
Cassava pone, 264–265
Channa, 236–237
Cheese rolls (see pastries)
Chicken
  Baked, 126–127
  Curry, 132–133
  Roast, 186–187
Chinese cake (see cake)
Chips
  Breadfruit, 231
  Plantain, 256
Choka
  Coconut, 204–205
  Eggplant, 108–109
  Potato, 114–115
  Salt fish, 218–219
  Smoked-herring, 220–221

Tomato, 121–122

Chow mein, 134–136

Chutney

    Green Mango, 212–213

Christmas cake (*see* cake)

Cinnamon (*see* tea)

Coconut

    Bake, 106–107

    Bread, 314–315

    Choka, 204–205

    Drops, 274–275

    Ice cream, 276–277

    Milk, 325

    Roll (*see* salara)

    Shortbread

      cookies, 278–279

Coconut milk (*see* coconut)

Conkies, 280–283

Cook-up rice (*see* rice)

Cou-cou, 140–141

Curry

    Chicken, 132–133

    Egg, 150–151

    Eggplant-potato, 152–153

    Gilbaka, 158–159

    Hassar, 160–161

    Katahar, 165–166

    Paste, 322–323

D

Dhal

Okra, 145

Spinach, 145

Split-peas, 142–145

Dhal puri, 146–149

Drinks

    Five-finger, 232–233

    Ginger beer, 244–245

    Golden apple, 246–247

    Mauby, 250–251

    Peanut punch, 257

    Sorrel, 260–261

E

Egg

    Balls, 242–243

    Curry, 150–151

Eggplant

    Biganee, 228–229

    Choka, 108–109

    Eggplant-potato

      curry, 152–153

F

Fish

    Bajan fish cakes, 97–98

    Flying fish tomato-onion

      sauce, 154–155

    Fried fish, 206–207

    Gilbaka curry, 158–159

Hassar Curry, 160–161

    Salt fish (see salt fish)

Five-finger drink (see drinks)

Flutee, 284–285

Flying fish (see fish)

Foo-foo (see plantains)

Fried rice (see rice)

Fried salt fish, 110–111

G

Garam masala, 326–327

Garlic pork, 156–157

Gilbaka curry, 158–159

Ginger beer (see drinks)

Golden apple

    Crumble, 286–287

    Drink, 246–247

    Stewed, 310–311

Gooseberry syrup, 288–289

Ground provisions (see mettagee)

Guava

    Cheese, 290–291

    Stewed, 312–313

H

Ham, 128–129

Hassar curry, 160–161

I

Ice cream

    Coconut, 276–277

    Nutmeg, 292–293

    Soursop, 309

J

June plum (see golden apple)

K

Karila

    Kalounjie, 162–164

    Sautéed, 190–191

Katahar (see curry)

M

Macaroni and cheese

    pie, 167–168

Mango

    Achar, 211

    Chutney, 212–213

    Sour, 214–215

Mauby (see drinks)

Mettagee, 169–171

O

Okra
 and salt fish, 172–173
 in tomato-onion
  sauce, 174–175

P

Paratha roti, 176–179
Parsad, 294–295
Pastries
 Cheese rolls, 238–239
 Mini quiche, 252–253
 Patties, 245–255
 Pine tarts, 298–299
Pastry dough, 320
Patties (see pastries)
Paynoos, 296–297
Peanut punch (see drinks)
Pepperpot, 180–181
Pepper sauce, 216–217
Phulourie, 258–259
Pig-tail (see rice and peas)
Pine tarts (see pastries)
Plantains
 Boil and fry, 99–100
 Boiled ripe, 202–203
 Chips, 256
 Foo-foo, 182–183
 Fried ripe, 208–209

Plantain chips (see plantains)
Potato
 Choka, 114–115
 Roti, 116–118
Pound cake (see cake;
  sponge cake)
Pumpkin and shrimp, 192–193

R

Rice
 and peas, 184–185
 Cook-up, 137–139
 Fried, 196–197
 Steamed, 321
 Vegetable, 198–199
Rice and Peas (see rice)
Rice pudding
 Vanilla Cardamom, 302–303
Roast chicken (see chicken)
Roat, 304–305
Roti
 Dhal puri, 146–149
 Paratha, 176–179
 Potato, 116–118
 Sada, 119–120

S

Sada roti (see roti)
Salara, 306–307

Salt fish
    Buljol, 101–102
    Choka, 218–219
    De-salting, 324
    Sautéed, 110–111
Smoked-herring choka
    (*see* choka)
Shrimp
    Bora and, 188–189
    Pumpkin and, 192–193
Sorrel drink (*see* drinks)
Sour
    Mango, 214–215
    Souree, 214–215
Souree (*see* achar; sour)
Soursop ice cream (*see* ice cream)
Spinach
    Dhal, 145
    Vegetable rice, 198–199
Sponge cake (*see* cake)
Sautéed squash, 194–195
Star fruit (*see* five-finger)
Steamed rice (*see* rice)

T

Tamarind balls, 316–317
Tea
    Bay leaf and
        cinnamon, 226–227
    Cocoa-stick, 240–241
    Lemongrass, 248–249
Tomato
    Choka, 121–122
    Vegetable rice, 198–199

V

Vegetables
    Bora and shrimp, 188–189
    Eggplant choka, 108–109
    Eggplant-potato
        curry, 152–153
    Fried rice, 196–197
    Katahar curry, 165–166
    Okra and salt fish, 172–173
    Okra tomato-onion
        sauce, 174–175
    Pumpkin and
        shrimp, 192–193
    Rice, 198–199
    Sautéed karaila, 190–191
    Sautéed squash, 194–195
    Tomato choka, 121–122
Vermicelli cake, 318

W

Washing rice, 328